The Wandering Ascetic Life of Acharya Satyananda Avadhuta

My Thirty-Five Years with Baba Anandamurtijii

The Wandering Ascetic Life of Acharya Satyananda Avadhuta

My Thirty-Five Years with Baba Anandamurtijii

Acharya Satyananda Avadhuta
(The First Avadhuta of Ananda Marga)

InnerWorld Publications
San Germán, Puerto Rico
www.innerworldpublications.com

Copyright © 2017 by Nityananda Mandal

All rights reserved under International and Pan-American Copyright Conventions. Published in the United States by InnerWorld Publications, PO Box 1613, San Germán, Puerto Rico, 00683.

Library of Congress Control Number: 2016959840

Cover Design: Devashish Donald Acosta

No part of this book may be reproduced or transmitted in any form or by any means, electronic or mechanical, including photocopying, recording, or by any information storage or retrieval system, without permission in writing from the publisher, except for the inclusion of brief quotations in a review.

ISBN: 9781881717560

For Baba

Contents

Preface   1

Part One: 1955–1961 Sadhana

1	Renunciation	5
2	Childhood	8
3	From Village to Town	9
4	My Initiation	10
5	First Ananda Purnima Dharma Maha Chakra	11
6	The Kali Temple Hill	14
7	Kamalakanta Mahapatra and Anandamurtijii	15
8	Baba's Keshavpur Residence	16
9	Kalpataru, 1956	17
10	Indication	18
11	Guru and Disciple	19
12	Opposition	20
13	Gaya Parey and Baba.	22
14	One Evening with Baba	22
15	Alipur Dharma Maha Chakra	24
16	Dignity and Self-esteem	24
17	Free from Bondage	25
18	Bhakta Batsal	26
19	Supaul Dharma Maha Chakra	27
20	Ac. Shiva Shankar	28
21	The Indas DMC	28
22	Arraha DMC	29
23	The Flow of Kulakundalini	31
24	A Test	31
25	Death Demonstration	33
26	Transfer of the Jagriti	34
27	Bhaktadhin Govind	35
28	Expression of Different Sounds	35
29	Blessings	37
30	Supreme Attraction	38
31	Stealing	40

32	Sahakarmi	41
33	Kalpataru II	41
34	Bethia Tattvasabha	42
35	Amrah DMC	44
36	Vishesh Yoga	47
37	The Strictness of Yama and Niyama	48
38	Construction of the Jamalpur Jagriti	50
39	Omniscient Baba	52
40	Vision of a Siddha (1957)	53
41	Vanity is the Downfall of Life	55
42	The Role of Active Margis in Prachar	56
43	Ranchi Dharma Maha Chakra	58
44	Svapratibha Samadhi	60
45	Subhasita Samgraha	61
46	Cooperative	62
47	Antaryami	63
48	Kundalini Tattva (1957)	64
49	Widespread Publicity of Ananda Marga	68
50	Baba's Talk in Allahabad University	69
51	Bhaktir Bhagabata Seva	70
52	Samyoga	72
53	Sarvananda	75
54	Krishnagar Dharma Maha Chakra	78
55	Ideal Marriage	81
56	Learning Sanskrit Shlokas	82
57	Tantra Sadhana	83
58	Upward Flow	87
59	Ashram Room	90
60	Ravin-da Prasanga	92
61	Kirnahar Dharma Maha Chakra	94
62	Volunteer Social Service	96
63	The Mystery of Birth	99
64	Antaratma: An event of 1956	101
65	Organization	104
66	Restoration of Life	107
67	Gaonoha and Dumka Central VSS Camps	109
68	Piithasthan	112
69	Phullara Piitha	114
70	Baksheswar Piitha	115

71	Sitakunda	116
72	Tarapiith	117
73	Panchamakara Sadhana	120
74	A Mysterious Event	125
75	Raja Yoga	126
76	Renunciation	128
77	Omniscient Baba	129

Part Two: 1962–1966 Prachar

Preface		133
1	Miracles of Baba	133
2	Angle of Vision	135
3	Karma Yoga	139
4	Preparation	142
5	Omnipresence	143
6	Calamity	146
7	Dejected State	151
8	Avadhutaship	152
9	Panic	154
10	Will Power	155
11	Navagraha Yoga	156
12	Baglata	157
13	Assam Tour	159
14	Revenge	163
15	Removal of Crucial Danger	164
16	Hari	167
17	Compromise	168
18	Inspiration	169
19	New Year's Day	169
20	Renaissance Universal Club in Delhi.	170
21	Central Volunteer Social Service Camp	171
22	More Wholetimers	173
23	Sympathy Becomes Enmity	174
24	My individual Prachar Programme	175
25	Return to Jamalpur	182
26	West Bengal Work	183
27	Malice	185
28	North India Tour	185

29	Disaster	196
30	Calcutta	197
31	ERAWS	199
32	Interview	199
33	Malaria	200
34	Tattvika Class at Calcutta	201
35	Penance	202
36	Asansol	204
37	Shantiniketan	205
38	Baglata Post Office	205
39	Gorakhpur Dharma Maha Chakra	207
40	Anandanagar High School Building	207
41	Jabbalpur Dharma Maha Chakra	208
42	Ara Dharma Maha Chakra	209
43	Hostel Construction	210
44	Mitigation of Sorrow	211
45	Gopenjii	213
46	Anandanagar VSS Central Camp	214
47	Behind the curtain	214
48	Anandanagar High School	215
49	Control	217
50	Forest Department Case	217
51	Ghazipur Dharma Maha Chakra	218
52	Removal of Doubts	219
53	Seva Dharma Mission	219
54	Orissa	220
55	Madras	221
56	Kerala	224
57	Madras	226
58	Mysore	226
59	Goa	227
60	Maharastra	227
61	Gujrat	229
62	Rajasthan	229
63	Punjab	231
64	Jammu	232
65	Ambala	232
66	Vrindavan	233
67	Delhi	234

68	Dehradun	235
69	Laxmanjhula	235
70	Lucknow	240
71	Raipur Dharma Maha Chakra	241
72	Jammu Dharma Maha Chakra	242
73	Transfer	243
74	Printing Press	243
75	Ananda Purnima Dharma Maha Chakra	243
76	Varanasi Office	245
77	Central Office at Anandanagar	245
78	Maha Mahopadhya Sri Gopinath Kabiraj	246
79	Touring Bihar, UP, and Bengal	249
80	Vox Populi	252
81	Lucknow Dharma Maha Chakra	252
82	Siliguri Dharma Maha Chakra	253
83	Inquiry	255
84	Jaipur and Bombay Dharma Maha Chakra	256
85	Dhurua Dharma Maha Chakra	259
86	Salem Dharma Maha Chakra	261
87	South India and Kerala	263
88	Vivekananda Rock	264
89	Mysore	266
90	Brindavan Gardens	267
91	Srirangapattanam	268
92	Telegram	269
93	Uttar Pradesh and Punjab	271
94	Ludhiana Dharma Maha Chakra	272
95	Tattvasabha at the Colliery Area	274
96	Workshop	276
97	Ananda Purnima Dharma Maha Chakra	277
98	Loss of Good Judgment	277
99	Prasadjii's Request	278
100	Ladies Section	279
101	Driver	280
102	Chalking out the World Prachar Programme	282
103	Baba's Ancestral Village	282
104	Bhabua Dharma Maha Chakra	283
105	Steering Committee	283
106	Indecent	284

107	Dharma Maha Chakras in North India	285
108	Delusion	287
109	Third South India Tour	289
110	Claimant	290
111	Pratapgarh	291
112	Akola and Amaravati	292
113	Nagpur	292
114	Hyderabad	293
115	Kurnul and Anantapur	293
116	Madras	294
117	Revenge	294
118	Bangalore Dharma Maha Chakra	296
119	Cochin Dharma Maha Chakra	296
120	Bombay Dharma Maha Chakra	297
121	Tribunal	297
122	Dumka School	299
123	Change of Strategy	300
124	Admission of Students	302
125	None Can Kill Those to Whom the Lord Gives his Protection	303
126	Advent	304
127	At Bardhaman with Baba	305
128	Doing Mischief to Others Invites one's own Destruction	305
129	Baba's Departure for Anandanagar	307
130	Influence	308
131	Conclusion	309

Baba in 1958

Preface

WHEN THE EARTH is subject to the wheels of the chariots of vice, injustice, and sin; when men under the influence of their attachments lose their common sense and forget Satyam, Shivam, and Sundaram; the advent of the Lord in human form occurs.

To destroy injustice and sin, he brings back the eternal virtues by liberating humanity from illusory attachment and creating spiritual effulgence in people's minds through devotion to the Lord.

Age after age, God incarnates on earth, whenever it is required, though the ordinary human being does not realize it. The infinite knowledge, the infinite attractive personality, the Creator, Preserver, and Destroyer of the universe, without beginning, and without end — few spiritualists recognize him when he comes.

The offices of Ananda Marga were sometimes attacked and even destroyed by antisocial elements or government machinery. Due to this most of the old records, including our daily diaries, have been lost. Therefore I was not always able to record the year and date of the following events. The information I am giving about the different spiritual expressions of Baba Anandamurtijii and other things related to his organization are through my personal experience.

Baba told me, "The day will come when you will be able to write books." I laughed and said, "Baba, I have no literary knowledge and no knowledge of any subject. How I shall write those books?" In reply Baba said, "In spiritual matters, no literary knowledge is required. People want to know the reality of spiritual feelings and their expressions. You have acquired that knowledge through your long association with me."

Due to such inspiration from Baba, during my seven years in custody in Bihar from 1971 to 1978, the thought developed in my mind to write this history. I started writing in my mother tongue, Bengali, in the Phulwari Sharif camp jail at Patna. Since then, I kept my writings protected despite so many difficulties, by the grace of Baba.

After seven years, when I came out from jail custody, I was heavily engaged with organizational work, trying to set right our ruined organization so as to return our robbed glory; thus I did not get the time to write.

After Baba's physical departure, and after surviving the greatest calamity of my life, fighting for my life, Baba allowed me to live for this purpose. The total time of Baba's organizational work was thirty-five years, from 1955 to 1990. I have divided this period into seven parts. I have completed each part in Bengali and then translated them into English.

Part One

1955 – 1961
Sadhana

1
Renunciation

*I*T WAS 1961. I was an employee of the Jamalpur railway workshop. I was very busy with my work in the workshop but in my inner heart I always felt restless for the Supreme. I was moving toward the unknown infinity where my Ista Deva resides. O Lord, I wanted to know, when is God going to appear in my thirsty heart and remove all my sorrows and pains forever.

At the time I had a strong desire to perform spiritual practices in the solitude of the Himalayas. I started to prepare myself to go to Rishikesh. That place is full of divine vibrations, sanctified by the dust of the feet of many sadhus and saints for centuries. During the Durgapuja holidays the railway workshop would remain closed for fifteen days. I took a free railway pass and prepared to go.

Baba was an accountant working in the accounts office. Everyday I used to go to his office at 1:00 p.m. for half an hour during his tiffin break. Putting my elbows on his table, face to face with Baba, I would talk of my inner feelings without hesitation. It appears now as a dream. Before him I expressed uncountable piques and other childish things that I never expressed to anyone else.

If I did not see him at least once a day, I felt uneasy. One can ask why I expressed my desire to go to the Himalayas if I had that attachment to Baba. The malice, delirium, and hustle and bustle of society compelled me to think about going to a solitary place for meditating on Anandamurtijii for the rest of my life. That desire was in the inner core of my mind.

As on other days at the time of tiffin, I went to Baba's office but this day I found Baba in a grave mood. Baba asked me, "During the Durgapuja holidays, what is your programme, what you have chalked out?" I replied that I had taken a railway pass for Rishikesh and would visit that place. But I would first attend the DMC programme that would be held at Lucknow during holidays. After attending that DMC, I would proceed to Rishikesh. I did not express all my plans to Baba, but omniscient Baba knew the nooks and crannies of my inner thought.

After knowing my programme he scolded me and said, "Without thinking of the liberation of the distressed and downtrodden people you are thinking for your own salvation? You are so selfish." I became ashamed and a thought came in my mind: oh Lord, fulfil your desire through me. I placed a sheet of paper before him and said, "Kindly make my tour programme for these fifteen days." Baba made the following tour programme: Jamalpur to Lucknow to attend the DMC and then from Lucknow to Allahabad to Raipur to Tata to Calcutta. Then back to Jamalpur. I thought that while in Lucknow, I could visit Rishikesh for one day and then go on to Allahabad as per the scheduled programme. But man proposes and God disposes. A few hours before it was time to leave for Rishikesh, a severe fever attacked me. I was going to Rishikesh secretly, ignoring the instructions of Baba, and that is why I was being rightly punished. During my illness, some Margi brothers offered me medicines and tried to take me to a doctor. I did not allow them to do so because I knew it was Baba's play. When the time to leave for Rishikesh had passed, I knew I would be OK and I was.

It was October 30, 1961, when I reached Baba's office. He said, "November 7 is a pious lunar day. That day I can give avadhuta initiation. If anybody is ready, inform me." I asked Baba the meaning of avadhuta, its rules and regulations. Unless and until I knew that, how could I search for a proper person? Baba explained to me the definition and rules and regulations to be avadhuta. I noted it down. Baba said that those who are married must take permission from their wife to become an avadhuta. I studied the rules thoroughly and the next day in his office I told Baba that the rules he had given were for an avadhuta who lived in the jungle. To serve the society, one-third of them should be omitted. Baba accepted my proposal.

After getting instruction from Baba, I decided that for the welfare of society I was ready to dedicate my life. I proceeded to my village home at Amrah in West Bengal to obtain permission from my wife, Srimati Anuja. After reaching there, I explained my desire. Surprisingly, she gave me permission without hesitation, saying that I was going for the great cause of our Paramaradhya Baba. She wished me an auspicious, successful, and pleasant journey. When I remember Anuja's sacrifice I am really astonished. Sometimes I think that such an ideal, glorified woman is rarely seen in Indian history. For the welfare of human beings, she put aside her own comfort with a smiling face and accepted the worldly sorrows and pains. Anuja fulfilled the desires of her husband

and left behind her worldly comfort. She went to live with her father-in-law along with our five-year-old child, Satyabrata. She left her child's future in Baba's hands and became an example of sacrifice. That is why I forever salute the fair sex.

Though Anuja allowed me to go work for Baba's mission, my worldly relatives tried to keep me from the path of sacrifice. They wanted to confine me within their walls. They pressured Anuja not to give me permission but with firm determination she remained faithful to almighty Baba.

The news that I would leave my worldly family spread quickly. My relatives came from different parts and tried to place obstacles in my path. All were weeping just as the village of Ayoddhya was weeping when Ram Chandra left his house for the forest. No consolation could be found and my suppressed heart was weeping for them also.

Then a good-looking sannyasi came to my house. Pointing his finger toward me he said a few sentences. His words touched my heart. The moment I understood his advice, he left the place without saying anything to anybody. He disappeared and nobody knew where he went. I thought that an invisible power in the form of a monk had come to me to remove my anxiety and bring me a new sense of ideology.

Many relatives and neighbours assembled at my house, trying to postpone my programme, but none were able to deter me. At times certain weaknesses crept in my mind but the thought of going back to Jamalpur gradually converted my mental thought into spiritual vibration.

I was due to leave for Jamalpur the next day at 10:00 a.m. When the time of my journey neared, people from different parts of the surrounding areas assembled in my house to see me. I came out from my room and was surprised to see that nobody was weeping. All were motionless. There was a grave atmosphere. My affectionate niece Radha garlanded me on behalf of the people assembled there and blessed me for my journey. With smiling face and folded hands I did pranam to all of them and with a prayer to achieve my goal I started for Jamalpur.

I crossed the Mayurakshi River at the village of Abadanga, from where I would catch the bus. Hundreds of people assembled by the side of the path, weeping with folded hands. That scene is still in my mind. From a little distance my loving father blessed me for the success of my mission. Then he addressed the people and said, "Your goodwill will help him to be successful in his path. I pray to Baba that more selfless fathers like me offer their sons for the cause of suffering humanity."

2
Childhood

ON THE WAY to Jamalpur I remembered my past events, one by one, from childhood. I was born in the year 1930 on the occasion of Shravani Purnima at midnight in the village of my maternal uncle in the Panpara district of Murshidabad, West Bengal. I grew up in my father's house in the village of Amrah. Later Baba would hold DMC there. When I was five years old, I dreamt every night for a week that I was floating in the current of a devastating flood, swimming to try to reach shelter and save my life. Ultimately, I caught hold of a wooden log floating nearby. Another big wave came and again I was carried away. Out of fear I cried loudly and the dream ended. Then on the seventh day Lord Krishna appeared before me in the form of glorious spiritual effulgence and said, "If you take the shelter of anything in this illusory relative world, like in your dream, then you will remain in trouble every moment of your life. Take the shelter of the Absolute One who is unchangeable. I am that personality, that Old Purusha. Take my shelter and surrender unto me. *Sarva dharmam parityaja mamekam sharanam braja.* I shall be responsible for you and thus you will remain unaffected by any stimuli." I accepted him as my spiritual guru and prostrated unto the feet of the Lord of the Creation, Sri Krishna, who from that day forward gave me guidance and shelter at his sweet feet. Since then, I felt that an invisible power was guiding me in each and every moment on the path to supreme realization.

At the age of eleven I developed firm faith that the Lord himself in his physical form had already incarnated on this earth. At this time I began sitting in a solitary place to meditate on my Ista Deva, Lord Krishna. I was anxiously waiting to come in contact with him. Night after night I wept for his sweet physical presence. When I sat for meditation, tears would roll down from my eyes. I did not know the cause. Once a sadhaka, Sri Mangal Biharijii, asked me why tears would roll down from my eyes whenever I saw Baba, and Baba himself once told me, "Since childhood you have been weeping for me."

This childhood eagerness for the Lord gradually waned under the influence of worldly life, but my firm faith and devotion to my Ista was not disturbed. I faced different struggles and disasters during that period. But in all of those adverse situations I felt his sweet touch and his abiding presence. His boundless grace showered me. As I grew older and fell under the influence of worldly objects, this feeling gradually started to become hazy. Eager to recover this feeling, the inspiration came in my mind to do sadhana in a lonely place and thus I developed a desire to go to the Himalayas.

3
From Village to Town

*I*N DECEMBER 1951 I got a chance to become a mechanical engineering apprentice in the Jamalpur Railway workshop. It was a five-year course and I stood first among the seventy-five students every year during that five-year course.

In Jamalpur the hopes and aspirations of innumerable oppressed persons, the maker of the age, Lord Anandamurtijii, was working in the railway workshop in the accounts office. The dust of his feet made Jamalpur a holy place. The very name of this hillside town is so beautiful that at the time of sunset, when the crimson light falls there, our heart becomes delighted just to see the scenery. The divine ordainer of the fortunes of the universe, Anandamurtijii, worked for many years in Jamalpur and there are innumerable stories of those years. It was in this holy place that Baba started Ananda Marga.

In Jamalpur I lived in the Bandhab Sawmilani mess on Monghyr Road. One of the other residents was Sri Hara Prasad Haldar. He took initiation from Baba in the year 1951. Baba did many miraculous demonstrations on him. Between 1951 and 1954 Sri Hara Prasadjii and many others were initiated. Then on January 1, 1955, Baba assembled all of his disciples at Jamalpur and founded an organization, which he named Ananda Marga Pracharaka Samgha. On January 9 the first Dharma Maha Chakra (DMC) was held there. I learned this from Sri Hara Prasadjii. The birthday of Ananda Marga is celebrated on the occasion of Shravani Purnima, dating from the year 1954.

After that, another two persons from our mess took initiation: Sri Hara Govinda Mandal and Sri Birendra Bihari Banerjee. Those three persons used to talk to me everyday about the importance of yoga sadhana. I was very interested in yoga and thought about the matter seriously. They explained to me that Anandamurtijii was the guru of Ananda Marga and Sri Prabhat Rainjan Sarkar was the president and that they were separate personalities. They also said that Anandamurtijii was from Madras and I believed them.

4
My Initiation

I WAS EAGER TO see Prabhat Rainjan Sarkar. Through my friend Sri Jiten Mandal, I learned that Sri P. R. Sarkar used to enter the workshop through gate number six each morning, coming from his rented house in Keshavpur. I worked in a brass-finishing shop very near to gate number six. On April 27, 1955, at about 10:15 a.m., I went to meet Jiten, and on the way I saw a gentleman entering gate number six with a small tiffin box and an umbrella in his hand. I looked at him and him alone as he walked toward his office. His gait, his gravity, and his personality charmed me. I entered my shop and asked Jiten about him. Jiten told me that he was Sri Prabhat Rainjan Sarkar, the president of Ananda Marga. Then I came out from the shop and looked again at him. I thought that if the president of Ananda Marga was so attractive, then the personality of Anandamurtijii must truly be extraordinary. I thought how fortunate I would be if I could meet Sri Anandamurtijii. The next day at the same time I went to gate number six to see P. R. Sarkar and he passed very close to me. He looked at me and that look I found highly attractive. His unparalleled personality and spiritual attraction removed all my vanity and other mental complexities and I bent my head.

The next day I saw him again entering gate number six and that evening in my mess I told Hara Prasad Haldar that I had decided to take initiation. He arranged for my initiation with lightening speed. The very next day I accompanied him to the railway quarter number 334 at Rampur Colony, which at that time was the jagriti and central office of Ananda Marga. Acharya Arun Kumar Mazumdar came to the jagriti to give me initiation. He was an inhabitant of Monghyr Lal Dwaraja and was working in the same accounts office as Sri P. R. Sarkar.

When Ac. Arun Kumarjii sat to initiate me, he told me to prostrate before the *pratik* (emblem of Ananda Marga). I briefly explained my past experience: how Lord Krishna had appeared before me when I was five years old and asked me to surrender before him; that since I had prostrated before him and accepted him as my Ista, it was not possible for me to do sastaunga pranam to anyone else. Only if I realized that Sri Anandamurtijii was the incarnation of Lord Krishna would I be able to prostrate before him and no other. I said, "Lord Krishna told Arjuna, 'If you want to know me, then know me through yoga.' Therefore, I am interested to learn yoga only." Ac. Arun Kumarjii went into the next room — by then Anandamurtijii had come and was sitting inside that room. After two minutes he returned and said that there was no need to prostrate now. I told him that whenever my faith developed I would prostrate before my Ista, but in the meantime I would practice the lessons of yoga regularly. He agreed and I took initiation from him.

5
First Ananda Purnima Dharma Maha Chakra

THE FIRST ANANDA Purnima DMC was held on May 6 at Monghyr Chotto Rajbari. The followers of Ananda Marga enthusiastically assembled that morning to attend. All were extremely busy to receive Baba. At noon I came to know that Baba had arrived and would give personal contact to the new sadhakas. I felt an infinite blissful flow dancing in my heart because I was going to have my first darshan of Baba. I was surprised to feel such an attractive wave vibrating my heart. Perhaps my adorable Lord of so many past lives has come to give me darshan, I thought, and that was why I was feeling such a vibration. Some fears were also peeping in the door of my heart.

About one hundred devotees were sitting enthusiastically in the hall. Ac. Chandranathjii was at the door to Baba's room, allowing the devotees to enter one by one for personal contact with Baba. Ac. Shiva Shankar Banerjee was fanning Baba with a hand fan and the doors and windows in Baba's room were open. The devotees entered one by one, did sastaunga pranam to Baba, and exited by another door. The moment I entered Baba's room, he directed Ac. Chandranathjii and Ac. Shiva Shankarjii to leave the room and close the doors and windows.

Before coming to Ananda Marga I had heard that the guru of Ananda Marga was Sri Anandamurtijii and he was a Madrasi, while Sri Prabhat Rainjan Sarkar was the president of Ananda Marga. Now, upon entering the room, I found that personality whom I had seen at gate number six was one and the same. Due to this I became fearful and stood like a stone statue, unable to go near him. Baba told me to approach him but I stood there frozen, with my eyes glued to the floor. Then Baba affectionately caught my hand and pulled me near him. That day I could not understand that the soul of my heart eagerly wanted to meet me. Baba embraced me and told me that I was going to do auspicious work for the universe. He said that I had wept much for him. Then he blessed me and wished me all-round development in my life. On that day Baba graced me without my knowing it. Now, when I remember those events, my head bows down unto his feet.

After my personal contact, I spent the whole day in a depressed mood. Many weak points flared up and my mind was filled with reaction. My friends had told me that Anandamurtijii was a Madrasi, though later I would see that P. R. Sarkar and Anandamurtijii were singular in spirit but dual in theory, having a dual role in the organization. All through the day everybody tried to remove my doubts and confusion.

The DMC was scheduled to begin at 7:00 p.m. and the devotees had decorated the room beautifully. All were eager to receive Baba. Baba entered at seven and sat on the dais. His presence flooded the room with spiritual vibration. The moment he sat on the dais I was surprised to see spiritual effulgence coming out from his physical body. There was no similarity between the Baba I was seeing now and his daytime presence. I found him now in the night as a bright delightful icon. Though I was surprised to see this light, I was still not fully satisfied. However, half of my reactions were now removed.

Baba explained in his discourse about the five kosas and seven lokas. I did not understand most of the speech. At the end of the discourse he gave a practical demonstration. Baba directed a devotee named Kestopal to sit near him in full-lotus posture, closing his eyes. Then Baba commanded the kundalini of Kestopal to gradually cross the different chakras and ultimately merge with Paramashiva in sahasrara chakra. When the kundalini reached the sahasrara, Kestopal fell down in an unconscious state. Baba extended his leg and put his heel on Kestopal's navel, giving him the strength to reply to his questions.

1) At this time there was a lot of publicity about Hillary and Tenzing's successful ascent of Mount Everest. Baba asked Kestopal, "Was it true?" He said, "I find it is difficult to enter this peak. It is an unknown mysterious place."

2) Malenkov was the head of Russia. Baba asked Kestopal what Mr. Malenkov was thinking at that moment. Kestopal said that he was

thinking about doing mischief in the world. In a grave mood Baba said, "Tell him to remove all such evil thoughts from his mind; otherwise as per the desire of Yogeshwar Anandamurtijii within a week he will be dethroned from his present position." I found that within a week, on May 11, 1955, Malenkov was demoted.

3) Baba directed Kestopal to go back 322 *crores* of years and describe the condition of the Earth at that time. Kestopal replied that it was a fireball. Baba then asked him to come back to this Earth and go back 3220 years ago and say what age was going on. Kestopal said it was Dwapar Yuga, the age of Lord Krishna. Baba asked him what Krishna was doing. Kestopal replied that Lord Krishna was walking on the bank of the river Yamuna with a flute in his hand. Baba asked, "Is there is any similarity between his physical body and the pictures we see?" Kestopal said, "No." Baba then asked him to describe the appearance of Lord Krishna. Kestopal described him as follows:

> *Navina megha sannivam sunil kamalachhaving*
> *Suhasa ranjitadharam namami krishna sundaram*
> *Yosoda nanda nandanam surendra pada bandanan*
> *Suvarna ratana mandanam namami krishna sundaram*
> *Bhabavdhi karna dharakam bhayartha nasha karakam*
> *Mumukshu mukti dayakam namami krishna sundaram*

> Salutations to Krishna the Beautiful, like the new-blue sky, cloud-coloured, soft-hearted, with beautiful body and red-lipped smiling face.
> Salutations to Krishna the Beautiful, who was an object of delight to Mother Yashoda, whose lotus feet were worshipped by the gods, and whose body was adorned with precious gems.
> Salutations to Krishna the Beautiful, who was the most reliable helmsman on the ocean of this universe, who removed the fear of annihilation, who granted salvation to aspiring souls.

The voice of Kestopal was barely audible so Baba started to explain his words. Baba became absorbed in samadhi while explaining the physical appearance of Lord Krishna. His body fell down in an unconscious state. The general secretary, Sri P. K. Chatterjee, made no move to set right the physical body of Baba so I took Baba on my lap and laid him down on the cot. The moment I touched him I felt an electric current throughout my body. My mind became charged with spiritual vibrations and I became abnormal for several minutes. A supernatural effulgence and the sweet smell of an attractive flower were emanating from Baba's body. His entire body was a play of such waves. Baba opened his eyes after twenty minutes and closed them again. He did this two or three times and then he signalled for us to help him sit. He asked for a cup of hot milk. Someone ran to fetch the milk and gradually he became normal. Meanwhile Kestopal was still lying on the floor in an unconscious state. Baba touched his heel to the navel point of Kestopal and said, "Be a human being." Kestopal then sat up. Baba gave instructions to massage him because the functions of his body had been suspended for a long time. Baba also said to give him a cup of hot milk.

After that Baba left for Jamalpur by car. The spiritual atmosphere of the Ananda Purnima DMC was over. All my reactions had vanished like clouds in the sky of the autumn season. This was first and last time in his organizational life Baba became absorbed in samadhi in a public place.

6
The Kali Temple Hill

I WANT TO SAY something about the Kali hill as I heard it from Baba. The Kali hill is situated at Jamalpur and it was known as a famous Tantra piitha. On the hill there was a temple of Kali, the deity of Tantra; this is the reason it was called Kali Hill. It was a dense jungle and many wild animals lived there, especially tigers.

During British rule, one Englishman went to this jungle to hunt tigers. He came upon a tiger and shot him but the furious tiger jumped on him. They fought with each other and both died. Now that spot is a large field. In the middle of the field, the bodies of the man and the tiger are entombed some twenty yards apart. A pitch road encircles the field. The Kali temple is situated on the top of a hill at the eastern edge of the field and at the foot of the hill there was a spring. It was rumoured that the water of the spring cured acidity and indigestion. Just below the temple, there are two small lakes and a reservoir. Between the two lakes a small valley goes up to where the two hills join. This valley was known as Death Valley. There was no path to the valley. Nobody dared go to this solitary place alone, even in the daytime. Death Valley was also known as a famous Tantra piitha. There was a tamarind tree in the middle of the valley. Baba wrote many mysterious articles having to do with this tree in his *Vicitra Abhijinata*.

On the top of the hill there was a valley near the Kali temple and it was also a famous Tantra piitha. In this lonely valley, Baba passed many evenings. There was a big boulder that looked like an altar, about fifteen yards from the Kali temple. Baba used to sit on it. One night I went to perform kapalik sadhana in this valley. When I passed near the Kali temple, I felt some fear. But the moment I crossed the temple area and entered the valley, my fear vanished and I was dancing with spiritual vibrations. I thought that there was some mystery involved and I wanted to ask Baba about it. I performed my kapalik puja and came back to my quarters at 2:30 a.m.

The next day, when I went to Baba's office at the tiffin hour, I told Baba about what I felt that night at the top of Kali Hill. Baba explained about the boulder and the glory of that valley. Baba said that to reach a joyful state, one must face some obstacles, and that is why I felt fear. The person who is able to overcome those obstacles will be victorious. Baba said that Lord Shiva once came to that place with his first kapalik disciple, his son Bhairava. Lord Shiva used to sit on that stone while Bhairava was performing his kapalik sadhana. Kaoveri (Kali), the mother of Bhairava, also watched the kapalik from a distance. The Tantra piitha with the Kali temple protects the sadhaka in all respects.

7
Kamalakanta Mahapatra and Anandamurtijii

*B*ABA ONCE TOLD me in his office why he was known as Anandamurtijii. While Baba was studying in Vidyasagar College in Calcutta, he went to Bankura District in West Bengal to attend the marriage ceremony of a friend. After reaching Bankura, he went to a cremation ground at the dead of night. While Baba was there, a young man singing a devotional song approached him. Baba asked him his name. He replied that his name was Kamalakanta Mahapatra. Then he said with tearful eyes that his guru had directed him in a dream to come here to this cremation ground to take tantric initiation. Baba very affectionately said to him, "I am that guru who directed you in your dream to come to this place for initiation and tonight I shall initiate you as per the rules of Tantra." That night Kamalakanta got initiation from Taraka Brahma Baba.

After taking initiation, Kamalakanta got the feeling of Parama Purusha. He started to dance and cried loudly, "ananda, ananda." Due to the influence of these spiritual vibrations, Kamalakanta said, "You are Anandamurti (the embodiment of bliss)," and from that auspicious moment Baba was popularly known as Anandamurti. The name of Anandamurti came from the mouth of Kamalakanta Mahapatra but actually it came from the spiritual attainment and the spontaneous flow of ananda that Kamalakanta experienced in his inner heart.

After that, Baba placed his head on the lap of Kamalakanta and slept there. Kamalakanta took advantage of his sleep to go to his feet. Longing for salvation and by the grace of Baba, Kamalakanta attained mahanirvana. Baba went to Bankura to give salvation to the most fortunate Kamalakanta.

8
Baba's Keshavpur Residence

*I*N 1955 BABA lived in a rented house with his family in the Keshavpur neighbourhood of Jamalpur. Baba used to stay alone in a small room. One holiday at noon Baba directed me to go to his residence. When I reached there Baba told me to sit on his cot where he was lying in *anantashayanam* mudra. I sat on his cot with him. Affectionately putting his hand on my back, Baba started to narrate different stories. This went on for hours. In the middle of his talk, Baba directed me to lie next to him on the small cot. I followed his order. I thought: the guru is so near and dear, like a worldly father who mixes with his small child without any distinction. That is why God incarnate in the form of the guru is known as *sakha*. This sort of relationship was previously established between Krishna and Arjuna. *Sakha* means *samaprana sakhasmritam* — where the same vibration of prana radiates in both bodies.

At the end, Baba said, "today a person came to argue with me on a spiritual matter, but after entering my room, he had no mind to argue with me." That person became spellbound and took initiation from Baba. After taking initiation, when he was doing sastaunga pranam to Baba, he became absorbed in samadhi. Afterward he was so overwhelmed, he was not able to get up and needed the help of others to sit. Then he started weeping, saying again and again that he had not been able to perform guru pranam. His name was Sri Gopen Mukherjee. Later on, he was known as our beloved Gopen-da. At that time he was working in the Central Excise office at Patna.

Baba also related another incident when Sri Chandranath Kumar was working at Nathnagar (Bhagalpur) as Sergeant Major. He had a little vanity. If any Margi said to him something about initiation, in reply he said, "I shall take initiation when the time comes and when a real guru is available." One day Chandranathjii came to meet Baba in his Keshavpur residence. The moment he entered Baba's room, Baba said, "Chandranathjii, has the time come?" He caught Baba's feet and started weeping. Then he took initiation from Baba.

9
Kalpataru, 1956

AFTER COMPLETING HIS evening puja, Baba used to go to the Kali hill field to walk in the fresh air. He would sit on the tiger's tomb with some disciples who used to come for his darshan from different parts of the country.

It was May 5, 1956 and I was sitting with Baba on the tomb. All of a sudden Baba became very grave. His face and voice changed. It appeared as if he had come from a supernatural world. He took the pose of varabhaya mudra and said, "Your guru is now in the form of Kalpataru; you can have any boon from him you wish."

First of all Baba asked Bindeshwarijii, "What do you want?" In reply he said, "Baba, that you will remain physically with us for a long time for the interest of Ananda Marga." Baba said, "*Tathastu* (so be it)." Then he asked Harisadhanjii the same question. In reply, he said, "I want *parabhakti* (intense love for the Lord)." Baba said, "Tathastu."

I was puzzled because I did not know what type of boon I should ask for from my great guru. In the meantime, Baba turned his face toward me and asked, "What do you want?" I told him, "I want to realize all sorts of experiences and expressions of spiritual feeling in this physical body during the period of your physical presence." Baba said, "Tathastu."

Then Baba gradually became normal. That evening for me was a blessed one, full of transcendental feelings.

At this time there were very few Margis. Baba used to sit on the tiger's grave every evening. I came to know through those conversations with Baba that Baba was omnipresent. If ever I did anything wrong during the day, knowingly or unknowingly, even in my puja, Baba would point it out in details and punish me accordingly during those evenings. Every day except holidays Baba used to go for evening walk and sit on the tiger's tomb. Sunday noon and evening he used to come to the jagriti (a small room in railway quarter no. 334 at Rampur Colony) where devotees assembled from different parts of the country to have his darshan. He was surrounded by his devotees and their devotional songs. That was known as *Hariparimandal*.

10
Indication

MANY SADHAKAS RECEIVED a direct indication about the arrival of Baba at the jagriti. In my personal life, whenever I went to jagriti, I found that Baba was there. I knew that Baba wanted me for a certain purpose. I shall explain a few of these indications through which I came to know that Baba had come to jagriti and wanted me.

At this time I lived in the Bandhab Samilani mess on Monghyr Road, about one kilometre from the jagriti. I lived in a small second-floor room. When Baba came to the jagriti I would begin to perceive the sweet smell of flowers and sandalwood, gradually increasing. Later on that smell started to come out from my physical body also. Even when I was on the road the smell came out from my physical body. The moment I received this smell I would eagerly rush toward the jagriti and I would find that Baba was there.

In the next phase, whenever Baba wanted me for any urgent work the smell became intense and I found a reflection of light around me. A beam, as if from a flashlight, would fall on the earth from my forehead. Then I would run to the jagriti. The moment I reached there, Baba would say very affectionately and sweetly, "Yes, I wanted you for some urgent work." This continued until Ananda Marga was properly organized.

At that time there were no printed books, just a sheet of paper that explained yama and niyama. *Caryacarya Part I* and *Ananda Marga Elementary Philosophy* were in manuscript form. Baba was our philosophy, our Ista, and the goal of our life.

11
Guru and Disciple

ONE DAY WHEN Baba was in the jagriti, Gopen-da came to have his darshan. Gopen-da had attained samadhi at the time of his initiation so he knew the importance of the guru more than we did.

On this day Gopen-da became absorbed in samadhi while doing sastaunga pranam. The general secretary and I entered Baba's room and we found Gopen-da lying there in an unconscious state. Baba looked like the personification of the great ideal. We stood in the room silently, observing the mystery of guru and disciple. Baba said something to Gopen-da after half an hour to bring him back to normal condition. Gopen-da returned to a conscious state but the flow of trance continued. He embraced Baba again and again. The spiritual atmosphere I witnessed there cannot be described in words.

At 10:30 p.m. Baba's mother was waiting to give him his meal so the GS told Baba that he should go home to take his meal. Baba was ready to go but it was nearly impossible to separate Gopen-da from him. Finally the GS separated Gopen-da from Baba with great difficulty and he went home. An emotional Gopen-da told us that inside the great Mahapurusha the whole universe was dancing. GS made a joke about his trance and Gopen-da said in a grief-stricken mood, "You may be the GS of Ananda Marga, but in the spiritual world you are nothing but a child. You are not able to see the almighty Parama Purusha. Do sadhana, sadhana, and more sadhana."

Baba gave Gopen-da the power to see the past, present, and future. This news spread among the disciples of the Marga. Gopen-da said many things to the disciples about their future but there was a doubt in my mind about his powers. The next Sunday, when Gopen-da came to the jagriti to have Baba's darshan, I tried to remove my doubts. Baba was not in the ashram, so I asked Gopen-da if Baba was coming to jagriti. Gopen-da saw the motivation behind my question and did not want to use his powers to answer me. I insisted and after a few seconds he closed his eyes, smiled, and said that Baba was on the way to the ashram at that moment and that he was just entering the market lane on his way to Rampur Colony. I rushed there and found that it was true, exactly as Gopen-da had said.

Whenever Baba came to the jagriti he would mix with the disciples while keeping himself in a certain elevated spiritual state. One day a sadhaka touched Baba's feet while doing sastaunga pranam and an electrical shock passed through his body. He fell down unconscious. I had a similar experience. One Sunday at the Rampur Colony jagriti, Baba came and sat on his cot. When I did sastaunga pranam and touched Baba's feet I felt a spiritual charge pass through me. I lost all sensation and did not have the strength to get up. Tears were streaming from my eyes. Baba took me in his lap, embraced me, and blessed me with a trance state. It took me three to four hours to come back to normal. Since that day, due to the love and affection of the Supreme Lord, a sense of honour has flowered within me.

All the jagriti work was done by sadhakas. Outsiders were not allowed in when Baba was present. Only sadhakas could see the *liila* of Baba. If a person wanted to know about Ananda Marga, he was allowed to come when Baba was not in the ashram. Ananda Marga is against all sorts of superstitions, such as idol worship, the sacred thread, casteism, communalism, and anything that leads to the path of contraction or the fragmentation of human society. Selfish men went against Ananda Marga. The orthodox religious followers blamed Ananda Marga in many ways.

I faced much trouble getting a vegetarian diet in the mess so I was compelled to leave. I shifted to a railway quarters at Rampur colony along with two Margis named Sushil Dhar and Ramakant Bagchi, who lived with me in the same mess. This made it much more convenient for us to do the work of Ananda Marga.

12
Opposition

IN JULY 1955, three months after my initiation, I was made an acharya and was allowed to initiate others. There was a rule that on Sundays and holidays the acharyas would go to the surrounding areas to spread the teachings of Ananda Marga. If an acharya went on long leave to his village or anywhere else, he would do prachar work (propagation of the teachings) in that area. The prachar programme began at the village level, among relatives and friends. Then it was expanded to towns. Accordingly I went to my village, Amrah, and did prachar there. Many young men joined Ananda Marga. I directed them to hold dharmachakra once a week, where the sadhakas would sit together in a room, perform collective meditation, and discuss different issues such as future prachar work.

The outlook of Ananda Marga is *harar pita gouri mata svadesha bhubanatrayam*, which means, "Parama Purusha is our father, Parama Prakrti is our mother, and the entire universe is our motherland." Since Ananda Marga did not allow superstitions, we began to face opposition from other groups. The scientific character of Ananda Marga clashed with their beliefs.

I went to my village, Amrah, during the Dashahara festival, and as per the system of Ananda Marga, I organized a celebration with dharmachakra, collective meal, public kirtan, and the distribution of clothes to the downtrodden. To break the casteism I put a young man from the untouchable caste in charge of the meal preparation. All the young men with their wives and children ate together, breaking the social norm. The elderly and the superstitious became angry and tried to eject us from the village. They said that everybody must follow the social system that had been in force for fourteen generations, that the breaking of that system was not going to be tolerated. They were united against Ananda Marga. When I think about it now, tears and a smile come to me. Human beings, the highest creation, had been tortured by orthodox upper-class Hindus for centuries. On this day those young men boldly faced the adverse situation and were able to overcome it. Their ideological boldness set an admirable example.

That same evening the devotees passed through the village singing kirtan. Nobody dared protest. The old persons surrendered before the Lord, who comes from time to time to rescue the downtrodden.

Sri Ram Avatar Sharma, who was the owner of the Navajivan Press at Jamalpur and also the editor of a small magazine, expressed his opinion when he saw the knowledge, devotion, and service to humanity of the Ananda Marga devotees in Jamalpur: "Ananda Marga is the child of a poisonous snake. If it is not killed now, in the future Ananda Marga will swallow the entire world." I thank Ram Avartarjii for his forecast about the spreading of Ananda Marga throughout the world.

13
Gaya Parey and Baba.

ONE EVENING A policeman named Gaya Parey was walking with me and Baba. As we were getting ready to return from the tiger's grave, Gayajii said to Baba that due to the puddles that had accumulated from the recent rains it would be difficult for him to walk up to the paved road. "Baba," he said, "please let me carry you on my back." Baba replied affectionately, "No, Gaya, it is not practical and it will be difficult for you." Gayajii said, "Baba, I weigh more than three mounds (120 kg). Besides I am a wrestler. I defeated many big wrestlers. I can easily carry you up to the paved road." Baba smiled and agreed. Gayajii took Baba on his back but after proceeding only a few steps, he was not able to move. He felt the weight of a hundred mounds on his back and had trouble breathing. Baba said, "You are facing much difficulty carrying me." Then Baba said, "As per my desire, you can now carry me very easily." Just after that, Gayajii felt his load lighten. He carried Baba up to the paved road.

14
One Evening with Baba

AS ON OTHER evenings, Baba and I were sitting together on the tiger's grave. In the meantime rain clouds covered the sky and after a few minutes, it started raining cats and dogs. We had no umbrella so we took shelter in the tin shed situated at the western end of the field. The British used to play golf in this field and the shed was used as a club for their rest and relaxation. There was a mango garden next to the shed, which made it very dark and grave.

Baba said that he was not feeling well and wanted to lie down, but there was no place for him to lie down. Ultimately, he lay down on the cement floor and placed his head on my lap. Then he started to explain the rules of dead-body sadhana. He said that once a disciple of a certain guru started performing dead-body sadhana here in the mango garden with his guru remaining a little distance away. The disciple sat on the dead body and started intoning mantras. After some time the dead body started to move and he became afraid. Then the guru started saying, "*Ma voi ma voi.*" ("fear not, fear not," in Sanskrit). Baba narrated the story in such a way that it was as if everything were going on just in front of us, and in that grave atmosphere I was affected.

Then Baba changed the topic and said, "In the field, if any fear complex develops in your mind, go to the three palm trees." I asked Baba why. He said, "Though you already know very well, still I shall make you understand more clearly. When you sit for puja, *brahmajyoti*, *devajyoti* and *atmajyoti* are expressed within you. But there is one more *jyoti* (effulgence), an evil spirit. White-coloured jyoti is *brahmajyoti*, golden-coloured jyoti is *devajyoti*, blue-white jyoti is *atmajyoti* and blue-black jyoti is an evil spirit. Seeing these jyotis ,Vidyapati said:

Sthir vijari ankhi nirakhia chinitey narinu kay.

During the time of meditation I visualized with my inner eyes the motionless bright light inside me but seeing that light I am unable to understand what it is.

"At the same time all the jyotis are also moving in the external atmosphere. Those who see the internal jyotis can identify the external jyotis also. Now look around you. What kind of jyotis are here?" I found that innumerable different-coloured jyotis were leaving this area and in the vacated spaces white-coloured jyotis were encircling us along with *devajyoti* and *atmajyoti*. Then Baba said, "Where we are sitting is the place of evil spirits. Due to our presence they are leaving this place and in their place other jyotis are coming. We sit regularly on the tiger's grave; therefore that place is full of *brahmajyoti*. If a sadhaka anywhere in the field becomes afraid he can go to the tiger's grave and his fear complex will be removed."

After this day it became easy for me to identify the favourable areas for sadhakas through those jyotis.

15
Alipur Dharma Maha Chakra

*A*T JAMALPUR IN Alipur (the neighbourhood where the jagriti would later be constructed), on the roof of the newly constructed house of advocate Mahadev Babu, a Dharma Maha Chakra was held. There was a remarkable incident that happened at the end of DMC while guru puja and varnarghyadana were going on. A sadhaka who was sitting about ten yards from Baba flew over the ground, fell on Baba's lap, and embraced him. Intense love and great emotion attracted that devotee to his Ista, like a magnet to iron. The moment varnarghyadana was over, we saw the union of guru and disciple and we became surprised. At last, the fortunate sadhaka became lost in samadhi and fell down in an unconscious state. That day an unimaginable spiritual atmosphere was created in my mind and this incident arose in my memory again and again.

16
Dignity and Self-esteem

*I*T WAS 1956. My daily routine was to meet Baba in his railway office at noon, and again in the evening when I accompanied him on his field walk where we would sit on the tiger's grave up to 10:30 p.m. I was allowed to meet Baba at any time.

One day our general secretary, Sri P. K. Chatterjee, came to me and said, "If anybody wants to meet Baba they will have to take permission from me."

When I heard this, I was reacted. I thought that there should be a sweet relation between guru and disciple that should not be disturbed by any means. I was not ready to accept such obstacles to meeting Baba. I could not leave it to the whims of GS. Accordingly I informed GS about my mental reaction and decided not to meet Baba. As a result my mind became restless. Without seeing Baba at least once a day I couldn't sleep properly.

Due to my pride and self-esteem I did not meet Baba for two days. If I was not able to see him even for one day I felt great mental tension and could not sleep. For that reason I went secretly to catch a glimpse of him passing by. One day I expressed my feelings to Ac. Dasarathjii. He was the headmaster of Jamalpur High School. He replied that he also felt the same mental agony. Every day when school was over he would rush to meet Baba, so great was his desire to see him physically, and now he was also being prevented.

17
Free from Bondage

*M*Y RELATION WITH Baba was from time immemorial. I loved him from the inner core of my heart. He was my balm whenever I felt sorrow or pain. Now permission was needed to see him? How could I adjust with this rule?

Every Sunday devotees would come to Jamalpur from different parts to have darshan of their beloved Baba. Every devotee came to see him at least once a week. Each Sunday the jagriti would be filled with devotees. Many of those sadhakas faced obstacles and sufferings to reach there — financial difficulties, complaints from their wives and children, physical discomfort, and so on. But the great attraction of beloved Baba enabled them to overcome these obstacles.

Once a devotee named Nat Khat Kedarjii of Saharsa faced heavy obstacles to come to Jamalpur. Out of his intense love for Baba he wrote a song in Maithili:

> *Ham tho jaibei karbei Baba ke sharanama unke darashana mana*
> *Oto chhatin brahma swarup Anandamurti nam anup*
> *Darshan bhailey khuloto nayanama unke darashana mana*
>
> I must go to the shelter of Baba to have his darshan. He is the Lord incarnate, known as Anandamurtijii, Seeing him, the eyes of knowledge are opened. Therefore I must go for his darshan.

Since I was not going to meet him, Baba asked the other devotees about me. "Where is Nityananda? He has not come to me for the last two days." He expressed this to the other Margis working in his office.

When I came to know of this, I went to a lonely place and wept, feeling the pain of physical separation. Two days passed in this way. At last, when the pain of separation became unbearable, the GS came to me and said, "Baba wants to see you. The rule of taking permission from GS will remain, but it was withdrawn in your case. You can meet with Baba in your usual way. Nobody will put any obstacle in your way." He requested me to meet him in his quarters before going to the field so that if there was any urgent work he could send it to Baba through me.

I presented myself like an accused at the dock of my beloved Baba. The uncontrolled flow of my tears rolled down and washed away my pride. Baba said, "Whenever I came with a mission on the earth in the past, you also came with me. You have forgotten but I remember. Our relationship is from time immemorial. Therefore separation from each other is painful." I told Baba I was thinking to take a transfer from Jamalpur to Calcutta. Baba said, "You cannot remain without me. To transfer from Jamalpur will cause you unbearable pain. If you did it you would be compelled to resign from your service to return to me."

18
Bhakta Batsal

*I*FOLLOWED THE ADVICE of the GS. Every day I used to go the field with Baba. One day the GS told me that some fifteen devotees had come from outside for field contact with Baba and since I was a local person, it would be better if I didn't go, so as not to increase the number of people in the field with Baba. That evening during my puja I received some special spiritual feelings for which association with Baba was very important for me, hence GS's words affected me deeply. I came back to my quarters with tearful eyes, bolted the door, and lay down on my bed weeping. Then someone knocked on my door. When I asked who was knocking, there was no reply. Again they knocked. This time I got up, put on the light, and opened the door. It was Baba. I could not believe that he had come. Was it not a hallucination, Baba coming to my quarters in answer to my heart's call? I remembered a line of a poetry of Kabiguru Rabindranath Tagore: *Jiivan yakhan shukheya jai karuna dharai aso hey* (When the mind becomes dry, O Lord, come to me with graceful showers).

O Lord, you have appeared in my vacant heart in your blissful Kalyana Sundaram form. O Lord, no one can understand your liila or your limitless grace. I was surprised and said, "Baba, you have come?" With smiling face Baba said, "Yes, I have come. I always watch the feelings in the heart of my devotees and act according to their needs. I will remain here for two minutes. Change your clothes and come with me." I put a blanket on the floor for Baba and he sat there. In the meantime, I changed my dress and accompanied Baba to the jagriti, one furlong from my quarters.

After we reached there, Baba sat on his cot and told me to bolt the door so that nobody could enter. I was sitting on the floor and embraced Baba's waist by putting my head on his lap. I forgot myself for two hours. When my consciousness returned I remembered that Baba needed to go to Keshavpur, where he lived with his family. I requested Baba to go and went with him. When we reached the Jamalpur market we met a group of devotees from Bhagalpur who were returning disappointed from the field since Baba had not shown up. They accompanied Baba from the market to his Keshavpur residence and I returned to my quarters after leaving Baba with them.

19
Supaul Dharma Maha Chakra

MANY DEVOTEES ACCOMPANIED Baba to the Supaul DMC by train on the occasion of Kartiki Purnima. I went as Baba's attendant. We passed through Barouni and reached Saharsa, where we changed trains for Supaul. In the railway station, devotees received Baba with garlands and bouquets. Many of them had come from different parts to attend the DMC.

As per system, Baba gave personal contact to those devotees who were getting their first darshan. I was guarding the door and one by one I allowed them to enter Baba's room. A devotee named Bindeshwari entered Baba's room and moments later I heard him shout from inside. I became surprised. Then I heard Baba calling me. When I entered the room, I found that Bindeshwari was shuddering. With folded hands he was saying, "O Lord, forgive me, forgive me." Baba motioned for me to remove him, which I did.

When he became normal I asked him about his abnormality. Bindeshwari explained that as soon as Baba started to speak, he saw spiritual effulgence coming from his mouth. He was dazzled by that light and then he saw the entire universe revolving inside his mouth. When he saw this he became afraid. His body started to tremble beyond his control and that's when he cried out. I told him that he was fortunate. The whole DMC was charged with spiritual waves.

20
Ac. Shiva Shankar

Ac. SHIVA SHANKAR Banerjee was a police inspector in the Bihar Military Police. After taking initiation from Baba he became a very good devotee. He used to accompany Baba on evening walk and sit on the tiger's grave with him. There he listened to Baba expound the philosophy of Ananda Marga. Every day he took notes of what Baba said and then he prepared the manuscript of the first Ananda Marga book: *Ananda Marga Elementary Philosophy*.

At that time the divine power of Baba was expressed among the devotees through different spiritual feelings, especially during their meditation. Baba watched everyone's thought and expression. Nobody could hide anything from him. Almost all the sadhakas realized that he was an All-knowing Entity.

When he saw the different spiritual expressions of different sadhakas in the jagriti, Ac. Shiva Shankar Banerjee became disappointed. He embraced Baba in the jagriti, overwhelmed with emotion, and cried out, asking why he was deprived of the spiritual feelings that other sadhakas were experiencing. He wept like a child. Baba's face looked like the personification of bliss, irresistibly charming, awakening great emotion among the devotees who were present there. The day passed in a spiritual atmosphere.

21
The Indas DMC

THE VILLAGE OF Indas is situated in West Bengal under Labpur police station. Ac. Sachinandanjii lived in this village. He was Baba's classmate in Jamalpur. His father, Sri Kumarish Mandal, worked in the Jamalpur workshop, so Sachinandanjii went to school in Jamalpur and eventually became a doctor. He took initiation from Baba and through his efforts many people in Indas took initiation and they soon formed an Ananda Marga unit there. His devotion and sacrifice for Ananda Marga was the eyesore of his father, who disinherited him after failing to convince him to leave Ananda Marga. Dr. Sachinandanjii opened a dispensary in his village and within a short period of time he became popular among the surrounding villages. Later he left Indas with his family and came to Anandanagar where he opened a small hospital for the service of suffering humanity. He was very popular in Anandanagar and became known as Doctor-da.

Under the supervision of Dr. Sachinandanjii, a DMC was organized in Indas in 1956. Baba came by train from Jamalpur to Maheshpur Station, three miles from Indas. From the station Baba went to Indas by bullock cart. An unforgettable supernatural flow of devotion took place in this DMC. When Baba's discourse was over and guru puja began, every sadhaka by a certain spiritual power became unconscious with devotion, tears rolling from their eyes. I sat about seven yards from Baba's cot. Due to the great attraction I was feeling, I approached Baba, embraced him, and became senseless. When I came to my senses, I found that Baba was no longer on the cot. All around me the sadhakas were rolling on the ground with devotion. The divine attraction of Baba flooded Indas and created a heavenly atmosphere. It took me at least a week to become normal again.

After DMC was over we returned to Jamalpur by train. As usual I went to the field each day with Baba. One day I was sitting near Baba with my eyes closed. He touched my forehead and inside me an effulgent stellar region opened up. At that moment, I discovered Baba's purpose for coming to this earth and the relation between us from the past lives. I came to know that Baba is the Purusha Purana, the Lord Incarnate.

22
Arraha DMC

ARRAHA IS A small village situated in the district of Saharsa in the state of Bihar. Ac. Nat Khat Kedarjii lived in this village and was one of the main forces behind this historic DMC. We started with Baba by train from Jamalpur and reached Arraha Station at about 9:00 a.m. Hundreds of sadhakas were eagerly waiting in the station to receive Baba. As soon as the train reached the station the devotees started shouting "Anandamurtijii Ki Jai, Parama Pita Baba Ki Jai." They had arranged several elephants to carry Baba from the station to the village and a band to play music during the procession. Innumerable people from the surrounding villages gathered near the station to see this scene.

Baba got down from the train and the world smiled with fascination as he looked around at everybody. A spiritual wave spread out over all. Nat Khat Kedarjii requested Baba to ride on the lead elephant. Those who had accompanied him from Jamalpur rode on the other elephants. The elephants were moving in slow motion and Baba's body was swaying very gently while he rode. It appeared as if the whole universe were dancing to Baba's rhythm. I will never forget that historic reception and Baba's supernatural beauty.

On the way to Arraha both sides of the road were lined with people observing the procession and the shouts of triumph. In accordance with Maithili culture, when the elephants reached the village of Arraha, the lady devotees greeted Baba by waving lamps around him and singing devotional songs. Then Baba went to take rest.

On that day the orthodox Maithili pundits could not tolerate the triumph of Ananda Marga. Ananda Marga intended to establish an ideal society, removing all kinds of superstitions, such as the sacred thread, idol worship, casteism, etc. and the Maithili pundits could not tolerate that. To damage the image of Ananda Marga in the eyes of the public they erected a tent by the side of the Ananda Marga jagriti and challenged us to a debate on spiritual philosophy. They hired a pundit from Varanasi named Bhayankaracharya for the debate. Ananda Marga accepted the challenge. From our side a professor of Katihar College, Sri Indradeo Gupta, was selected to take part. At first, the argument started in Hindi. When Indradeojii defeated their superstitions through logic and reasoning, the pundits felt offended and ashamed before the public. Then Bhayankar proposed that since they were pundits, the debate must be in Devabhasa (Sanskrit). Indradeojii agreed and started debating in Sanskrit. Again he badly defeated Pundit Bhayankaracharyajii in all respects. As a result they did not hesitate to use filthy language and physical force against us.

23
The Flow of Kulakundalini

*A*T THAT TIME in Jamalpur there was a small unit of the Bihar Military Police. An Ananda Margi acharya named Ram Bahadur Singh was posted as the District Superintendent of Police of that unit and he organized a DMC in his Monghyr Road quarters. Many devotees came to attend. In the morning, at the time of Ishvara Pranidhana, a sudden wave of the kulakundalini passed through me. The serpent power rose up from the muladhara chakra and passed through the spinal cord inside the hollow passage of the sushumna nadi (brahmani nadi), creating a tremendous vibrational flow heading toward the sahasrara chakra, the seat of Paramashiva. As a result my body and mind lost their balance. A thrilling vibration gave rise to continuous forceful breathing. Outwardly it appeared as restlessness but internally it was a feeling of bliss. I did not have the capacity to digest silently that startling spiritual vibration. I understood that it was the miraculous play of our beloved Baba.

In the following days the kulakundalini rose at odd times with the same thrilling vibration, even during sleep. My body was flooded with infinite thrilling spiritual vibrations and my I-feeling merged into the blissful state of anandam. It was like Vaisnaviya Radha running to meet her beloved Shrii Krishna. When I reached Baba's railway office during his tiffin hour, Baba told a story about kulakundalini and its movement in the body and mind of a sadhaka. Baba looked at me with a mysterious, gentle smile, appearing as Antarjami, the omniscient one. O Lord, only you know the feelings of the inner core of my heart. O Lord, let your will be fulfilled through me.

24
A Test

*A*T THIS TIME the total number of Margis was about six hundred. Baba said that in the coming week, he would watch every sadhaka to see whether they were following the principles of yama and niyama or not. If needed he would punish them but their fault would not be exposed to the others. The GS informed the Margis of Baba's desire and so we, the local Margis, became alert.

During this period Baba remained silent in the evening when he sat on the tiger's grave. No discussion was allowed. If a devotee asked Baba a question, he expressed his annoyance and said, "During this one-week period I am observing every individual Margi so I don't want to be disturbed."

One day during the week, Goba-da, Dwarikanath, Uma-da, and I were standing in the open field behind the jagriti talking about Baba's test. In the middle of our discussion, I requested Dwarikanathjii to give me his snuffbox. The moment Dwarikanathjii placed the snuffbox in my hand, he became Baba and started to warn me, "I always remain with you and watch your each and every action in every moment; if required I appear in physical form also. Nobody can do any secret action without my knowledge." Goba-da ran inside the jagriti and excitedly started telling everyone that Dwarikanathjii had become Baba. Then he came back and did sastaunga pranam to Dwarikanathjii as Baba.

Seeing this transformation I became afraid. Without taking any snuff, I put the snuffbox back in the pocket of Dwarikajii. After ten minutes he became normal and again we started talking about the test of Baba. I asked Dwarikajii about the cause of his abnormality. He replied that he did not know about it. My doubtful mind could not accept this so easily. I thought that because we were talking about Baba, he must have been feeling Baba in his subconscious mind and thus acted accordingly.

After some time all left for home and I requested Dwarikajii to come to my quarters. Once we were inside my bedroom we started to talk about Baba. It was about 10:30 p.m. To test him, I requested Dwarikajii to give me the snuffbox. The moment I took the snuffbox, he became Baba again and started saying, "I always remain with you and watch your actions in every moment; if required I will appear physically before you. Nothing can be hidden from me, neither your actions nor your thoughts." As soon as he said this I threw the snuffbox out the window. My doubts and confusions were removed and I was convinced that Baba was an all-knowing, omnipresent personality. After ten minutes Dwarikajii became normal again. When I asked him about his abnormality, he said that he did not know what I was talking about. After one week GS posted a list of the punishments on the jagriti wall. My name was not on the list.

25
Death Demonstration

ONCE A REMARKABLE demonstration took place in the Jamalpur railway quarters. Baba came to the jagriti like other Sundays. Just after reaching there, he said, "Those who wanted to know the trouble one faces at the time of death, come here." Everybody was looking at each other and out of fear none dared approach Baba. When Baba saw that no one was coming forward, he chose one disciple and directed him to lie down in the middle of the room and remove his shirt. Baba showed the locations of the five internal *vayus* — prana vayu, which controls from the neck to the navel point; *apana* vayu, which controls from the navel to the rectum; *saman* vayu, which remains at the navel maintaining the balance between prana and apana; *udana* vayu, which controls the vocal cords; and *vyana* vayu, which controls the circulation of the blood throughout the body — and explained their function.

Baba then said that he was going to break down the boundary of each vayu and that all should observe the movements of the body. Movements began from the neck to navel and from the navel to the rectum. Prana and apana vayus were working like a pendulum of a watch, with saman vayu maintaining the balance between them. Baba then ordered the boundary of saman vayu to be broken and from the rectum to the neck the vayus were working without any obstacle. Baba said that now the three vayus were mixed together. Baba then gave an order to udana vayu to break its boundary and from the neck a wave producing the sound of *ghar ghar* could be seen. Then he ordered vyana vayu to mix with the others. The sadhaka's whole body started shivering. Finally Baba ordered the united vayus to go out the door of an organ. All his functional movements stopped and his lifeless body was lying on the floor.

The devotees became afraid and with imploring eyes they silently looked at Baba, wondering if he would return life to the body or not. Then Baba directed them to shift the body to the side room. After it was shifted Baba started narrating a funny story, but at that time none were in a mood to laugh. After half an hour Baba asked them to bring the body back. Then he asked in dramatic style whether the life of the body was going to come back or not. All were surprised. They became even more nervous when Baba said, "I am not finding his departed soul anywhere in this atmosphere. Still, I shall try my best to get back his departed soul."

After this Baba ordered the departed soul with the five vayus to enter the body and the body started functioning. Baba then ordered the vayus to occupy their respective places. Gradually the sadhaka became normal. Then Baba said, "Behave like a human being." Now his mental and physical functions started to work in the usual way. He got up and sat properly.

Baba said that the sadhaka still felt uneasy because he had remained lifeless for a long time with no circulation so he asked someone to massage his body and another to bring him a glass of hot milk. Then Baba left the jagriti. After he left, the devotees asked him what he had experienced. He replied that gradually he had gone into a deep sleep and did not feel any difficulty on the way.

26
Transfer of the Jagriti

DUE TO THE jealousy and the conspiracy of some selfish people, we were compelled to shift the jagriti to another quarter of the same colony, about one furlong from the previous one. After some time, for the same cause, we had to again shift the jagriti to a rented house in the Machopatty area of Jamalpur Bazaar. The place was undesirable and except for weekly dharmachakra no other work was possible there. GS kept the office work in his own quarters. Baba's Sunday sitting and other functions were held in my quarters. At that time Baba was so close to me that though physically we were two, internally we were one. Therefore, Baba's arrival in my quarter was no problem for me. Like a worldly father, Baba used my bed and utensils. He did not hesitate to eat with me. There was no need to make any separate arrangements for him. Baba and I were an inseparable part of each other in the three strata: physical, mental, and spiritual. This close physical proximity with Baba did not last for long but the mental and spiritual proximity has remained. He has always remained with me, in visible and invisible ways, and he will always remain with me in the future, as he foretold.

In those days I saw the simplicity of Baba, but later on, when I realized that he was the Lord Incarnate, almighty, omnipresent, and omniscient, I became surprised at how Parama Purusha hid his advent, playing with me freely and frankly, without any difference. Alas, Lord, nobody can understand your liila. I am lucky that you have given me your supreme grace. O Lord, let your grace continue.

27
Bhaktadhin Govind

ONCE A FARMER came to have Baba's darshan from the other bank of the Ganges, just opposite Monghyr. He was so emotional that when taking the name of Baba tears rolled down from his eyes. At that time there was a rule that before a person could come in contact with Baba they had to pass a test on yama and niyama, to see whether or not they understood the principles and followed them.

The farmer could not pass the examination, so he was not allowed to see Baba. He was weeping like a child and begging GS to allow him to see Baba from a distance, but GS would not allow him. Lamenting his separation from his Ista, he returned home. GS was also moved to see his departure.

After one month, the same farmer came back to the ashram to have Baba's darshan. This time he was not as eager to see Baba as he had been. The GS offered to give him a gate pass without having to take a test. He replied that he was an illiterate farmer. Then he said, "Dada you did not allow me the other day to see Baba. But after one week, Baba came to my house. I offered him a sweet drink and did sastaunga pranam to him. He blessed me and I knew that he was the Lord incarnate."

28
Expression of Different Sounds

IT WAS THE year 1956 and at the time of my evening practice I often heard different types of sounds: sometimes insects, *arati* bells, anklets, or flutes. I did not understand the cause of these sounds and I was eager to find out. I knew that Baba would have the answer to my questions. Earlier Baba had granted me a boon to experience different spiritual realizations and feelings during my sadhana. When I reached Baba in his office (where I used to go everyday), he started to explain, one by one without my asking, the different sounds I had heard during my evening sadhana. After hearing his explanation I understood that those sounds were nothing but my internal physico-psycho-spiritual vibrations expressed in different ways. They were not from outside. One evening when doing sadhana I heard somebody in the adjoining quarter dancing in a very nice rhythm with ankle bells. I felt a heavenly rhythm within me. Out of curiosity, I got up and searched for him in the area outside my quarter, but all was silence. I came back and sat for sadhana and again the same rhythmic dance with anklets started. I got up and searched again. Now all my doubts were removed. I realized that it was the sound of the inner core of my heart, created by constant incantation of my Ista mantra during the period of my sadhana.

On another occasion my body and mind was vibrated with the sweet sound of a flute. But still I had a doubt, so once again I got up from my seat and searched the area from where I had heard the sound coming. Again there was no sound. I came back and sat for puja. The sound of a flute merged with the supreme flow and I enjoyed the fruits of my sadhana. I understood that the sound of flute was the sound of Lord Krishna in my heart, playing his flute in Vrindavan on the banks of the Yamuna. The sound intoxicated my mind and attracted me toward its source.

The moment Radha, the kulakundalini shakti, hears that sound, she cannot remain in the *kula* (the nadir point of the spinal cord where kundalini resides). Leaving the kula, she runs upward to meet Lord Krishna. Those who hear that sound can't remain in kula. They run to unite with Parama Purusha, Lord Krishna. That is why in the temple of the heart there is so much thrilling attraction. The combination of all sounds is omkara. The source of sound is Parama Purusha. Therefore all sorts of sounds attract the sadhaka in a special rhythmic way toward him. In this connection the Upanishad says:

*Pranava dhanu sharajhatma brahma tallukshya muchatey
Apramoktena bedhyabyam sharvat tanmaya bhavet.*

In sadhana, *pranava* (the sound of omkara) is the bow, atman is the arrow, and the target is Parama Purusha. Like an arrow flying with full concentration toward its target and hitting its aim, similarly, through the help of omkara, the concentrated mind moves toward the source of omkara, ultimately unifying itself with Parama Purusha. This is the summum bonum of life.

At that time I was experiencing different sounds within me. As a result, I heard less external sounds though I did not yet know the cause. I heard less and less and gradually became nearly deaf. I became worried and went to Baba to explain my condition, how I was constantly hearing inside me a sound like a village market coming from a distant place and how I was becoming externally deaf.

After listening to me, Baba smiled and said, "I know exactly what you have been experiencing these last few days." He then went on to describe one by one everything I had experienced during the past one month of sadhana. "What you are hearing now," he said, "will become denser until the sound of omkara gains full expression inside you. Do not be afraid. After some days you will become normal. Yogis and rishis sit in divine contemplation for long periods to be able to hear the omkara sound, but rarely are they able to hear it. But by the grace of Parama Purusha you are hearing this and other related sounds while sitting in a room of your railway quarters. Due to intense love for Parama Purusha you have got this opportunity." He concluded by saying, "Don't be afraid; you are not going deaf."

I was submerged in spiritual bliss for the next two months. After that time I became normal. I realized through this experience that the sadguru unifies the devotee with Parama Purusha, observing everything while sitting in the inner core of the devotee's mind and heart. Nothing can be hid from him: the past, present and future are dancing before his eyes. After realizing that nothing could be thought or done without his knowledge, I prayed to the Lord to free me from the realm of Maya, to take my entire existence completely as his own.

29
Blessings

DURING THIS TIME I was working as a mechanical apprentice. During the previous four years I had stood first in my class, but as I entered my final year, due to sadhana and the work of Ananda Marga, I was not getting sufficient time to prepare for my exam. This made me uneasy. I knew it would be difficult for me to pass the exam. On the other hand, I did not want to neglect Baba's work. I was caught between the two, whether I should continue to work for the Lord and do sadhana or pay greater attention to my future career. I did not express this to anyone, but little did I know that Baba was observing every inner feeling of my heart.

Six weeks before the exam, I went on evening walk with Baba to the tiger's grave. Around 10:00 p.m., as we were preparing to return from the field, we prostrated before Baba as per the rule. When I did sastaunga pranam, Baba was sitting in a special pose. He blessed me, saying, *sakaler shrestatha arjan karo* — be superior to all. Then we started walking back. The moment Baba blessed me my clash vanished like a cloud in autumn. I threw myself into Baba's my work with enthusiastic zeal.

When I sat for the examination six weeks later, I found that I knew the answers to all the questions on the examination sheet. When the result was declared, I stood first in the exam. After this experience, I came to the conclusion that it was better to throw myself at the feet of Parama Purusha and work fearlessly as per his desire. Everything goes as per the desire of Parama Purusha and is fulfilled through different media. That is why Lord Krishna said to Arjuna, *nimitta matra bhava sabyasachi* — "be an instrument to fulfil the desire of the Lord."

30
Supreme Attraction

IN THOSE DAYS DMC was held every full moon in different places. Baba would appear before the devotees and explain the importance of jinana, karma, bhakti and so forth in a simple, lucid way. He gave us many examples so that we could easily understand. These discourses were later on published under the name of *Subhasita Samgraha*. At the end of the DMC talk, Baba would bless the disciples with his varabhaya mudra. Hundreds of devotees assembled and passed their time singing spiritual songs. From time to time Baba would also come during the kirtan and as a result many sadhakas fell into trance and became unconscious as their small selves merged into the Supreme Flow. In Vaishnava philosophy, when one's individual flow merges with the supreme flow of Lord Krishna it is known as the *rasaliila*. Lord Krishna would join the gopis during the full moon and their hearts would be flooded with the Supreme Flow, the Paramarasa. During DMC the devotees experienced the Paramarasa and lost their individuality. The poet has said:

Sei ananda charan patey
Shara rupu jey nritey matey
Plavan baye jai dharatey
Baran giiti gandherey.

After touching the feet of Parama Purusha, the devotee is overwhelmed with joy. The six cardinal passions start dancing and the mind merges with the universal rhythm. The aspirant becomes abnormal by its influence.

When the devotees returned home after DMC, the flow of the Paramarasa continued for a long time. They were relieved of worldly tension. Many sadhakas became abnormal due to the spiritual intoxication. Baba's blessing aided the disciples in their spiritual practice and this feeling continued from one DMC to another. Baba spiritually charged and revitalized them, which was not only helpful for their spiritual practices but for their prachar work as well.

For this reason sadhakas were eager to attend, forgetting their pains and sorrows. Rabindranath Tagore has said:

Antara glani shansaya bhar, palaka feletey holo akakar,
Apanar majhey svarupa tomar, dekhibarey jena pai.

When Parama Purusha glances toward a devotee, the devotee's internal mortification and uncertainty of mind are removed and the devotee visualizes the presence of Parama Purusha within himself.

During the time of Lord Krishna, the gopis ignored all obstacles to be with Krishna, their beloved Ista, singing devotional songs and dancing. That history was repeated in our DMCs with Baba.

Once a DMC was scheduled to be held at Saharsa, but due to unavoidable reasons I could not attend. I saw off Baba at the Jamalpur railway station and returned to my quarters in a depressed mood. As that feeling of depression grew, my mind became restless. I was not able to work. I felt that my soul had fled and left an empty cage within me. Without delay, I changed my dress and without informing my office I hired a taxi for Monghyr. Crossing the Ganges at Sahebpur I caught the same train in which Baba was going to Saharsa. I could not meet Baba at that station due to the short stoppage but I met him in Khagaria Junction. Smiling, he said, "You told me that you would not be able to come." I told Baba that if I would have been guided by my own will, it would not have been possible for me to come. But an invisible power drove me as per his will, and to fulfil his desire I was compelled to come. In a sweet voice Baba said, "It is true. You are guided by an invisible power. He is always with you. You are never alone."

31
Stealing

WHEN BABA SHIFTED to Rampur Colony from Keshavpur, he was living with his two brothers and his mother. Both brothers were also railway employees. Therefore, two railway quarters were allotted to them, just in front of each other. At this time they were all unmarried. Baba, his younger brother Manas Rainjan, and his mother lived in one quarter. His brother Shudhansu Rainjan lived in the other quarter. Each quarter consisted of two equal-size rooms, a small kitchen, a verandah, a bathroom, a latrine, and a courtyard. Baba lived in one room. Manas and his mother lived in the other room. The door between the two rooms remained open.

One night a thief entered his mother's room and took a trunk and some money from the pocket of a shirt. Manas and his mother were sound asleep. They had no idea what was happening. Then Baba called Manas softly and said that perhaps some thief had entered his room and stolen some articles. Manas woke his mother and they checked their valuables. When they saw that a trunk and some money were missing they raised a hue and cry. Then Baba said, "I think they left all the belongings by the side of the colony wall and escaped. Perhaps they only wanted the money." Manas went to the colony wall and found the open trunk with all their belongings lying there.

32
Sahakarmi

SRI AMAR BABU was a railway employee who worked in Baba's office. He lived in the Rampur Colony railway quarters, about a hundred yards from Baba's quarters. Every Sunday morning between 8:30 and 9:00, Baba used to go to Amar's quarters, unable to avoid his cordial invitation for breakfast. One day I saw that Amar was anxious because Baba had not arrived. He went out to the road many times to see if Baba was coming or not. He was not a Margi but Baba never refused his invitation. His devotion compelled Baba to take a little quantity of his devotional offering, even though Baba took his breakfast in his house before reaching there. Baba did not go to anybody's house on Sundays other than Amar Babu's house. Though he was not a Margi, his devotion to Baba was the equal of any Margi.

33
Kalpataru II

ON OCTOBER 15, 1956, Baba stopped at the jagriti, as he would do from time to time. This day there was a special atmosphere. After Baba entered his room, he sat on his cot in a grave mood and nothing was discussed. Ac. Dasarath, Harisadhanjii, Jitendranathjii, Pranay Kumarjii, and I entered the room and sat down on the floor near Baba's cot. There was an inexpressible spiritual atmosphere inside the room.

Suddenly Baba adopted the pose of varabhaya mudra and said, "Your guru is now in the form of Kalpataru for the attainment of your objective; ask any boon you wish from him." He started to ask us one by one what we desired. Somebody said *parabhakti*; another said *atmamokshartham jagat hitayaca*, and so on. At last Baba asked me what I wanted. I could not decide. I was thinking that Baba was the controller and owner of the expressed and unexpressed world. I wanted Baba only. Knowing my inner feeling, Baba said, "You want me and you will get me; so be it." In that spiritual atmosphere we remained with Baba up to 10:00 p.m.

34
Bethia Tattvasabha

*A*T THAT TIME Ananda Marga had only one published book: *Ananda Marga Elementary Philosophy*. Our philosophical knowledge was limited to that book and Baba's talks in different DMCs. Thus our philosophical knowledge was scant, but we were preaching the ideology among our relatives, friends, and neighbours. The Margis organized a *tattvasabha* (public conference) in Bethia (subdivisional headquarters of Motihari District in Bihar), and the Bethia committee requested the Jamalpur central office to send a *tattvika* (one versed in the philosophy) to address the tattvasabha.

When GS selected me to address the conference, I told him that I had never addressed a meeting before. Nor had I ever taken part in a debate, mostly because my philosophical knowledge was limited. Nor did I know Hindi properly. I wanted to go as a representative of Ananda Marga, but I did not want to address the conference since I had so many weaknesses.

The next day at 1:00 p.m., I went to Baba's office as usual. Baba told me to go to Bethia to address the tattvasabha. I told him the same thing I had told GS. Baba said, "The work of the Lord will be done by the Lord himself. You will be a mere instrument in that drama. Remembering your Ista, stand on the stage and through you he will do according to his need."

After getting this assurance from Baba, I became confident and started for Bethia. But before starting, Baba advised me how best to make the journey. As a result I did not face any difficulty on the way. I also had an authorization letter from GS.

After I left, GS sent a telegram to the Bethia unit secretary, Sri Ananda Kishore Singh, with the details of my arrival. When I reached there I found a group of devotees waiting with a Jeep to receive me. I accompanied them to the house of Sri Ananda Kishore Singh. I showed him my authorization letter and soon the local Margis began arriving one after another to meet me. Some of them went around town with a loudspeaker announcing the evening tattvasabha. This created a spiritual atmosphere.

As the tattvasabha drew near, my heart started beating faster and I became worried that I was not going to save the prestige of Ananda Marga ideology. A good crowd was expected and I knew that I knew neither Hindi well enough nor Ananda Marga philosophy. I was afraid that I would tarnish Baba's image and damage the reputation of Ananda Marga. Externally I was smiling but inside I was anxious.

A tastefully decorated stage was erected on the grounds of the district library. I reached there at 7:00 p.m., accompanied by the local Margis, and found that Dr. Nagendra Srivastav, the advocate Sri Sakaldeo Singh, and an officer of the BMP, Sri Kishanjii Singh, had already reached there to address the tattvasabha. They were all acharyas of Ananda Marga. When I saw them I became very happy.

We sat together and decided what we would talk about. By then the grounds had filled with spectators. We decided that Dr. Srivastav would explain about glands and chakras first, then Sri Sakaldeojii would talk about superstition in society, I would explain about Ananda Marga and social justice, and lastly Sri Kishanjii would talk about devotion. I inaugurated the conference by reciting the collective meditation mantra:

Samgacchadvam samvadadhvam samvomanamsi janatam
Devabhagam yatpúrve samjanana upasate
Samanii va akuti samana hrdayanivah
Samanamastu vo mano yathavah susahasati

Let us move together, let us sing together, let us come to know our minds together.
Let us share like sages of the past so that all may enjoy.
Unite our intentions, let our hearts be inseparable.
Let us be of one mind so that we can become one.

After reciting the mantra I became thirsty and started sweating. I was very nervous and tried to remember Baba's assurances. When it came time for me to give my speech, I remembered my Ista as per Baba's directions. I told them that my discourse was about Ananda Marga and social justice, and within a second I lost myself. An invisible power entered my body and started to deliver the speech, which lasted forty-five minutes. During that time I did not know what was going on. I wasn't even aware of the subject matter.

After my speech was over, I came down from the stage and some devotees embraced me and said that it was like Baba's speech during DMC, the same tone of voice and the same Sanskritised Hindi. But I did not disclose the mystery of my lecture.

After my discourse Ac. Kishanjii Singh started his speech. After completing his lecture, he came to me and said that during his discourse somebody took possession of him and gave the lecture. Rather than comment, I simply laughed.

When I returned from Bethia, I went to Baba's office to meet him. He did not ask about the tattvasabha but instead talked of other subjects. I remembered a few lines from the poet Ram Prasad:

Sakali tomari ichha
Ichhamayee tara tumi
Tomar karma tumi karo ma
Lokey boley kori ami.

Everything in this universe happens as per Your desire. You are doing your work through different media. But people say, I am doing.

35
Amrah DMC

IN ORDER TO hold DMC in a particular place, there were some rules to be observed: Baba will stay in the house of a local acharya, and there must be a unit committee. That committee will send the invitation to GS with assurances that the unit secretary will be able to arrange the DMC site and a place for the guests to stay and also free food for them. After GS is satisfied, he will give his approval for the DMC, and at the same time he will inform all the unit secretaries of Ananda Marga about the scheduled programme.

A DMC was scheduled to be held at Amrah, a small, attractive village in the district of Birbhum, West Bengal, on the banks of the Mayurakshi River. It had a silk factory named Ganutia Kuthi that had been opened by a British company. A brick wall surrounded that area to protect it from flooding. There were coconut trees, fruit trees, and flowers inside the compound. In front of the gate there was a big playground. The village had a high school and a post office. I heard a rumour that originally the Mayurakshi River did not pass there. In order to obtain water for the silk factory, the British dug a canal to connect it with the Mayurakshi. Later on this canal became the main tributary, separating the village Ganutia from the factory.

The Sainthia railway station was ten miles to the west and the Labpur railway station five miles to the south. A small bus ran between Labpur and Ganutia ghat, except during the rainy season. I grew up in this village.

Baba came by train from Jamalpur to Labpur, then from Labpur to Ganutia ghat by bus, and finally by bullock cart to the village.

The moment Baba reached the village, hundreds of devotees of all ages started to shout "Baba Anandamurtijii Ki Jai." Conch shells were blown and a thrilling spiritual wave vibrated the atmosphere. The devotees were weeping with spiritual emotion and the surrounding area became vibrated. Devotees came from different parts of the country to attend the DMC, from Punjab, Delhi, Rajasthan, MP, UP, Bihar, and different parts of Bengal. The young devotees of the village played an important role in organizing the programme.

Baba stayed for three days. As per Baba's desire, a local folk dance known as *raibasey* was performed and a musical debate known as *kabigan*. Those events were new and interesting for the devotees who came from other parts of India. Kabigan is a favourite of the village people in that area. The programme, which began at 9:00 p.m. and would not end until 9:00 a.m., was announced by drums and soon some five to six thousand people from the surrounding area gathered there. The subject of the musical debate was Ananda Marga ideology versus the old rituals, and this helped to spread the ideology of Ananda Marga to the surrounding villages. They understood that the old rituals were holding us back. To become a full-fledged man one must adopt the new scientific method of development. The heads of the two parties were Keshori Kora from Dwarka village, representing Ananda Marga, and Shankar Mandal from Moodighi village. Keshori Kora was initiated in Ananda Marga. Baba gave him personal contact and briefed him on some points about our ideology. The Kabigan was so interesting that even Hindi-speaking people watched in pin-drop silence throughout the twelve hours. An interpreter was provided so that they could understand without difficulty.

Ac. Hara Prasad Haldar was working in the Jamalpur workshop and lived in my room in the Bandhav Samilani mess. Baba initiated him four years before starting Ananda Marga. He was the subject of many miracles. He was born in Krishnagar in West Bengal and he brought a group of devotees from Krishnagar to attend the DMC. After reaching there, Baba gave him personal contact and infused him with a certain spiritual power. Hara Prasad then influenced the devotees with his spiritual vibration, creating a spiritual tidal wave in their minds. They started dancing and singing spiritual songs. For three days it was like a village fair.

After coming in contact with Baba, Hara Prasadjii developed some occult powers through which he could easily know the feelings of others, and accordingly he gave them advice. Baba did not come in contact with non-sadhakas, therefore through Hara Prasadjii he exposed his spiritual power and attracted the village people toward the spiritual path. By seeing Hara Prasadjii, the village people understood that Anandamurtijii was the Lord Incarnate, the maker of the age. Many devotees besides Hara Prasadjii were laughing, weeping, dancing and becoming unconscious. It appeared that the devotees had merged in the universal rhythm of the Supreme Father.

The DMC was held outside the courtyard of our house in a fenced-off area. Baba said that Shrii Chaitanya Mahaprabhu had visited this place five hundred years earlier and had stayed here for three days to preach his *harinama* kirtan. Now the place became supernaturally revitalized by the coming of Shrii Shrii Anandamurtijii. About eight hundred devotees attended. Thousands of non-Margis from the surrounding villages came to hear Baba's discourses. Nice arrangements were made for them outside the fenced-off area and a loudspeaker was used so they could hear. Thus the public did not feel any difficulty.

Before the DMC there was collective meditation. When I was conducting the collective meditation, my whole existence suddenly became vibrated with spiritual emotion and I fell to the ground and remained unconscious for half an hour. When I came back to my senses, a flow of bliss flooded my mind. I realized immediately that it was late so I ran to bring Baba to the dais. After a song Baba started his discourse.

The next morning, at the time of our departure for Jamalpur, Baba again came to the dais to give darshan to the devotees for five minutes. When Baba's bullock cart started moving, the devotees started weeping and running behind his cart. It was like the scene when Lord Krishna departed for Mathura from Vrindavan.

Two days later I went to Jamalpur to rejoin my work. The emotions I had felt during collective meditation continued. Day and night I was spiritually intoxicated. When I found that my daily duties were being disturbed due to those feelings, I went to Baba's office and told him everything. Baba smiled and said, "Do not worry about it. Everything will be all right and you will become normal." The next day I was completely normal.

36
Vishesh Yoga

The yoga of Ananda Marga is divided into *nama* mantra, *praramb-hika* yoga, *sadharan* yoga, *sahaja* yoga, Tantra yoga (performed in the cremation ground), and *vishesh* yoga, the highest yoga. The purpose of yoga is to achieve the spiritual goal of life, unification with the Supreme Lord.

Acharyas are allowed to teach nama mantra, prarambhika yoga, sadharan yoga, and sahaja yoga. Only Baba teaches the Tantra yoga, which is practiced in the burial ground. Vishesh yoga is taught by an authorized purodha. At that time there were no purodhas, so Baba was teaching vishesh yoga. A sadhaka could become eligible to learn vishesh yoga only after completing all the above systems of yoga.

At the time of teaching vishesh yoga to Arjuna, Lord Krishna said that he had taught this rarely available yoga to Surja and now he was teaching it to him. Arjuna said, "Surja took birth several generations before and you are a man of the present age. How could you have taught this yoga to Surja?" Lord Krishna replied, "We both were there at the time of Surja but you are under the control of Maya and I am the controller of Maya. That is why you have forgotten those past events, but I know everything, past, present and future." Now after 3500 years the master of all yogas, Shrii Shrii Anandamurtijii, has again started to introduce vishesh yoga.

Baba was living at Jamalpur at the same time I was living there, but I did not get the first initiation from him and this left a pain in my mind. I eagerly prayed to Baba that he would allow me to learn vishesh yoga directly from him. Baba in his own style started to test me. He said that I would have to pass the tests of intelligence, talent, and knowledge of geometry before I could be considered. After hearing this, I said that the sadguru was omnipresent and omniscient, so why was there any need for him to test the candidate? If he knew everything, then why so many formalities? Baba replied that his physical body was not going to be here forever and he needed to introduce certain rules through which one could be selected.

That same week, when I reached his railway office, Baba suddenly said, "Come to the jagriti this evening with paper and pencil. From today your vishesh yoga training will begin." Accordingly I went to the jagriti and Baba started to teach me. All my pains and sorrows were removed from my mind.

37
The Strictness of Yama and Niyama

*H*UNDREDS OF DEVOTEES would attend DMC, vibrating the venue through devotional songs and dance and filling it with joy. And every Sunday, sadhakas from different places came in groups to have Baba's darshan at the jagriti. Everyone knew that the basic principles of yama and niyama must be followed strictly by every Margi, but thus far Baba had not said anything directly to any sadhaka about the strictness of yama and niyama.

Then Baba asked me to see to the matter. "Many sadhakas come here," he said, "and take part in devotional songs and dance, joining the *hari-parimandal*. But they do not follow yama and niyama properly. I shall be stricter in this connection; otherwise when the number of disciples increases it will be very difficult to control them."

After reaching this decision, Baba started to make them understand about yama and niyama. "Follow yama and niyama strictly," he would say, "and tell others to be strict." Some days passed and Baba observed that a few devotees were secretly violating yama and niyama while still attending collective bhajan and kirtan. Baba told me about it and said, "Now I shall be strict in this connection. I shall give them some punishment."

The work of the guru is not only to give blessings but also to give punishment for the welfare of the disciples. Without punishment one cannot follow the spiritual path properly. Maharishi Patanjali said, *atha yoga anushasanan*. The meaning of *anushasanan* is *hitharthe shasanam*, punishment for the welfare of the disciples. The definition of guru is:

Shanta danta kulinashcha viniita shudhavesaban
Studhacara supratistha suchirdaksha subudhiman
Asharmi dhyana nishchestha Tantra mantra bisharada
Nigrahanu grahe shakta gururitya vidhiyate

He is calm and quiet, noble, humble, pious, virtuous, well-reputed, careful throughout and sensible. Living in a hermitage, firm in meditation, well versed in Tantra and mantra, he strictly punishes any misdeed of a sadhaka but at the same time he is gracious and merciful. These are the formal traits of a guru.

Now Baba began to take measures against those who were violating the principles of yama and niyama. As a result the amount of devotees that came to the jagriti decreased. Those who did not follow yama and niyama did not dare come before Baba. Only those devotees who were trying their best to follow the principles of yama and niyama came to the jagriti to have Baba's darshan. They knew that nothing could be hidden from Baba. He knows all our thoughts and actions. In this connection, Lord Buddha once said in Pali:

> *No antarikshey no samuddamajhey no pabbatanang bibaram prabishya*
> *No bijjati so jagdipya desha yatta titha manchajja papa kamma*

> While doing sinful work you cannot hide yourself anywhere in this universe. If you hide in the sky, under the deep ocean, in the mountain cave, or any other place in the universe, two eyes are watching you.

That is why Parama Purusha is known as the Witnessing Entity. Sitting within the heart of every living creature he witnesses each and every action of all individuals.

Once Ramakrishna Paramahansa told his favourite disciple, Swami Vivekananda, that he had a desire to eat the meat of a pigeon. He told him to take the pigeon to a solitary place and kill it where nobody could see him. After some time Swamijii came back with the pigeon alive and told Ramakrishna that he could not kill the pigeon because he could not find any solitary place. Swami Vivekananda said that everywhere two eyes were always watching him.

This leads us to the conclusion that the sadguru knows the past, present, and future. He is omniscient, omnipresent, and always accompanies every individual. Trying to hide something from him is foolish.

After that Baba gave me the duty to see whether or not the sadhakas were following yama and niyama. I used to go to the jagriti and the devotees listed their names to be tested on yama and niyama. Every evening in the jagriti I taught classes about yama and niyama. Those who learned well were allowed to have personal contact with Baba. This system continued for a long time. As a result, the Margis were eager to follow yama and niyama.

38
Construction of the Jamalpur Jagriti

*A*T THAT TIME all the work of Ananda Marga was going on in my railway quarters, other than weekly dharmachakra. The weekly dharmachakra was held at a rented room in the Mechho Patti area but it was an unsuitable place. There was no jagriti or land for a jagriti. The Rampur Colony railway quarters were too small; thus we needed to find another place to accommodate the expansion of the prachar work. The neighbours on both sides of my quarters were family men who did not appreciate the constant coming and going of outsiders. Thus we were compelled to shift the office of Ananda Marga to another place. We found a rented house in the middle of the market area and left the room at Mechho Patti.

Around this time a piece of land was bought in the Alipur neighbourhood. The owner of that land obtained legal ownership of it from the high court but he did not dare take possession of the land, so he sold it to Ananda Marga. We also had a lot of trouble taking possession of the land.

We were using the rented house in the market area for different activities of Ananda Marga, such as Sunday sittings, holiday sittings, weekly dharmachakra, etc. We invited Bachhu Mandal, the person who had illegally occupied the land, to inaugurate the foundation for us. After getting the invitation he responded by erecting a makeshift temple on the land in which he installed some pictures of deities there, declaring it a place of worship and thus making it difficult to evict him.

On the date fixed for laying the foundation stone, the general secretary along with some Margis went to the land and saw the temple. The wife of Bachhu Mandal was in the temple. Baba was in the jagriti and I was alone with him. Everyone else had gone to the land with the general secretary. I took permission from Baba and went there. I found everyone waiting for Bachhu Mandal to inaugurate the programme. Then Bachhu Mandal arrived with a lathi and a spear. He was furious. He attacked us and expelled us forcefully from the land. We were all unarmed and none dared face him. The general secretary directed us to go back and we all left.

After some time Acharya Dasarathjii reached there and Tara Mandal, the son of Bachhu Mandal, jumped on him with a short spear aimed at his chest. Ac. Dasarathjii closed his eyes and remembered Baba, waiting for certain death. Tara Mandal tried to stab him but two inches from his chest an invisible power held the spear and it did not touch him. Tara Mandal was frozen like a statue.

Soon afterward, Ac. Dasarathjii came to the jagriti. The moment he reached there, Baba said, "Dasarath, the spear almost ran you through, but it stopped a few inches from your chest, is it not?"

Dasarathjii replied with tears in his eyes: "It was your magic play that saved my life; otherwise I would have died on the spot. Tara Mandal was thrusting his spear at my chest, but when it was one inch away he suddenly became paralysed. It was nothing but your magic play, Baba; you saved my life."

After this the general secretary fixed a date for construction of a boundary wall. He sent a circular to the unit secretaries of Ananda Marga to come on that date with as many devotees as they could muster so we could face the situation properly. Especially police Margis were instructed to come, taking at least one-week leave.

On the date announced by the GS for the construction of the boundary wall, we were prepared to take possession of the land. Bricks and other necessary materials had been collected and Ac Kedarjii of Ranchi and Ac Chandranathjii (both police DSPs) were in charge of the project. Bachhu Mandal and Tara Mandal came with spears and axes to fight us. Ac Kuldeep Singh and Ac Baban Tiwary, both officers of the Bihar Military Police were also present to help us face the battle. They compelled them to abandon the land forever. The boundary wall was completed that night and the next day an iron gate was fixed to the entrance. The jagriti area was now protected.

During the construction of the boundary wall a remarkable atmosphere prevailed. Literate and illiterate, officers and labourers, were working together without any distinction of post or position. One person was mixing clay, somebody else was carrying bricks, another was preparing food, and so on. Some units supplied flour, some ghee, some rice, some vegetables. Many sadhakas with great joy were dancing, singing, and playing musical instruments. It appeared that the Lord himself was doing the work through different media. Everyone worked hard and instead of being tired they had a look of spiritual effulgence on their faces.

Baba said that if by December 28 we were able to complete the construction of the jagriti and hold a DMC there, then we would not face any problem in future. We had only fifteen days to build the jagriti and hold the DMC. It seemed impossible to complete it in such a short span of time so we begged Baba to give us more time. Baba said that if it were finished after that date, we would face trouble with the land in the future. Then all the local Margis under the supervision of Ac Vivekananda Singh of Jamalpur started to work day and night. Many Margis took leave from their work for that purpose. The roof was cast on the twenty-sixth, the remaining work was completed on the twenty-seventh, and on the twenty-eighth a pandal was set up in the courtyard of the jagriti for DMC. It was a great joy when at 7:00 p.m. the DMC programme began and Baba reached the dais. This was the first jagriti of our own.

While the DMC discourse was going on, the district magistrate of Monghyr came to inquire about the legal case. Seeing the protected area and the hundreds of devotees listening to Baba's lectures in pin-drop silence, he did not proceed further and returned back to Monghyr. The case was dismissed and after this the activities of Ananda Marga went on smoothly in the jagriti.

39
Omniscient Baba

*A*c. Dasarathjii was a very honest and good devotee of Baba. Baba conducted numerous demonstrations through him where he gave him some occult powers through which he could visualize the propensities in the mind of others through the colour radiating from the glands that carried those particular propensities.

Once Ac. Dasarathjii desired that Baba should come to his residence. Ac. Dasarathjii lived in Rampur Basti in Jamalpur. He was an assistant teacher of a government high school. He wanted Baba to go to his house, but there was a rule that Baba would only go to that house where all the members of the family were Margis. But the family members of Dasarathjii were not Margis. So there was pain in his mind for that reason.

But the guru found a way to satisfy the devotional sentiment of that great devotee. One evening after completing puja in a room with the door closed, Dasarathjii opened his eyes to find Baba sitting in front of him in a chair, looking at him with a sweet smile. Dasarathjii prostrated in front of Baba and left the room to bring something for him. When he came back the chair was empty. He felt very sad because Baba had left without taking anything. Afterward Dasarathjii went to the tiger's grave to see Baba.

When Dasarathjii reached the grave, Baba said, "You had a strong desire for the past one year that I should go to your house, and that desire was fulfilled today, was it not?" With tearful eyes Dasarathjii said, "Yes, Baba, but why did you leave without taking anything? I follow yama and niyama strictly and I do not know what fault I have committed that would cause you to leave my house without taking anything." Baba told him that the guru works according to the need and welfare of the disciples, so he should not feel any sorrow or pain in this connection.

Baba always watched over the spiritual, mental, and physical needs of the sadhakas, even when they were living in distant places. One day Baba came to the jagriti and I did sastaunga pranam. Then he said,

Yoginam hridayambuje nritanti nrityamonjusa,
Adhare sarvabhuteshu sphuranti vidyutakriti.

When a yogi is doing spiritual practice, divine spiritual effulgence dances in his mind and sparkling lightning lights up his heart. The sky visualized by his inner eyes is filled with electric vibration.

After hearing this shloka I understood what Baba wanted to say. During my evening puja, I realized that *akash* was converted into *mahakash*; stars and planets were sparkling like lightning in my mental arena. To understand the meaning of these mysterious feelings, I had gone to the jagriti to be near Baba and through this shloka he illuminated my feelings.

40
Vision of a Siddha (1957)

TODAY BABA WAS discussing the spiritual world and its inhabitants. Many creatures inhabit that world, but some of them, such as *yaksha, kinnar, siddha, gandharva, vidyadhara,* and *pishach,* like to remain in spiritual company. Baba explained that they were from different spiritual worlds but that now they sitting around us. "Perhaps you are not able to see them, but like you they also prostrate in front of me before sitting.

Their bodies are made of three factors. The liquid and solid factors are absent. That is why ordinary men cannot see them." Baba touched the forehead of Ac. Dasarathjii and directed him to see them. Dasarathjii was then able to see those luminous bodies. Elevated sadhakas can see them. They like spiritual environments, spiritual discussions, bhajans and kirtan, and they are attracted to places in which those activities take place.

Baba further said that those siddhas were once highly elevated sadhakas. During their sadhana they took a certain *samkalpa* (vow or firm determination) and until the samskara of that samkalpa is over they will remain in those bodies. To attain salvation they must acquire a human body and perform sadhana under the guidance of a sadguru. They feel great repentance for their past samkalpa. They are caught in a state from in which one can go neither up nor down; they have to wait. Therefore to get the grace of Parama Purusha they came to Baba, so they could be freed from their bondage.

Baba said that spiritual aspirants should always remain alert, because in a weak moment that kind of samkalpa can come into their minds. Sadhakas must always remember their Ista and their ideology. They should never wish to acquire occult powers unless they destroy the eight fetters and control the vrittis; otherwise it will be a curse for them. The use of occult powers under the influence of vrittis and for self-interest will be the cause of spiritual downfall. These siddhas have to face mental affliction.

Hearing this, I remembered a story about a great Tantric, Bamakhepa, who lived at Tara Piitha in Birbhum District. He left his physical body in the year 1918. Two dogs always remained with him. Their names were Kelo and Bhulo. Bama loved them very much, ate with them from the same pot, and slept with them. They were as obedient as servants. When people came to know that Bama was a siddha purusha, they started to come to him with different problems. But he called them sinners. Once a gentleman said, "Baba, you live with two dogs but you do not allow human beings to visit you. Are human beings below the rank of dogs?" Bama told him to watch the dogs and see the people sitting around him. Bama touched the forehead of the gentleman and he showed him that the two dogs were great yogis in their past lives. Due to certain mistakes they were reborn as dogs. The dogs knew that they were yogis in their past life. He said that some of the human beings that were sitting there were below the rank of human beings. Bama said that the dogs were like lightning-struck trees with the physical bodies of dogs. To get the grace of Parama Purusha they were living with him. The gentleman apologized to Bamakhepa for his foolishness.

Afterward, Baba said that there are many things around us that are not visible to human beings. People are not usually able to see the reality of things. To understand reality one must obtain the grace of Parama Purusha. This illusory world is nothing but a playground of Mahamaya. Mahamaya has covered the reality of the universe with her illusory veil. Lord Krishna said:

*Daevyesa gunamayii mama maya duratyaya,
Mameva je prapadyante maya metang tarantite*

According to my desire, Maya has covered the reality of the universe. Therefore nobody can cross the realm of Maya by his own effort. If a devotee surrenders to me with intense love, I shall rescue him from the illusory world.

41
Vanity is the Downfall of Life

ONCE A SADHAKA in Jamalpur came in contact with Baba and became a good philosopher. He became a popular and attractive personality. The unit secretary used to call him for prachar work and Baba performed many practical demonstrations through him. Baba loved him very much, therefore the Margis liked to associate with him. Gradually he started to think that he was an extraordinary man and that he had been a great man in his past life. He thought that because he was not like the others, he had no need for association with a guru. He created another universe in his mind and did not respond properly to what Baba wanted. He forgot *shive ruste gurustrata gurau ruste na kaschana* (If Lord Shiva is angry then the guru can rescue you, but if the guru is angry then no one can rescue you).

Still Baba went to his house to set his mind right. We also tried to make him understand, but we did not succeed. Then Baba turned his face from him. He became a guruless man moving around the street, an ordinary man lost in the darkness of society. The idea and ideology continues to move in its own rhythm destroying all obstacles. The person who runs with the spirit and rhythm of Ananda Marga will be the fortunate one.

42
The Role of Active Margis in Prachar

HOUSEHOLDERS AND ACHARYAS were doing prachar to establish the ideology of Ananda Marga. Some of their names were: Ac. Sachinandanjii from Birbhum District; Ac. Hara Prasadjii and Ac. Sukhendra Nayek from Krishnagar; Ac. Kedar Sharmajii and Ac. Amulya Ratanjii from Ranchi; Ac. Satyanarayanjii from Gaya; Ac. Arun Kumarjii, Ac. Taradasjii and Ac. Jagatjii from Monghyr; Ac. Mahadevjii from Bhagalpur; Ac. Indrajitjii from Katihar; Ac. Kedarjii and Jainarayanjii from Saharsa; Ac. Dipnarayanjii from Supaul; Ac. Sakaldevjii, Ac. Dr. Nagendrajii and Ac. Gangasharanjii from Muzaffarpur; Ac. Sarjuprasadjii from Motihari; Ac. Ananda Kishorejii from Bethia; Ac. Giridharijii and Ac. Shyamananda Laljii from Darbhanga; Ac. Gopenjii and Ac. Prema Bahadurjii from Patna; Ac. Kishunjii and Ac. Babanjii from Ara; Ac. Sachidanandajii and Ac. Raghunathjii from Gorakhpur; Ac. Keshavjii, Ac. Vindhyachaljii and Ac. Indrajitjii from Ghazipur; Ac. Ratneshjii from Allahabad; Ac. Chamandaljii and Ac. Om Prakashjii from Lucknow. Other acharyas were Ac. Pranay Kumarjii, Ac. Sukumarjii, Ac. Shiv Shankarjii, Ac. Naginajii, Ac. Virendrajii, Ac. Chandranathjii, Ac. Hari Sadhanjii, Ac. Sushiljii, Ac. Ramakantajii, Ac. Hara Govindajii, Ac. Nityananda (later on Ac. Satyananda Avadhuta), Ac. Dasarathjii, Ac. Jitendrajii, Ac. Vivekanandajii, etc. Many of the above-mentioned acharyas were high-ranking government officers. Wherever they were transferred they formed an unit of Ananda Marga. The combined efforts of the Margis for the expansion of Ananda Marga helped to spread our ideology, which gradually covered the entire globe.

At that time there was a different system to make people acharyas. Those sadhakas who exemplified the qualities of honesty, simplicity, courage, devotion to Ista, and ideological dedication got the chance to become acharyas. No importance was given to educational qualifications. After becoming an acharya, they started doing prachar work within their own circle. When they were able to initiate a sufficient quantity of sadhakas, they were considered for tattvika training. That is why the number of tattvikas was less than the number of acharyas.

Baba was the focal point of the devotees. The only book we had was called *Ananda Marga*. All the intellectual sadhakas were tongue-tied seeing the spiritual expressions of Baba. Baba's supernatural powers were beyond the ambit of the intellect. Those intellectuals surrendered unto his feet without any questions.

Baba gave nirvikalpa samadhi to Ac. Gopenjii. After getting all-knowing power from the guru, Gopen Mukherjee started to tell the past and future to many of the Margis who came in contact with him. He was working at Patna in the Central Excise Department. His great devotion and clairvoyant powers attracted the Margis. They would rush to Patna on Sundays and holidays so that he tell them their past and future. He instructed them to develop intense love for Baba because he is everything and by his grace life becomes significant. The devotion of Gopen-da was unparalleled but he discouraged the workers to do Baba's work. As a result the speed of prachar slackened.

One day Baba told me, "Under the influence of Gopen, General Margis are becoming organizationally inactive. You should meet with him and make him understand that I have come with a mission. Sadhana and work are both equally important for me." As per Baba's instructions, I went to Patna and conveyed Baba's message. In reply he said, "He will do his own work. How much capacity do we have to do the work?" I told him that if we ignore the reality of existence by not working, we cannot move in the devotional world. Baba has come with a mission, and as his devotees it is our first and foremost duty to cooperate with him in order to establish his mission on earth. A few days after my meeting with Gopen-da, he was transferred to Calcutta.

Most of the Margis came to know that Baba had given nirvikalpa samadhi to Gopen-da, which was why he had become an extraordinary man. He had gone beyond time. He lived in Behala area of Calcutta with his family. There was an Ananda Marga unit there. Here he started acting as he had done in Patna. Once again Baba sent me to talk with him. The Margis of that unit, after hearing my message, changed the name of the weekly dharmachakra to madhuchakra and cut off all connection with Ananda Marga. Baba became annoyed and withdrew both Gopen-da's spiritual powers and his acharyaship. He became an ordinary man and never again came in contact with Margis. He lost his spiritual power forever.

Soon afterward DMC was held in Birla Dharmashala in Camac Street in Calcutta. I accompanied Baba as his attending secretary and as such I oversaw the personal contacts. A Margi barrister named Sri Niharendu Dutta Mazumdar came to meet Baba. I asked him why he wanted to meet Baba. He said that Saulomari Sadhu wanted to meet Baba. I informed Baba and Baba said that there was no need since Baba was with him in every benevolent work. When I told him Baba's reply, he said he still wanted to meet with Baba. But Baba did not meet him. There was a rumour that the sadhu was actually Netajii Subhash Chandra Bose.

Baba asked me if I knew where Gopenjii lived. He wanted to see him secretly. I told Baba that Manoharlal Gupta knew where Gopenjii's residence was. I then asked Manoharlal to accompany us to Gopenda's house. We went by car and Baba stayed in the car while I informed Gopen-da that Baba was waiting in the car to meet him. When he heard this he ran toward the car weeping and prostrated in front of Baba, saying, "Baba, you have forgiven me again and again." He did not have the strength to get up due to his emotion. I picked him up and carried him to his house.

43
Ranchi Dharma Maha Chakra

A DMC WAS GOING to be held in Ranchi. On the way to Ranchi, Baba told me to go to Purulia for prachar. He also told me the best way to get to Purulia and from Purulia to Ranchi. As per Baba's instructions, I reached Purulia and contacted a number of well-known persons with whom I discussed the philosophy and spiritual cult of Ananda Marga. I also contacted the secretary of the Lok Sevak Sangha, Sri Arun Kumarjii, and with his help a meeting was organized at the Haripada Memorial Hall where I explained the ideology of Ananda Marga. Then I went to Ranchi to attend the DMC.

The DMC was like a spiritual playground for Parama Purusha. Most of the acharyas attended. Baba created a spiritual atmosphere with his blissful countenance. Every devotee had an attractive facial expression full of emotion and spiritual glow. It appeared that they had come to earth from the supra-mundane world. When the outsiders saw them, many were inspired to take initiation and see Baba. A great poet said:

Jay Mati Dipika Ujaley Adhika Bhitarey Anala Shikha
Patanga Asia Paraye Ghuria Puria Maraye Pakha

When insects see the bright light of the lamp, they lose their senses and run toward the light and lose their existence. Similarly under the influence of the spiritual effulgence of Parama Purusha, the little existence of the devotees merges with the spiritual effulgence and they start dancing blissfully with the universal rhythm. Seeing that scene, some started to laugh, saying that they had become mad.

A sadhaka poet has said:

Jey Torey Pagal Baley Tarey Tui Balishna Kichhu
Ajkey Torey Pagal Bhabay Angey Ray Tor Dhulo Dabey
Kal Sey Pratey Mala Hatey Asbey Ray Tor Pichhu Pichhu

The devotee, when merged with bright spiritual effulgence, starts dancing with the universal rhythm in a blissful state. At that time the general people see the scene and say that he has become mad. Thinking him mad they throw dirt at him. But don't say anything to those who call you mad. When they will realize the truth of your condition tomorrow, they will come up behind you with a garland and try to put it on you out of respect.

Really we all became mad because we got the goal of our life. *Pa* (get) + *gal* (goal) = *pagal* (mad). Parama Purusha is the supreme reality of life. We got him physically and our individual vibration merged with the supreme spiritual vibration. We got a chance to dance to the rhythm of Parama Purusha. From the beginning of the creation, we had come travelled the centripetal path crossing so many lives. Ultimately we got a human form and in this human form we have been fortunate enough to be physically associated with Parama Purusha, who is the ultimate goal of human life. If anybody says that we are mad, he is telling the absolute truth, because we have reached the goal.

44
Svapratibha Samadhi

IN A SADHAKA's life different clashes and cohesions arise in their minds that help them to convert their crude mind into subtle mind and the subtle mind into atman. In this connection Lord Buddha said:

> *Tula Dhuni Dhuni Ansu Ray Ansu*
> *Ansu Dhuni Dhuni Nira Bareysu*
>
> By beating coagulated cotton, the fibres are separated from each other. Beating those fibres, they merge into the atmosphere.

Similarly, when Ista mantra strikes the crude mind it converts it into subtle mind and that continued striking converts the subtle mind into atman. This atman is the absolute entity of the individual. By reaching that state one goes beyond the scope of rebirth. Atman merges into Paramatman. That is why a sage has said:

> *Sanyogo yoga ityukto jiivatma paramatmana*
>
> Yoga is the union of the unit consciousness with the Cosmic Consciousness.

To achieve that state one must perform sadhana regularly with intense love for one's Ista. During the period of the practice of yoga, different trends of thought will be experienced in the mind. If a certain highly spiritual thought arises in the mind at the time of performing sadhana, it will bring balance, and a flow of bliss will flood one's entire existence. This state of mind is a kind of samadhi or trance expressed in different ways. This state was expressed in the life of Mahaprabhu Sri Chaitanya; he was the embodiment of emotional trances.

In the supreme state of samadhi a sadhaka unifies with his Ista. The feeling of "I" is converted into the feeling of the Lord. The unit mind becomes one with the object of meditation. When it is of a permanent nature it is called *moksha* or salvation. This is the ultimate goal of life.

If a sadhaka performs sadhana, service, and sacrifice under the guidance of a guru and is able to please him, the guru will give him grace, and by the grace of the guru, his life will become significant. The Lord is watching all the physical and mental actions of the sadhakas. Kabiguru Rabindranath Tagore said:

> *Aman aral diye lukiye galey chalbey na go chalbey na*
> *Amar hriday majhey lukeye boso, keyo janbey na keyo balbey na*

The devotee always wants to keep his Ista in the inner core of his heart. He always thinks that his Ista is his own personal property. He cannot share it with anybody. Devotees, by their intense love and devotion, bind the Lord to them as they surrender themselves at his feet, making their arrival in this mortal world significant.

I will explain a little about my experiences with these sorts of trances. Once I lost myself and instead of me, Baba Anandamurtijii appeared in my physical structure. That feeling continued for a long time. I thought that it could have been a hallucination and hence many questions arose in my mind. There was a spontaneous flow of peace, tranquillity, and bliss in my heart. Outsiders treated me as a madman. I went every day to Baba's office at his tiffin hour, from 1:00 p.m. to 1:30 p.m., but I did not get any chance to discuss those feelings with him. One day omniscient Baba started to say that when Kabiguru Rabindranath was writing with devotional feeling, another Rabindranath was reflected before him. It was difficult for him to identify which was the real Rabindranath. "This state of mind is *svapratibha samadhi*," Baba said. "If this state of mind comes to you, do not be afraid of it. Adjust to that feeling. If somebody feels the advent of Parama Purusha within his physical structure, you will know that it is nothing but the unconditional grace of the Lord. It is a result of his past deeds."

Hearing this from Baba, I laughed inside and said, "O Lord, please fulfil all your desires through me."

45
Subhasita Samgraha

During Baba's discourses he explained the science of Brahma and how to attain him. The responsibility to note down the talks was given to professor Indradeo Gupta of Katihar College. He was a great pundit in four subjects: Hindi, Bengali, Sanskrit, and English. He was the man who argued in Sanskrit in the debate with the Pundit Bhayankaracharya, who was brought from Varanasi by Maithili pundits at the Arraha DMC to fight against Ananda Marga. Indradeojii defeated him and established the superiority of Ananda Marga. Most of the DMCs were held on the occasion of full moon. They were usually held on Sunday so that the maximum number of devotees could attend, since most of the sadhakas at that time were government servants.

After returning to Jamalpur from DMC, Baba in his leisure time would take the notes written by Indradeo Gupta during the DMC and re-dictate the discourse to Ac. Sushil Kumar. These were collected into a book named *Subhasita Samgraha*. Ac. Sushil Kumar was a railway workshop clerk and a good devotee. He went to Baba's office everyday at a fixed hour to take Baba's dictations. He prepared the manuscript.

46
Cooperative

THE MAIN OBJECT of Ananda Marga is *Atma Mokshartham Jagathitayacha* — self-realization and service to suffering humanity. We were preaching dharma and giving initiation to deserving candidates, but at that time there was no social work. Then the Jamalpur Margis took the initiative to open a cooperative grocery shop at the entrance to the road that led into Rampur Colony.

Many gave contributions and purchased shares so that we could open it. The aim was to make materials available at their cost price. Margis and non-Margis alike were eager to purchase articles from that shop. Cheap items were brought from different parts of Bihar through the Margis of those places when they came to Jamalpur for Baba's darshan.

Within a short period of time our cooperative gained a good reputation in the adjoining area of Monghyr. Many people came from the surrounding areas to purchase goods in that shop. But man proposes and God disposes. The honest man who was running the cooperative got a job in the railway and was posted at Alipurduar. There was no one else available to run the cooperative and thus we faced many difficulties. Ultimately it closed.

47
Antaryami

*I*HAVE ALREADY MENTIONED that at that time there was only one Ananda Marga book available. Baba and his miraculous spiritual powers were the sole attraction and inspiration in our spiritual path. He was the answer to all our questions. If a devotee had a unexpressed question, Baba used to give the answer in his Sunday discourse after seeing the state of mind of everyone who attended. That is why there was no necessity to ask questions. The sadhakas of that time realized in their hearts that Baba was an omniscient and indwelling personality. Through his different supernatural expressions he compelled the devotees to realize that he was the Lord Incarnate. Before him there was no distance, subtle or crude; any thought that arose in the minds of devotees, Parama Purusha came to know it. That is why his other name is the Indwelling Lord. He is the Witnessing Entity (Sakshi Chaitanya). The existence of the conditioned soul and the mind depends upon his existence. If you try to hide anything from Parama Purusha, it is foolishness.

Brihatcha tad-dibyam achinta rupam
Sukhacha tad-sukham starang bivati
Duratshu durey tadi anti kechu
Pashyat sihaiba nihitam guham.

Parama Purusha is so vast that he is beyond the thought of human beings.
He is so subtle that one cannot imagine.
He is so far that he is unfathomable.
He is so near that he remains in the inner core of the heart of every individual.

Nothing can be hidden from him. Two eyes are always watching the actions of every individual. Baba established himself as the Lord Incarnate. If any doubt appeared in anyone, Baba would wash it away through his demonstrations. From his talks and expressions of spiritual mystery, it became apparent that this universe is nothing but the magic play of a great magician. Everything is under his control. He explained the truth of death and rebirth, past and future, the feelings of samadhi, etc., in the form of stories. If required he also showed the devotees through practical demonstrations. He gave answers to different types of questions beyond the scope of worldly knowledge. A shloka of the Upanishads says:

> *Yo eko he jalavana shata ishanibhii*
> *Sarvan lokani shata ishanibkii*
> *Ya abaikay ud-bhabey sambhabey cha*
> *Ya atad bidura mritastey bhabantey*

This creation is nothing but the magic play of a great magician, who through his thought projection created this universe. He lives within it simultaneously in his *ota* and *prota* yoga. He watches and controls each and every particle of this creation, those that have been created and those that will be created. The sadhaka who is able to know this mystery attains salvation.

Some Margis believed that the sadhakas he used for his practical demonstrations were elevated souls. The idea that they were not ordinary men was a reason for their downfall. I prayed to Baba not to demonstrate on me in my immature state of mind. One must be alert during a sadhaka's life. The sadhaka realizes so many spiritual feelings. He must keep his mind under the control of consciousness; otherwise the selfish world will ruin his spiritual gains. Keeping the Lord in the inner heart, the devotee will be guided by devotion. One should direct all one's propensities toward the Lord and be engaged in welfare work. By doing this he will be entitled to get the grace of Parama Purusha.

48
Kundalini Tattva (1957)

IN THOSE DAYS the devotional outbursts of kundalini and the omkara sound were expressed in many sadhakas. Different expressions were seen during puja, such as restlessness, smiling, dancing, rapid breathing, etc. Newly initiated sadhakas were surprised to see such expressions. Baba explained that the awakening of kundalini creates those feelings during puja, so new sadhakas should not feel fear.

Here I shall tell you something about kundalini. At the nadir point of the spinal cord there is little bend in the tail bone that is known as *kula*. In spiritual science this whole area is known as the muladhara chakra. There is a spiritual power named kundalini lying in a dormant state in every human being. Its condition is expressed in the following shloka, the dhyana mantra of kundalini:

Dhayet kundalini sukhsamam muladhara nivasinim
Tvam ista devata rupam surdhatri balayanitam
Koti sondamini bhasam svayambhu lingabestitam

O subtlest kundalini, residing below the nadir plexus of muladhara chakra, please get up . You are like the Ista Devata, like a serpent coiled three and a half times around the *svayambhu linga*. Crores of lightning radiate from your body.

Inside the kula are the *kama piitha* and *kama biija*. Crossing the *kama piitha* and *kama biija* there is the sushumna nadi and the last portion is known as *svayambhu linga*. From the last point of *svayambhu linga* there is a hollow passage up to the sahasrara chakra called brahma randhra. The last portion of the kundalini's tail is inside the nadir point of brahma randhra and the rest is bent three and half times round the *svayambhu linga*. The mouth of the kundalini bites its own tail. It is lying in a dormant condition in every human being. Kundalini is just like a snake. It is subtle like 1/10,000 of a hair, its colour is golden and the brightness coming out from her body is like *crores* of lightnings. Kundalini cannot be seen by the open physical eyes. The sadhaka can see it at the time of sadhana through his mental eyes or through spiritual vision. Different scriptures have given different names to kundalini: in Tantra it is known as kundalini and Ishvara; in Vaishnava scripture it is called radha shakti and hladinii shakti; in the Vedas it is called parashakti and jiiva shakti. Only the Mahakaul can teach its sadhana at the time of the advent of Mahasambhuti Taraka Brahma.

Once a spiritual wave created a sensation in my physical body. The feeling appeared mostly at the time of drowsiness. A thrilling sensation started in my body, and inside the spinal cord from the lowest part a flow of lightning arose, moving like a snake. My whole body was flooded with thrilling, unspeakable spiritual vibrations. A sadhaka poet has said:

Sei ananda charan patey shara rupu jey nritey matey
Plavan baye jai dharatey baran giiti gandhereyy matey
After touching the feet of Parama Purusha, the devotee is overwhelmed with joy. The six cardinal passions start dancing and the mind merges with the universal rhythm. The aspirant becomes abnormal by its influence.

This blissful state and flow of lightning flooded my entire existence and pushed me toward Parama Purusha. When the flow of kundalini reached sahasrara chakra and became associated with the Paramashiva, my whole existence merged with the Lord and I forgot myself. It was a state of samadhi, a state of eternal bliss. After some time she came down and then again rose up. I came to understand that my physical body was nothing but a playroom of Shiva and Shakti. A sadhaka poet has said:

Jaga ma kulakundalini muladhara nivasini
Shirasi kahasra daley parama shiveytey miley
Krira Kara ma kautuhaley nityananda dayenii.

Oh Mother Kundalini, inhabitant of muladhara, the nadir point of the spinal cord, please rise up to the culminating point of sahasrara chakra, the thousand-petaled lotus at the top of the head, the abode of Paramashiva, the supreme reality. Please reach there and mix with Paramashiva; play with him with excited curiosity and give me constant joy.

Without considering time and space, the lightning flow of kundalini vibrated my entire body. Occasionally, when the flow was uncontrolled, the sound of omkara came out from my mouth. My thoughts became introspective and I was extremely eager to sit for puja. If I did not sit for puja I felt uneasy. After sitting for at least one and a half hours I felt calm. This feeling did not depend on my will. It was the play of an invisible power.

I followed the path that Baba gave with intense love and devotion. I felt that either I was going to achieve the goal of life or I would die. On one side were my worldly affairs and on the other side my ideology and Ista. The goal of my life was Baba Anandamurtijii.

When Baba first became Kalpataru before me and granted me a boon, I asked that all sorts of spiritual feelings be expressed in my physical body.

Baba said *tathastu*, so be it, and embraced me with love and affection. I felt very fortunate.

Long before I learned vishesh yoga from him he taught me how to realize the union of kundalini with Paramashiva. There is a vast difference between the feeling of formal sadhana and the automatic flow of kundalini beyond time and space. When he desires, the speed of the rising of kundalini is a hundred times faster and reaches the culminating point within a short time. The sadhakas who gets his unconditional grace are fortunate. They can burn the past deeds of lifetimes by dint of their intense love for Ista. Those sadhakas are lucky and easily fulfil their human mission.

The practical process of kundalini sadhana is secret and cannot be told here. The striking of an awakened Ista mantra can rouse the dormant kundalini. Mantra is life, kundalini is soul, and the body is an instrument. The three of them are required for mantra sadhana. As per kundalini tattva, the serpent power is lying in a dormant condition in every human being. For the awakening of kundalini three things are required: mantra chaitanya, mantraghat, and mantra dipani. But without an awakened mantra there will be no results, even if you repeat the mantra millions of times.

> *Chaitanya rahita mantra prokta narnasthu kevalam*
> *Falong naiba prayaschanti laksakoti japai rapi*
>
> A lifeless mantra is nothing but letters of the alphabet; if one does incantation of that mantra millions of times one will not get any result.

Constant incantation of Ista mantra arouses the dormant kundalini and during puja it tries to go up the sushumna, which is like a hollow pipe connecting the muladhara to the sahasrara through the spinal cord. By dint of puja the path of sushumna nadi gradually becomes clear. Kundalini rises gradually and crosses the six chakras, passing through the various knots — *brahma granthi, vishnu granthi,* and *rudra granthi* — and ultimately reaches the sahasrara chakra where it unifies with Paramashiva. This is the unification of the jiiva with Shiva, the individual with the Cosmic. Permanent unification is the goal of human life.

49
Widespread Publicity of Ananda Marga

*A*T THIS TIME most of the acharyas of Ananda Marga were government servants. They formed unit committees with the help of the Margis in different parts of North India. Due to the limited number of acharyas, it was difficult to contact the unit committees properly and to continue to give the lessons to the sadhakas. Therefore, to solve this problem, it was decided that good sadhakas should become acharyas. In this way the number of acharyas was increased to fulfil the demand of the unit committees.

After completing their acharya training, they were given responsibility for prachar work as per the demand of the different units. Due to the scientific spiritual philosophy and the concerted effort of the Margis, many people from all strata of society took initiation. Thus the ideology of Ananda Marga reached the entire society: farmers, teachers, students, men and women. The extraordinary personality of Baba influenced the mind of every individual sadhaka. When the sadhakas came in contact with Baba they realized that he was not an ordinary guru — he was Ishvara; Brahma himself in the form of the guru.

After getting personal contact with Baba, the sadhakas forgot their material gains and did not hesitate to devote their time for the establishment of the ideology of Ananda Marga. Thus the ideology spread throughout the country. When Margis from different parts of the country came in contact with Baba and with other sadhakas at the time of DMC, a bond of love was formed among them. Ignoring their worldly relatives, they formed new ties with the ideological universal brotherhood and a society without superstitions, narrowness, envy, or selfish motives was created; there was only love, affection, universal brotherhood, and the desire to establish the ideology among all.

Up until now I have only mentioned acharyas, not tattvikas. I have already said that at that time the personality cult of Baba was everything. Those sadhakas who were saintly and did good work were selected for acharyaship. After getting acharyaship, when they qualified for tattvika training by giving initiation to a certain number of people, their names were recommended. That is why only good devotees got the chance to become acharyas. In spirituality devotion plays a vital role. Because the guru gives initiation through the acharya, only good devotees are able to work as a representative of the guru. Devotion helped the sadhakas to come in contact with the guru and merge with the Lord.

Bhaktir bhagavata seva
Bhakti prema svarupinii
Bhaktir ananda rupacha
Bhakti bhaktasya jiivanam

Devotion is service to God; devotion is love personified; devotion is the embodiment of bliss; devotion is the life of a devotee.

50
Baba's Talk in Allahabad University

A DMC WAS HELD at Allahabad and some highly qualified devotees of Baba requested him to deliver a lecture at Allahabad University, knowing that it would have big repercussions among the intellectuals. As per the desire of the devotees Baba agreed to deliver the lecture and the local Margis arranged the programme within an hour. Baba was scheduled to deliver the lecture in the philosophy department of the university. It would be Baba's first public lecture.

We arrived at 11:00 a.m. Professors of different departments, educated persons from the town, and about 350 students were waiting in the hall for Baba's arrival. The head of the department cordially welcomed him and offered him a chair. When Baba sat on the chair we found a spiritual effulgence radiating from his body. It appeared as if he were not a man of this earth, but rather a visitor from a transcendental world. The lecture lasted forty minutes and all were charmed with his speech. I and the other devotees were transfixed by the charming beauty of the transcendental image of Baba Anandamurtijii.

When the speech was over, the head of the department, Mr. Kaul, praised Baba's unparalleled personality. As far as I know, this was the only speech that Baba gave outside the Marga. After that, I never saw him speak outside the Marga again.

51
Bhaktir Bhagabata Seva

*H*ow did devotion help the acharyas with their prachar work? At the time there was a limited knowledge of philosophy among the pracharakas. They overcame this through their intense love for Baba. Those sadhakas who developed a strong degree of devotion and surrender felt the presence of Baba within them. When the sadhakas reached the climax of that feeling, they were able to forget themselves and work as machines of Parama Purusha. Most of the acharyas felt this during their prachar work. A sadhaka has said:

> *Sakali tomari ichha ichhamayii tara tumi*
> *Tomar karma tumi karo ma lokey boley kori ami.*

> Everything in this universe is going on as per your desire. You are doing your work through different media. But people say that, I am doing, you are doing, he is doing.

Those sadhakas who thought they were intellectuals or philosophers were deprived of those feelings due to their intellectual vanity.

Baba often said during his Sunday sittings that Parama Purusha always remained with us. He used to say that Parama Purusha cannot do two things: he cannot create another Parama Purusha and he cannot hate anybody. Parama Purusha is impartial. Suppose it is raining and somebody keeps an umbrella over his head. He will not be drenched, but that does not mean that it is not raining. If the umbrella of vanity is removed from the head, he will also be drenched. Similarly the grace of Parama Purusha falls on everybody, but unless and until intellectual vanity is removed, the devotees will not receive it. In this universe, innumerable stars and planets are moving in a mysterious way but people do not know the reality behind it. Many plants, insects, animals, and minerals exist on this earth that people know very little about. A person may have a masters degree in one subject, but he has no knowledge of other subjects. A little knowledge should not be the cause of vanity. If someone wants to acquire real knowledge, he must catch hold of the magician who is hiding behind the creation, playing the mysterious role of creator, preserver, and destroyer of everything. The devotee who joins the party of that magician, working sincerely and obediently, will gradually remove the veil of illusion that covers his eyes; he will be able to see reality. This is real knowledge. It is an endless spontaneous flow of consciousness.

Perhaps you have seen worldly magic. The magician plays a variety of games but the people seeing the magic show are not able to explain the mystery of those games by logic and reasoning. But those who work with the magician know the explanation; the magician cannot hide anything from them. Similarly, when a devotee surrenders to the feet of Parama Purusha with intense love, Parama Purusha cannot hide anything from him. That devotee will be able to know the mystery of his game. The devotee can see this reality because his eyes are no longer covered by a magic veil. A realized yogi has said:

Jey bujhechhey say majhechhey
Jey bojheni say achhey bhalo
Adh bujhanir pranta galo.

Those who understood the Parama Tattva are overwhelmed with joy.
Those who do not understand the Parama Tattva are okay.
But those who understood haphazardly are worried and upset.

To know Parama Purusha one must do sadhana. Through sadhana one will acquire devotion. Then you will see that in the depth of your devotion, in the inner core of your heart, the Lord expresses himself. You will understand that you are not alone. You will feel that Parama Purusha is inseparable from you, that he lives within you. One must perform sadhana and do service to humanity to reach this state. When by sadhana and service the distortions of the mind are removed, you will see Parama Purusha and your individual "I" feeling will be merged with him permanently. *Brahmavid Brahmeva Bhavati.* He who knows Brahma becomes Brahma himself.

When your *prarabdha* (past deeds) are exhausted you will merge permanently with Parama Purusha. This is the final goal of life. For this reason you have achieved human life. Keep Parama Purusha as the goal of your life. If a person always follows the path of ideology, he will succeed in achieving the goal.

52
Samyoga

THE WORK OF Ananda Marga during these days was fascinating. During my prachar work, I experienced many mysterious events connected with the incidents of previous births. Many people came to me whom I had never seen before but whom I felt were well known to me, near and dear. The attraction between people who had never seen each other was so strong that at the time of departure many were weeping because of physical separation. The cause of this attraction is beyond logic and reasoning. Cause and effect is the eternal mystery of creation. Worldly people are not able to understand this.

I had been working for a long time as an acharya when Baba said that I should become a tattvika. I did not want to acquire theoretical knowledge because I was afraid it would give me vanity. I felt that Parama Purusha was utilizing me as his machine, so there was no need to become a tattvika. I wanted to leave everything at the feet of Parama Purusha and work directly by the strength of the Lord. *Tomari garabey garabini ham rupasi tomari rupey*. "I am proud and beautiful due to your presence within me."

I did not want theoretical knowledge. I wanted to depend on him only. The poet Rabindranath Tagore has said:

> *Nishidin bharasa rakhis orey mon habai habey*
> *Jadi pan karai thakis say pan tor rabai rabey.*

> If one's mind depends on the Lord, working all the time, his promise must be fulfilled by his grace.

But omniscient Baba, knowing my inner feelings, often asked me which books I had read. He told me to read some books and I agreed. One day Baba told me that he would go to the jagriti that evening. I performed my puja early and went to the jagriti to wait for Baba's arrival. Baba reached at the scheduled time and sat on his cot in his room. After doing sastaunga pranam I sat near Baba. No other devotee was in the room. Baba told me to bolt the door from the inside so that no one else could come in. Then Baba said that he would give me the tattvika examination. I was surprised. Baba asked me only two questions. I gave the correct answers and he was satisfied. I had passed the exam. I told Baba that I did not know much spiritual philosophy. Baba said, "Whatever responsibility is given to you, lay everything on he who is giving you that responsibility. Thus you should not have any anxiety in this regard. You should work every moment remembering your Ista and that will help you to have success." After getting this assurance from Baba, I was satisfied.

A few days later Baba taught higher tattvika class for one week and told me to attend those classes. The higher tattvika classes were compiled in the book *Idea and Ideology*. After attending the classes, Baba made me the training secretary of the Tattvika Board and assistant training secretary of the Acharya Board. This compelled me to acquire proper understanding and knowledge of complicated philosophical ideas and scientific spiritual practice.

After becoming a tattvika, I undertook a programme to do prachar in North Bengal. First I reached Alipurduar, where one of my initiates, Subrata, was working for the railway. I stayed in his quarters and he organized a tattvasabha at the railway colony. After the tattvasabha was over, many people took initiation. Among them was a young, spirited boy named Ranjit Rudra who started to work with us. The next day was Sunday. I went with Subrata by train to Cooch Behar for prachar work. It was a completely new place for us and it was the first time that I had gone to North Bengal. After reaching Cooch Behar, I was not sure how to start. Ultimately I told some intellectuals about my programme. They advised me to organize a tattvasabha and invite some people and tell them about our mission. With their help I made a list of the reputed men of town and decided that I would meet each individual personally and invite them to join our programme. But before inviting them, I needed a place where the invited guests could come. One gentleman suggested that I contact Sri Sharat Babu. "He is the owner of a cinema," he said, "and in his residence he has a small hall. He is also a reputed man of this town. I think your problem will be solved." I approached Sharat Babu and he gladly accepted my proposal. We were allowed to hold a meeting in the hall attached to his residence.

After that I hired a rickshaw to contact the persons on my list. A few of them raised objections about going to a meeting in a private residence but I made them understand that it was a tattvasabha of Ananda Marga, not a programme of a certain individual; he was merely cooperating by allowing me to hold the meeting in his hall. There were about fifty names on my list, so it took the whole day. It was not only extending the invitation — many of those persons wanted to discuss about our mission.

The meeting was scheduled for 7:00 p.m. and I completed extending the invitations at about 6:00 p.m., without stopping to eat. By then I was quite tired. After inviting the last person I decided to go to a park for puja and tiffin and then proceed to the hall. However, the last person I met invited me to perform my puja and take tiffin in his residence so we could go together to the meeting. I accepted his proposal.

By this time Sharat Babu had decorated the hall and put out chairs and sofas for the guests. By 7:30 about forty people had arrived. I was only given twenty minutes for the lecture, so in that short period of time I explained the practical approach of yoga. When the time was up, they said that I could speak for as long as required, so I explained different aspects of the yoga of Ananda Marga for another forty minutes. I then invited their questions but they had no questions. Most of them wanted to take initiation but I had no time because at 9:30 I had to catch the last train for Alipurduar to attend the scheduled programme the next day at Alipurduar College.

After taking permission for departure I left the hall. One gentleman came out of the hall and embraced me with tears in his eyes. He asked me to give him initiation before leaving. I told him that I had to go, but he continued to request me for initiation with tears and folded hands. Seeing his strong emotion, I asked him why he was so eager for initiation. He said that in the afternoon, when I went to invite him at his house, he was weeping and doing pranam with devotion. That night he had seen me in a dream so when I came to his residence and he saw that I was the person in his dream, he thought that God had mercifully sent me to initiate him. "You are the guru from one birth to another," he said. "Kindly give me initiation and show me the path of liberation." I told him that if I initiated him, he would have to remove his sacred thread and as a result he would face trouble from his family and in his social life. However, he said that he was ready to face any trouble and again he requested me for initiation. I remembered Baba, as per instructions, and initiated him. His name was Radhika Mohan Bhattacharya. He was a teacher. Once he was initiated, a high school headmaster named Sri Radha Madhav Dutta also requested me with folded hands for initiation. I initiated him as well.

By then it was 9:00 p.m. and Subrata told me that we did not have time to catch the train. I told him that everything was going on as per the will of the Lord, so I was not going to think about it. On the other hand I did not want to misuse the time. I thought that we should make every effort to get the train. It was one mile from Sharat Babu's residence to the rickshaw stand, but the moment we left his residence we found a rickshaw waiting at the gate. When we reached the station, we found the train waiting on the platform. We bought two tickets and as soon as we reached the platform the train started. That day Subrata understood that everything in the universe is controlled by an invisible power.

The next day, after completing the programme in Alipurduar, we returned to Jamalpur where the office work resumed. During this prachar work I had realized an infinite energy and boldness. I felt that there was no strength in this universe that could surpass the ideology of Ananda Marga. I was sure that within no time we would establish the ideology of Ananda Marga throughout the world. I felt that my normal "I" feeling and the "I" feeling I felt while doing prachar were vastly different. There was no similarity. I told Baba about these feelings and he said, "Your actual identity was expressed in your prachar work; you have taken birth on this earth for that reason. You did not come for the work you are doing in the railway office. Do not think that you have less potential than Sri Chaitanya or Swami Vivekananda. You will do many works in this world." These were the same words Baba had told me at the time of my first darshan. After hearing this I remembered that Parama Purusha lived in my inner heart. I thought: O Lord, Controller of the Universe, you made me to fulfil your mission.

53
Sarvananda

BABA WORKED AS the head of the audits section in the accounts office at the Jamalpur railway workshop. It was known that nothing could be hidden from the eyes of Sri Prabhat Rainjan Sarkar. If by some unavoidable cause Baba went to inspect an office, the concerning officials would became afraid. Baba gave them the chance to rectify their errors before taking official action against the offending party, but he took the necessary actions against those who were deliberately doing wrong. There was an accountant in Baba's office named Sarvananda who was deliberately doing wrong. Sarvananda told Baba not to disclose the matter. Baba pointed out his fault and gave him a chance to rectify his habits, warning him to remain cautious in the future. Due to such advice, Sarvananda's vanity was wounded. He showed his annoyance and wanted to suppress the whole matter. He raised a protest and thus everybody in the office came to know about the scandal. Baba was very popular and almost all the employees came to him with different problems to ask him for a solution. It was well known to everybody that Baba was an intellectual and a truthful pundit. People held him in high regard. Even the head of the entire office used to come to him to discuss the office work. Everybody in the office was annoyed with Sarvananda. They censured him and many wanted to punish him.

Sarvananda became ashamed. He came to the office and would sit silently in his chair. He lost the courage to talk with others face to face. Due to his misbehaviour with Sri P. R. Sarkar, an Ananda Margi threatened him with dire consequences. His mental pain became unbearable and ultimately he resigned his service and left Jamalpur forever.

One day I went to Baba's office and found him in an abnormal mood. The whole office was grave and dreadfully still. I asked Baba why he was in that mood. Baba said that it was because of the incident with Sarvananda. Baba said, "The sinner was afraid and he thought about his past sins. I exposed all his improprieties and he was not able to work peacefully. But I shall not put anything in black and white. I shall give him time to rectify himself." Then Baba started to tell a story: "Once there a black cobra who lived in a certain place. The cobra killed everybody who passed along that road. One day God passed through and the snake ran after him. God stopped the snake and asked, 'Why you are killing all those people unnecessarily? You are not getting anything in return.' The snake stopped biting the people and the news spread. People started to use the road without fear and the cowherders started to play with the snake. They would catch its tail and throw it. Due to this ill treatment the snake became wounded and sick and was about to die. God came to the snake and asked him what had happened. The snake said that he was obeying God's order and now he was going to die. 'You did not understand the proper meaning of my advice,' God replied. 'I told you not to bite, but I didn't tell you to stop hissing. If someone wants to live peacefully, he must protect himself from wrongful acts. That is the practical way to live on this earth. You have not done that, so now you are facing this painful condition. You must live with dignity, but do not bite anybody.' After that the snake started hissing and the news spread in the surrounding area. From then on he was able to live peacefully."

When he finished, Baba asked me to explain the spirit behind the story. I told him that if a person shows his anger, that was enough to serve the purpose. There was no need to hurt anybody. If somebody is not able to do good to others, then he does not have the right to hurt them.

Within a week Sarvananda left Jamalpur but he tried to take revenge against Baba. With the help of the chief accounts officer at Calcutta, he arranged to have Baba transferred from Jamalpur to Calcutta. At that time Baba was guiding all the activities of Ananda Marga from Jamalpur. If Baba were transferred, the work of Ananda Marga would be severely hampered. Baba received his transfer order and took leave for one month. He did not find a solution for his transfer and thus extended the leave for another month. In the meantime the general secretary called a meeting with the acharyas and reputed senior Margis. They decided that Baba had no need to continue working. All his needs would be fulfilled by his disciples. When they communicated this to Baba, he said that he was in agreement with the proposal, but that the time had not yet come. "You should know that to do good work many obstacles will come along the way, but they are temporary. The Lord always fulfils the desire of his devotees; whatever they want will be done."

When the two months were over, Baba was unaffected. He said, "Let tomorrow come." We were anxious, wondering why, due to the conspiracy of a sinner, Baba was facing such difficulties. We went to the field with Baba for his evening walk to take his consent to pursue the alternative arrangement but Baba did not address the situation. He discussed another issue. That night, after returning from the field, I could not sleep properly due to anxiety. The next morning I went to the house of the general secretary and found him in a happy mood. He told me that in the night the railway office had received the news through radiogram that Baba's transfer order had been cancelled. We became very happy and distributed sweets to everyone present. We enjoyed the victory of truth.

It was decided that the 1958 New Year's Day DMC would be held at Trimohan in the Bhagalpur district of Bihar at the residence of Acharya Harendrajii on January 26. Devotees came from Bengal, Bihar, and other parts of India. A new section of Ananda Marga was opened named the Renaissance Universal Club. The club was for intellectuals and educated young devotees. The first secretary of the club was Ac. Dr. Nagendra

Srivastav of Muzaffarpur. Later on, the office of RU was shifted from Muzaffarpur to the New Delhi quarters of Sri Shashi Rainjan Sahu, at 93 North Avenue. Ac. Lalan was made the secretary of the RU Club.

In 1957 Baba agreed to get married under pressure from his elder sister. Baba got married at Bandel in the court. Long before, in *Caryacarya*, it was written that Marga Guru should be considered to be married. After the marriage, a function was organized in our newly constructed jagriti at Jamalpur in which Baba's wife, Srimati Uma Sarkar, played the sitar very nicely. There was a question among the Margis how we should treat the wife of Marga Guru. Most of the disciples were confused about this so I asked Baba about it. He said, "She is the wife of the guru and she will be treated as part of the guru." After that she accompanied Baba to the DMCs, but she was not allowed to sit on the dais during the DMC. Baba said, "In DMC Baba Anandamurti is a singular entity; there is no place for any dual existence."

54
Krishnagar Dharma Maha Chakra

*E*ACH DMC HAD its own characteristics. This DMC was particularly splendid due to the concerted efforts of the local Margis and acharyas. The acharyas did their prachar work and many sadhakas came to attend the DMC from the surrounding areas and from different parts of West Bengal and India. It was decided that Baba would travel to Krishnagar from Calcutta by the noon train. Due to an unavoidable cause, Baba reached Krishnagar by car one hour before the scheduled time but the sadhakas did not know this so they went to receive Baba at the railway station. The moment the train reached the platform, they started to search for Baba in the different first-class compartments. When they did not find him on the train, they were all disappointed. Then the unit secretary, Sri Manorainjan Sen (Balai-da), informed them that Baba had already reached by car. Everyone started dancing and shouting slogans after hearing the news. He told them that Baba wanted them to make a procession, chanting bhajans and kirtans through a particular part of town. They then assembled in rows and raised flags brought from the different units. The procession followed the specific route that Baba had given. After proceeding a little ways, the sadhakas became intoxicated with spiritual feelings and started dancing on the road. Even those who were hesitant to dance, highly educated devotees dressed in coats, pants, and tie, started to dance with the others. The local people were surprised to see these educated gentlemen raising their hands in Hari kirtan on a public road in an abnormal state of mind, tears streaming from their eyes out of devotion for Parama Purusha.

When the procession reached the middle of the town, one sadhaka who had taken part went to Baba and informed him about the different expressions of the sadhakas dancing on the road. I took permission from Baba and went to see that remarkable procession. There I found that all were intoxicated with spiritual feelings, dancing and chanting Hari kirtan. My physical body also became vibrated with spiritual feelings but I controlled myself and left because I had many responsibilities connected with the DMC. I felt that an invisible power was working behind the procession. The sadhakas merged their individual rhythms with the universal rhythm and lost their sense of self. The only exception was the unit secretary, Balai-da, who was guiding the devotees and controlling their activities. In his student life he had been an active worker for Netajii Subhash Chandra Bose, founder of the Forward Block. Balai-da was a very good devotee and his constant activity was a big influence on me.

After the procession was over, Balai-da directed the sadhakas to take rest in a school where lodging and food had been arranged for them. The DMC was scheduled for 7:00 p.m. in the Krishnagar town hall. Before the DMC a tattvasabha was organized for the public and there was a large turnout. Acharyas and tattvikas explained the ideology of Ananda Marga and many people asked questions, which the acharyas answered. Meanwhile the sadhakas performed their evening puja and obtained their gate passes to enter the hall. Baba reached the hall at the scheduled time and sat on the dais, which was beautifully decorated. As soon as he appeared the devotees started shouting in triumph, "Anandamurtijii ki jay," over and over again. Then there was an opening song and after that Baba began his discourse. The devotees who had obtained gate passes could see and hear Baba, but the public could only hear his talk through the loudspeakers set up outside the hall. They had been attracted by the procession and were not satisfied with only hearing the discourse — they wanted to see this Mahapurusha. The moment they heard Baba through the loudspeakers, they started demanding to see him, but the volunteers could not allow them inside, since that would violate the rules. The situation was soon beyond our control. We informed Baba of their desire and waited for his decision. Then Baba directed us to open the gates and allow them inside. When they entered Baba requested them to remain calm. Seeing Baba, they were spellbound. Baba delivered the lecture in his own spiritual style. Nobody was able to maintain his separate existence while seeing Baba's delightful, radiant figure, just as the stars are unable to maintain their existence in the presence of the sun. Before the Kalyana Sundaram figure of Yogeshwar Anandamurtiji, everyone lost themselves. It was a strange scene. Baba's rhythmic discourse attracted the heart of everybody and they unanimously said, "O Lord, your arrival in Krishnagar has made us fortunate; kindly give us your blessing so that we can get your compassion in every age."

After the DMC finished about 11:00, Balai-da, Ac. Sukhen, and myself went to the school where the Margi brothers and sisters were staying. After eating their dinner, everyone was engaged in bhajans and kirtans. They soon became intoxicated with spiritual feelings. Gopen-da was also there with his eyes closed, standing in a corner of the room. We brought him into the kirtan. He raised his hands and started to dance, and within two minutes he fell to the ground in a spiritual trance. Those vibrations affected me but I remained a certain distance away. Balai-da and Sukhen-da embraced me and brought me into the dancing. I quickly lost my emotional balance and started dancing with them. I realized that an invisible power by his universal rhythm had compelled everybody to dance according to his desire. After some time I fell to the ground and lost all awareness of the external objective world. My mind merged with Parama Purusha, reaching a blissful state of *anandam*. After some time I became normal.

At 1:00 a.m. we returned to where Baba was staying and took rest there. The next morning we told Baba about the Hari kirtan the previous night, how it appeared that he had inspired the devotees to dance in tune with the universal rhythm and helped them to realize Parama Purusha. Baba said, "Do you know, once Bhakta Shiromani Narad asked God a question about Hari kirtan: 'O God, where do you live?' In reply God said:

*Na aham tisthami Vaikunthey yoginam hridaye na cha
Mat bhakhta yatra gayanti tatra tisthami Naradah.*

I don't live in the so-called heaven or in the hearts of yogis, Narada; I live where my devotees sing."

55
Ideal Marriage

THE IDEOLOGY OF Ananda Marga influenced the society and the devotees realized the importance of creating an integrated society. We wanted to form a universal human society, removing all superstitions that went against the ideology, such as the exploitation perpetrated by the orthodox priests, the dowry system, untouchability, the caste system, etc. We wanted to cure the diseases of society, to remove the danger posed by persons whose self-interests were hampered. Once the construction of an ideal society has started, it will continue. Rabindranath Tagore has said:

Amader yatra holo suru ogo karnadhar tomarey kari namaskar
Tufan chutuk batas utukh firbo nako ar

Saluting you we started our journey, and no matter what adverse situation arises we shall not turn back.

This strong determination enabled the Margis to introduce intercaste, interprovincial, and intercontinental marriages, through which a real human society can be established — without the differences of caste, creed or colour. The likes and dislikes of the bride and bridegroom must be considered. The marriage board sent out a circular in this regard. When information reached our office regarding those issues, the office announced that those who came forward to marry a widow or abandoned lady would be rewarded with a special honourable title from Ananda Marga. Many young boys accepted the challenge. A poet has said:

Porey gelo karakari
Ke ba agey man koribek dan
Tari lagi taratari

Now scrambling started among the devotees. Who will dedicate his life first for the ideology? For that there is a harem-scarem situation.

Sri Shambhunath Verma of Motihari was the first boy to marry a widow. That created a great sensation in Bihar among the intellectual Kayasta society. Initially the reaction was negative, but in North Bihar there were many respected, educated Margis; therefore the reaction died down. After a few days there was an intercaste, interprovincial marriage at Darbhanga between Dr. Amarnath Chakravarty (Bengali) and Vina, the daughter of an advocate, Giridharilal (Kayastha). The marriage was celebrated before Baba. Revolutionary marriages in Ananda Marga became common and many of them were performed on the occasion of DMC. There was another intercaste marriage at Monghyr. A girl and boy wanted to get married, but the father of the girl was preventing it. The boy, Dilip Bose of Jamalpur, requested help from our general secretary. As per his request, a date was fixed and it was decided to hold the ceremony in Monghyr. Many reputed Margis and acharyas were present. Dilip took the girl on a date to the cinema and from there he reached Monghyr, where in the presence of a hundred Margis the ceremony was performed. Afterward, the bride and bridegroom unitedly wrote a letter to her father to inform him about their marriage and obtain his blessings.

Within a short period of time, both in India and abroad, people came to know that Ananda Marga was beyond any narrowness and was bent on breaking all superstitions in order to create a universal human society. Soon after, a great revolutionary marriage was arranged in Jammu. The bride was a Muslim and the bridegroom was a Brahmin. The ceremony was performed at the Jammu DMC. It created a great stir in the society. We can say that the only medicine for all social diseases is Ananda Marga.

56
Learning Sanskrit Shlokas

*B*ABA USED MANY Sanskrit shlokas in his discourses to illustrate his ideas. The sadhakas tried to memorize those shlokas and repeat them in the same tone and rhythm as Baba. But the tone and rhythm we used was not adequate. All-knowing Baba was watching our activities. One Sunday, Baba explained the history of language and then explained musical tempo, tone, and rhythm. After hearing this, we realized that we were taking a drop of water from the ocean. We measured our knowledge and came to know the depth of it. After that we stopped practicing shlokas, but Baba wanted us to learn the shlokas properly. He said, "How many people are trying to learn shlokas? You will all come to the tiger's grave in the evening and I will guide you in this matter."

I told Baba, "The whole day you are labouring much and in the evening you relax with the devotees; we should not disturb you at that time." Baba said, "I have come in human form. As long as my respiration continues, I will continue to work. When my respiration stops, then there will be no further scope to work and I shall take rest forever. If you people come to the field to learn shlokas, I shall be very glad."

As per the will of Baba, four of us started to go to the field to learn shlokas. Baba started to teach us from *Subhasita Samgraha*, but we were not able to get the rhythm right. We became disappointed and were waiting for Baba to tell us that there was no need to learn shlokas. Instead, Baba encouraged us to continue. Sometimes he would repeat a shloka as much as fifty times until we got the correct rhythm, tone, tempo, etc. After a few days, three of the sadhakas stopped coming to the field. I alone continued to attend. Baba continued the programme for more than one month. Then I told Baba that I had learned some shlokas that would help me in my prachar work, and if required, I would learn more from him later — there was no need to continue now. Baba agreed with my proposal.

During this period, I realized that Baba was taking much trouble to build me up as a full-fledged man. It is a debt I shall not be able to repay in this lifetime. Even worldly parents do not take such trouble for their most affectionate children. With unparalleled compassion, affection, and love, Baba wanted to exhaust himself by giving everything to me. Who is he? Very few persons came to know him. He is Parama Purusha, the devotee's devotional sentiment, our nearest and dearest relative, Baba, the pole star of our life. He has come to remove the darkness from our lives and ignite a flame of spiritual effulgence. He has come among us in human form. It is his gift. O Lord, Almighty Baba, our greatest desire is to get your love, affection, and grace, age after age!

57
Tantra Sadhana

THE MOVEMENT FROM crude to subtle is called Tantra sadhana. In a general sense, midnight sadhana in the burial ground is referred to as Tantra sadhana. In Ananda Marga different processes of yoga (spiritual cult) are known as Tantra sadhana. They remove mental complexes such as hatred, fear, etc., which are obstacles to the total expression of the mind. These complexes are obstacles for social service also. Unless and until they are removed, one cannot overcome the adverse situations that arise in individual life and in social service work. Therefore, to overcome such weaknesses, a part of Virachara Tantra sadhana is practiced in the burial ground at midnight as per the system of Lord Shiva. It is essential for the dedicated worker to be fearless. That is why Baba introduced the system of kapalik sadhana in Ananda Marga. Once this sadhana was practiced throughout Bengal, Mithila, Maharastra, and Gujarat.

Bangey prakashita vidya, maithilley prabalikrita, kachit kachit maharastray, gurjarey pralayongata.

Tantra sadhana first started in Bengal; then it predominated in Mithila (a district of Bihar), then in Maharastra and then in Gujarat.

In the year 1958, Baba first taught kapalik sadhana to two sadhakas of Mithila, Jatashankar Jha and Harivallav Thakur. After that, they attended the Bhagalpur DMC. They had a spiritual glow that attracted everyone, and a young group of people became inspired to learn kapalik sadhana. I was affected by their charming personality and decided that after returning to Jamalpur I would request Baba to teach me kapalik sadhana. When I reached Jamalpur, I started thinking about going to the burial ground in the dead of night, on the darkest night of the month, the new-moon night, with a human skull. Was it possible for me to perform sadhana in that fearful environment? This created doubt in my mind, but I thought that it was better to die for Parama Purusha than encourage fear complex in my mind. I took the firm decision to do or die, and then I was ready to approach Baba for kapalik sadhana.

One evening Baba took me with him on his evening walk. We were alone that day. After reaching the Kali hill, Baba did not go to the tiger's grave. Instead he went to the opposite side. Baba said, "In this field there is a world-famous Tantra piitha. We will go there." I thought that he knew my inner feeling and thus was going to satisfy my desire. I knew that the guru always thinks of the welfare of his disciples. Therefore, I accompanied him without any questions. It was about 9:30, winter season, and the surrounding trees made it quite dark. The closest habitation was more than a mile away. It was an extremely frightening place. Baba suddenly stopped and pointed. "This is the famous Tantra piitha. In the pre-British period many tantrics achieved the spiritual goal of life meditating in this place. Now you will perform sadhana on that piitha. I am going back to the tiger's grave. If the dance of skeletons starts, do not be afraid." I told him that I was surrendering myself unto the feet of the Parama Purusha. I would obey his order and would not care what happened.

Baba left the place. Just after his departure my whole existence was flooded with spiritual vibrations. I sat for puja as per the rules. My mind was completely fearless and I felt a strong energy coursing through my physical body; I felt Baba's presence inside and outside me. Instead of feeling fear, I was laughing with the flow of blissful anandam. Innumerable skeletons started to dance around me. I thought it was a hallucination but I opened my eyes and found that they were there. Nevertheless the dancing skeletons could not create any adverse effect in my mind. I was not afraid at all. I was completely unaffected. I forgot myself and instead I was only aware of the presence of Baba Anandamurtijii. The play of Parama Purusha had cast a spell over me. After performing my puja I went to the tiger's grave where Baba was sitting. Other devotees were there too. After some time we all came back to town.

Earlier Baba had told me that whenever fear arose in my mind, I should remember him and I would realize that I was not alone. I realized that Baba was omnipresent and that he was always with me.

After performing sadhana in that Tantra piitha I experienced many miracles that filled me with inspiration and increased my attraction to Tantra sadhana. Baba said, "Those who are practicing vishesh yoga have no need of burial-ground sadhana. Vishesh yoga is the highest process of yoga. Burial-ground sadhana is a lesser process." I told Baba that all those lower or higher processes are under the control of the guru and that I was extremely eager to know the mystery behind them. I asked him to teach me the burial-ground Tantra sadhana and thus fulfil my desire. Baba remained silent. After two days, Baba told me that before teaching Tantra sadhana it is essential to test the ability of the devotee. "If the candidate passes the test, then his case can be considered." I told Baba that I was not able to pass his examination. "You are the controller of the universe," I said. "You know every nook and corner of every individual. That is why for you there is no need to test anyone. In future I shall not disturb you any further for burial-ground sadhana. I will leave everything in your hands. Whatever I need, it is your choice."

Less than a week later Baba told me to collect the materials needed for Tantra sadhana and accompany him the next night to the Tantra piitha so that he could teach me. I collected the materials, except one particular item that was difficult to find. Baba told me the about a place in Jamalpur where I could get it. I went there and found that somebody had kept it there for me. Now in possession of all the necessary items, I went to the Tantra piitha and Baba initiated me into kapalik sadhana.

Kong sambritta bodhi chitta palaka iti kapalika

He who always controls himself by intuitional power is kapalik.

Each night at midnight during my kapalik sadhana I encountered many siddhas, pishachas, gandharvas, vidyadharas, kinnaras and apsaras, as well as many other mysterious supramental and spiritual entities along with the presence of Mahasambhuti. However, I am not allowed to disclose these miraculous experiences.

Every day, when I would go to Baba's office during his tiffin hour, he would explain to me the different miraculous experiences of Tantra sadhana, and accordingly every night when I went for my practice I would experience what he had hitherto described. Baba told me that sometimes during sadhana the individual rhythm of one's bhairavi chakra would merge with the universal rhythm and at that time it was not possible to maintain one's separate existence. One night while I was performing my puja at the sadhana piitha, I heard the sound of a small bell and felt a thrilling spiritual sensation. My bhairavi chakra started to move like potter's wheel. The speed increased and merged with the universal wheel. I lost my separate existence and started revolving in the cosmos with the planets and stars. I became afraid and cried for Baba. Suddenly everything vanished and I regained my normal condition. I do not know how much time I had remained in that state of samadhi. It was 2:30 a.m.; the flow of anandam was vibrating throughout my existence.

By the grace of Baba, I experienced hundreds of such mysterious miracles during my puja over the next month. Through those experiences I came to understand that Baba's words had opened the sevenfold transcendental realm. His lessons are sufficient to acquire all occult powers. He is the Lord Incarnate, present in a physical body so that we can understand what is sadhana. Every sadhaka knows that the hidden root is the grace of the guru. Sadhana is nothing but:

*Mantra mulam guru vakyam, puja mulam guru padam
Dhyana mulam guru murti, moksha mulam guru kripa.*

The root of mantra is the word of the guru; the root of worship is the feet of the guru; the root of meditation is the form of the guru; the root of liberation is the grace of the guru.

58
Upward Flow

THE FOOD THAT we eat is converted into fluid, then into blood, flesh, fat, bone, marrow, and semen. This constant transformation is necessary in order to maintain our physical structure. After the formation of seminal fluid, one-third goes to nourish the subtle nerves and two-thirds to nourish the brain cells. This is necessary for the development of the brain, and a strong brain is necessary for both worldly and spiritual work. I advise everyone to take proper care of this invaluable property, the instrument that controls the activities of human beings along with their conscious and subconscious minds. The preservation of semen is needed for both spiritual and worldly work. Ingesting intoxicants hampers the ability of the mind to project itself and thus should be avoided. Through proper thought projection one selects one's path in life and one's day-to-day work goes smoothly. The mind leads us down the path to hell or the path to liberation. Do not allow little weaknesses to spoil your valuable human life. *Mano abo manusyanam karanam bandha makshaya.* "Remember that the mind is the cause of downfall as well as cause of liberation."

Through the conscious mind we are able to maintain objective adjustment and enter into the subjective spiritual world. The mind can thus cross the different phases of the realm of darkness and reach the goal of life — *turiya loka.* Taking intoxicants perverts the mind; it is a kind of suicide. One must follow certain rules of discipline that will help maintain purity of mind. This will help you to reach the ultimate goal in this present human life.

Earlier I said that the conversion of food passes through different stages. The body takes what it needs and the rest is eliminated in the form of stool, urine, sweat, etc. If one takes food regularly, the food of twenty-eight days creates twenty-nine days of semen. The excess semen can then be utilized for giving birth to a child through sexual intercourse. However, this should not be indulged in more than four times a month; otherwise it will cause harm in the physical, mental, and spiritual strata. If householders are able to live in a controlled way, they will be respected by society and treated as ideal men and women. When the entire population lives in this way, then heaven will come down on the earth and society will become divine.

Those who have dedicated their life to the service of society and left their personal life behind, following *naistic brahmacharya* (celibacy), should strictly follow the rules of monastic life, such as fasting four times a month during the two ekadashis, full moon, and new moon, taking sentient food, practicing meditation, maintaining purity of mind and serving society with the ideation that human beings are expressions of God. One should follow one's conscience and protect the purity of one's mind by intense love for Ista. If one is still not fully able to control oneself, he should offer his weaknesses to his Ista during the practice of vanarghyadana. The propensities of the mind must be ruled by the conscience. If one practices ashtanga yoga as per the direction of the great guru and meditates in a lonely place, then by the grace of the guru the kundalini, which is situated in svayambhulinga, will rise up and the semen will also rise up through the brahmani nadi, the passage that links the muladhara chakra to the sahasrara chakra. Only intense love for the guru can help us reach the culminating point, the seat of Paramashiva. One who attains this state is indeed fortunate. He has crossed the mortal world and entered the immortal world. One may think that it is extremely difficult but in practice it is a way of life. That path is pure and blissful. The flow of life, like the Phalgu River, becomes introspective. The expression on one's face becomes divine due to an endless, eternal, spontaneous flow of bliss.

In the beginning, when I faced these problems, I became disturbed. It was difficult to maintain the balance between the strict observance of yama and niyama and the attractions of the material world. I depended on Parama Purusha and performed my sadhana regularly. I kept all the propensities of the conscious mind under the custody and control of my conscience. However dream and sleep were beyond my control. I prayed to Baba in solitude with tears in my eyes to remove my internal clash. I decided to dedicate my life for social welfare and found that *naistic brahmacharya* was essential. I expressed my inner pain to my beloved Baba. It is impossible to be established in *naistic brahmacharya* without the grace of Parama Purusha. Fortunately Baba blessed me. After getting the blessings of Reverend Baba my mental clash was removed. Since that day, at the time of my puja, the movement of kulakundalini rises up with the flow of semen through the brahmani passage to the seat of Paramashiva. In spiritual science this is known as the maithuna yoga of Panchamakar. For the sadhaka who experiences this, worldly enjoyment is illusory.

> *Kulakundalini shakti dehinam dehadharini,*
> *Taya shivasya samyogah maithunam parikirtitam.*

> The kundalini force resides in *svayambhulinga*. When, by dint of sadhana, it rises up the sushumna channel to the culminating point of sahasrara chakra and becomes unified with Paramashiva, this union is known as *maithunam* yoga.

Without the grace of Baba one cannot achieve such a state.

> *Mahat kripayaeva bhagavat kripa lesadhva.*

> For devotee even a bit of grace of the sadguru is sufficient for liberation.

One who gets a fraction of the grace of Parama Purusha is fortunate; his life becomes fruitful. One can perform sadhana with extreme effort and undergo many hardships therein, but at the last stage he will not be able to open the gate to the storehouse of knowledge without the grace of Parama Purusha. No one can open the third eye without the guru's grace.

> *Mukam karoti vacalam paungam launghayate girim,*
> *Jat kripa tvamaham bondey paramananda madhavam.*

> O greatly delighted Madhava, by the your grace a mute person can give a lecture and a lame man can cross a mountain.

The sadhaka by his individual effort can reach the hiranamaya kosa, but to experience the Satya Dharma, guru's grace is a must. The gate of the Satya Dharma is closed by the hiranamaya kosa. To open this gate, the sadhaka must pray to the Lord with intense devotion, with tears in his eyes, and say:

Hiranmayena patrena satyasyapi hitam mukham
Tattvam pushanna pavrinu satya dharmaya dristaye

The access to absolute truth is closed by the door of hiranamaya kosa. Oh merciful Parama Purusha, I pray to you to kindly open the door of hiranamaya kosa and allow me to see the absolute truth.

59
Ashram Room

*A*FTER COMPLETING THE construction of the Jamalpur jagriti, one small room was reserved for Baba. The room was kept neat and clean, and a mattress, a sheet, and pillows were kept on the cot for Baba's use. Baba used it every Sunday morning and evening and on holidays. The same system that was followed in the previous ashram continued in the jagriti. Everyone knew that Baba would come there without fail on Sundays and holidays, so sadhakas from different parts of the country used to attend Baba's sittings on those days.

The devotees would encircle the cot before Baba arrived and create a heavenly atmosphere by singing bhajans and kirtans. The moment Baba reached the jagriti, his personal assistant would direct the devotees to leave the room. Then Baba would sit on the cot and complete his organizational work with his personal assistant. After that, the devotees were allowed back in the room and again they would start to sing spiritual songs. Occasionally Baba would reply to their unexpressed questions during his discourse, and through demonstrations he made them understand the practical side of sadhana. Baba also showed his supernatural powers to encourage the devotees.

Those who had personal contact with Baba accepted him as the Lord Incarnate, even if they were crude or materialistic by nature. Most of the sadhakas understood that Baba was a Yuga Purusha, the teacher of the age. The moment Baba sat with the devotees, the place appeared to be heaven. Most of the devotees merged their existence into Parama Purusha. In this connection a poet has said:

Baba rey ghiriya yato bhakata brindo oai
Ananday du haht tuley nachey
Tara Baba paney chahi roy,
Nayaneytey dhara boy,
Tara hari parimandaley virajey
Balo Baba Baba balo Baba Baba,
Baba Nam Kevalam, Kevalam Baba Nam.

Encircling Baba, the devotees sing songs, raising up their hands and dancing around him. At the same time they are looking toward Baba, overwhelmed with joy as tears roll down from their eyes. This periphery is known as *hariparimandal*. In this stage they are reciting the kirtan Baba Nam Kevalam.

When Baba sat in the *hariparimandal*, the circle of the lord, he was the image of spirituality. It was completely separate from his ordinary life. His physical expression, colour, etc. were otherworldly. His spiritual expressions vibrated the minds of the devotees, attracting them toward merger with the Supreme Entity. After completing the sitting, when Baba was leaving for his Rampur Colony quarters, the devotees would start weeping and run after him. The scene looked odd to outsiders. They did not understand the feelings of the devotees toward their Ista and might be tempted to make jokes about it. Therefore, as per order of the PA, no one was allowed to go out of the ashram gate. Only five people were permitted to accompany Baba to his railway quarters.

At one point, the room Baba used became dirty because the devotees would eat there and take rest there. I was hesitant to say anything to them because they were all devotees. When I went to Calcutta for some organizational work, I visited Dakshinashwar, where Ramakrishna Paramahansa had lived. There I came across the advice of Swami Vivekananda: "If someone wants to know the truth behind a man, he will not find it in his lectures and other grandiose expressions. Observe his activities when he is free or unoccupied. Watch his movements and all his small expressions and the reality will become visible, the true character of the man." There I was able to see the bed used by Ramakrishna Paramahansa; it was kept in a very nice way with proper sanctity.

After coming back to Jamalpur, I decided that my first duty was to maintain the purity of Baba's room. But first I had to get Baba's consent. I told him that Ramakrishna Paramahansa had left his physical body about one hundred years ago but still today his cot was scrupulously maintained; its dignity was preserved. I told Baba that he was the Lord Incarnate living among us, but we were not maintaining proper purity. I requested his permission to maintain the purity of the room that he was using in the jagriti. Baba said, "I also feel that the room is not properly maintained. It is the duty of you people; whatever facility you give me, I shall adjust with that." After hearing this, I took immediate measures. The room was cleaned and decorated and I instructed the ashram manager to keep it closed. It should only be opened when Baba came. After that the room was cleaned everyday and made fragrant with incense. Nobody was allowed to use it for any extraneous purpose.

60
Ravin-da Prasanga

RAVIN-DA WAS A railway clerk in the Jamalpur workshop who worked in Baba's office. He was an Ananda Margi and very good devotee of Baba. Every evening after office hours and performing puja, he used to go with Baba during his evening walk and carry a water bottle for Baba. When Baba sat on the tiger's grave with the devotees he used to drink the water brought by Ravin-da.

Ravin-da was a Bengali. His ancestors had come from Bengal long ago and settled in Jamalpur. Ravin-da was much older than me but his mind was just like a child's. He always consulted me for everything and asked my advice in spiritual, psychological, and family matters. We took advantage of his childlike mentality and made so many jokes with him. He was a very simple and very good man. Simple, honest, and divine men like Ravin-da were hard to find.

Day by day the work of Ananda Marga was increasing and no suitable worker was available to control and manage those works, so that pressure came on my head. Without considering the hour, devotees came to meet me and expected me to solve their problems. As this increased, my evening puja was badly disturbed; thus I requested the devotees not to meet me during my puja time. Any other time was okay. But this did not suit them. They were not at fault because most of the devotees at that time were government servants. They came to Jamalpur for a short period and, after completing their work, they went back. Considering their difficulties I also sacrificed my likes and dislikes for the greater good, but my evening puja was a deeply ingrained habit. If I was not able to perform it properly, I felt uneasy. Being a government servant, I went to the office at 6:30 a.m. Thus I could not do my vishesh yoga properly in the morning. Now, due to the pressure of organizational work, my evening puja was also being disturbed. Due to this an internal clash arose in my mind. Finally I brought the matter to Baba. I told him that between my railway service and my Ananda Marga work, I was not getting time to do my personal puja properly. I could not leave the work of Ananda Marga so I had decided to leave my railway service. After hearing what I had to say, Baba smiled and said that the time had not yet come to leave my service. "When the time comes I shall tell you."

After that I decided that at least I needed to do my evening puja properly, so I chalked out a plan. I was living alone in a railway quarter of Rampur Colony so in the evening I started locking the front door from the outside and entering through the back door before I began my puja. Nobody knew about it. If anybody came looking for me they saw the locked door and left. They started asking me where I was at that time. I told them that at 8:00 p.m. they would find me in my quarters.

In this way more than a month passed. Then suddenly one evening I was performing puja and someone started rattling the locked door and calling me. I thought that after some time he would leave but he continued to rattle the door without pause. I realized that whoever it was, they knew I was there. Finally I went to the door and opened it. It was Ravin-da. Before I could say anything, he said, "I am coming from the tiger's grave. Baba sent me to call you for some urgent work. He said that you were performing puja inside your quarters and that to avoid disturbances you had locked the door from the outside so that people would think you were not at home. Excuse me for disturbing you during your puja time but it was Baba's instructions." I laughed loudly and invited Ravin-da in. I asked him about the urgent work, he said that all he knew was that Baba required my presence at tiger's grave and that I should accompany him there.

Once we reached the grave I completed the necessary talk with Baba. Then I requested Baba and Ravin-da not to disclose my secret to anybody; otherwise I would be disturbed during my puja. I explained that being a government servant I could not perform my puja properly in morning and thus needed to employ that subterfuge in order to perform my puja properly in the evening. "It is my earnest request to both of you, please help me maintain my secret." Hearing this, they laughed loudly.

61
Kirnahar Dharma Maha Chakra

KIRNAHAR IS A developed village situated in West Bengal in the district of Birbhum. It lies on the metre-gauge railway line between Katwa and Ahamadpur. The DMC was organized by Acharya Sachinandanjii of Indas, where under his supervision a previous DMC had been held. His father-in-law lived in Kirnahar, which is three kilometres from Indas. Ac. Sachinandanjii, with the help of his relatives, reserved the Kirnahar High School for the DMC. It was a big building with a big compound. All arrangements were made there, including Baba's stay and that of the other guests. This was the third DMC in this district, which is in the centre of West Bengal. Devotees throughout West Bengal and from other parts of India attended. There was no difficulty reaching there since it was on the railway line.

Like the Amrah DMC, a kabigan was organized. Kabigan was very popular among the rural farmers and it was the best way to preach the ideology of Ananda Marga among the villagers. We called the same kabigan parties and directed them to challenge each other as they had at Amrah — Ananda Marga versus the old rituals. The leaders were Sri Shankar Mandal from Moddighi village and Sri Kishori Kora from the village of Dwarka. In simple village language they presented the ideology to the audience, showing them through this kabigan how it would be helpful to accept the spiritual cult and lead an ideal life. In this connection Lord Shiva has said:

Svagamaeh kalpitaestainca janam madvimukhan kuru
Maincha gopaya yena syad sristireshottarottara

General people according to their choice worship gods and goddesses, but unless and until they acquire intuitional knowledge they cannot attain salvation. They will take birth again and again in this cosmological order according to their past deeds.

We made them understand that Ananda Marga was a way of life. In kabigan one party puts musical questions to the other party. That party replies and then puts their own questions to the first party. The performance continues for ten to twelve hours. For example one may take the part of Sri Krishna and the other Gandhari, and the questions and answers between them may last for an hour. This system is properly known as *bol katakati*.

This kabigan had a powerful influence on the village people. They continued to repeat the rhythmic kabigan songs for months afterward as they worked in the fields. That is why Baba suggested kabigan for the prachar work of Ananda Marga among the villagers. Kabigan was an important way to communicate our ideology to the illiterate rural people.

A powerful zamindar family lived in this village. Earlier they used to keep elephants and horses at their residences as a sign of their aristocratic standing. Though the zamindary system was abolished, they did not give up their aristocratic ways. Their half-educated descendants were passing their days attending opera and indulging in different intoxicating habits. They came to know that only disciples were allowed to meet Baba and participate in the DMC. Those who were not disciples had to stay outside the fenced-off area, though they could listen to Baba's discourses through the loudspeakers. This diminished the prestige of the zamindar family. Before then no one had dared to do anything like this, so they tried to disturb our programme in different ways.

In the evening of the first day Baba was scheduled to give his Renaissance Universal discourse at 7:30. Baba was staying in one of the school rooms. During the time of his evening puja, someone threw a firecracker into his room. Hearing the sound, we rushed in and found the room dark and full of smoke. There were several more small explosions. In the meantime Baba was standing on his cot. We asked him if he were hurt but he was not. Baba said that the windows were open and somebody had thrown the firecrackers inside. Considering the situation we did not take any legal action. The zamindars were oppressors but their friends and followers obeyed them, and for the welfare of the Margis we decided to let it go; however, from that moment we became alert.

The evening programme continued as scheduled but we understood that the disturbance was due to the zamindars not having been invited or consulted. The situation was alarming. Many Margis from different parts of India had come to attend this DMC, so it was necessary to proceed with caution. We talked to some of their elders the next morning and took their grievances to Baba. After hearing what we had to say, Baba said that five persons from their side would be allowed to meet him. Accordingly we informed them that they could choose five people to meet Baba. After they met Baba, the situation calmed down but still they were not fully satisfied. We decided that Kirnahar would not be safe for the night programme, so instead of conducting DMC in the evening as usual, we decided to hold the programme at two p.m. and leave for Jamalpur by the four-thirty train. That way there was no chance that the incident would be repeated.

The new schedule was announced and we left for Jamalpur at 4:30.

62
Volunteer Social Service

*A*FTER RETURNING TO Jamalpur, I pondered the matter of Baba's security. The incident in Kirnahar was a lesson for us. Baba was not only a preceptor but also a social reformer. Those who encouraged superstition in order to maintain their livelihood and their reputation would not tolerate him. There was every chance that they would physically attack Baba. We had not considered this before and hence had not made arrangements for Baba's physical safety. After the Kirnahar incident we came to realize the necessity of Baba's physical protection. Before doing anything I asked Baba what sorts of security arrangements should be made for the coming DMC. Baba replied that the decision of the Margis would be his decision.

I then called a meeting of senior, educated, and committed devotees to discuss Baba's security. In that meeting it was decided that we would organize a cadre of young devotees and train them to provide security for Baba and for DMC programmes in general. They were to work under my command with proper discipline. A few volunteers would be deputed as Baba's bodyguards. They would look after all matters related to Baba's personal security, such as checking his food and accompanying him at the time of his morning and evening walks. These volunteers would also look after the comfort and security of the devotees who attended the DMCs and guide them in a proper way. This new wing of the organization was named Volunteer Social Service (VSS).

The next DMC was held at Ranchi and beforehand we decided that VSS would be officially inaugurated by Baba at the DMC. We took permission from Baba and organized the programme, including a band and fireworks, and Baba inaugurated VSS. Since then VSS has been working for Baba's security, as well as for the all-round safety and needs of the devotees attending DMC. In conjunction with the Ranchi DMC we organized a one-week VSS camp. Around fifty devotees attended. During the camp, the attendees were trained in different aspects of social service, such as how to serve the society during natural calamities and wartime, fire-fighting, etc.

Afterward such camps were organized in different parts of India and abroad. Then we held a central VSS camp at Ranchi. Volunteers joined from throughout India. I was the commander-in-chief. Many different types of training were given, including how to safeguard the civilian population during wartime bombing campaigns. We also performed PT parade and decided that at such times VSS would be known as Vishva Shanti Sena (the army of universal peace). Baba visited the camp and took our salute as our supreme commander. He also gave a message:

> As a soldier you must not search for worldly pleasure or comfort.
> Be ready for all sorts of sufferings. Let sufferings be your asset. Suffering will help you in establishing the sadvipra samaj.
> You must not argue, you must not think twice. You should do or die.
> I don't want to see the face of a defeated son in flesh and blood.
> Yours affectionately, Baba

After the Ranchi camp, we began requiring a gate-pass for those who wished to attend DMC. Unrestricted meetings of devotees with Baba were no longer permitted — both at home and on tour security volunteers accompanied him — and a few Margis expressed their displeasure with the new arrangements, but eventually everyone understood that the new system was essential for Baba's security.

One may say that the maker of the age, Parama Purusha, by his thought projection, was responsible for the creation, preservation, and destruction of the universe, but despite being the controller of the creation, he kept himself hidden behind the curtain, watching all its activities. Nobody can hide any thought or action from him. Such a great personality is providing security to the entire universe and we are providing security for him? How ridiculous was this? Once a rishi said, "Nothing is necessary for him because the entire universe is his homeland. Parama Prakriti is his housewife. Whatever he wants, she prepares then and there." There is nothing in this universe that anyone can give him. Still he has said that when his devotees offer anything with devotion he gets pleasure. Our effort to provide security for him was nothing but an effort to give him pleasure. To give pleasure to Parama Purusha is the sadhana of the devotees.

I remember one story: A student lived in a hostel and his entire expenditure was paid by his father. His father liked apples very much and so, during the summer vacation, when the student was going home, he purchased some apples for him. When the student reached home with the apples, his father was very happy. He told his neighbours about it with pleasure, telling them that his son loved him very much, that he always remembered what he liked. However the money the son used to buy the apples was actually his father's money.

Similarly, Parama Purusha gave us the capability to provide him with security and a comfortable life, and like that worldly father this gave him pleasure. So we can say worship of God is nothing but to try to give pleasure to Parama Purusha. Baba also said that your sadhana is to please Parama Purusha. Our mind is given to us by Parama Purusha. We take work from this mind and through it we enjoy happiness and face trials and tribulations. Only through spiritual sadhana is it possible for a human being to surrender his mind to him. A sage has said:

Ratnákarastavagrham grhińii ca padmá
Deyam kimapi bhavate puruśottamáya
Ábhiiravámanayanápahrtamánasáya
Dattam manah yadupate tvamidam grháńa

O Parama Purusha, the universe is your homeland and Parama Prakriti (the operative principal) is your virtuous housewife. Beyond that there is nothing we can offer you. O Lord, I remember one thing that is mine — you have given me my mind. Thus, as an honorarium to the preceptor, I surrender to you my mind. Kindly accept my cordial offer and free me from all bondages.

63
The Mystery of Birth

*B*ABA HAD BEEN discussing about the mystery of the birth of different devotees over the course of a few days. Through demonstrations he showed the past lives of many of them. Baba would touch someone's forehead and direct him to see the past life of another person. He showed that one person had been a bird of prey, a kite, in his past life. As a kite he was flying in the desert with a piece of bread in his mouth. The piece of bread fell near a sadhu who had not eaten for several days and the bread saved his life. He blessed the kite wholeheartedly and as a result in the next life the kite got a human body and had the chance to perform spiritual practice under the guidance of Parama Purusha. After the demonstration was over, Baba asked that person, "Please tell us, do you sometimes think about flying in the sky?"

"Yes, Baba," he said.

In the same way Baba showed us the past life of another young boy who had been a wild pig in the jungle. Once in Jamalpur Baba was passing near a place where a pig was being roasted alive. The pig was crying loudly and Baba's heart was touched by its cries. As a result, he was reborn as a human being and became a good devotee of Baba, sitting in front of him at that moment (I shall not disclose his name because he has dedicated his life for the welfare of the society and become a respected avadhuta of Ananda Marga). Baba asked him, "When you are passing near the jungle, do you sometimes feel a sudden desire to enter it?" "Yes, Baba," he said. Hearing this, the assembled devotees laughed loudly.

After witnessing these things, I became curious to know about my own past lives. I was with Baba from the beginning, but Baba had not told me a single word about my past lives, apart from one sentence at the time of my first darshan — that I had come age after age to do social work with him, that our relation had spanned several ages. At that time he had said, "You are not able to recollect this, but I can." But he had said nothing more in this regard and a strong tendency had grown in my mind to know the mystery of my past lives. If by dint of sadhana it was possible to know thus, then hard sadhana was needed. This had caused a commotion in my mind but I could not disclose it to anybody. Nevertheless, all-knowing Baba was watching my thoughts. I knew that I could not even think without his knowledge.

One evening I went to my Tantra piitha to perform my evening puja, thinking that when Baba came to the tiger's grave I would go and sit with him. It was a dark night with a clear sky. As I sat for my puja in that Maha Tantrapiitha, the thought projection in my mind reached my innermost self, revealing a stellar region with delightful snow-white light throughout the vast firmament. I found that I was an inhabitant of that stellar region. Many other brilliantly lit beings were also living in that vast firmament. The entire stellar world was controlled by the Old Purusha (Purusha Purana). Everybody living there was his obedient servant. I saw myself in a particular place always doing puja. Suddenly that Old Purusha called me. There was a rule that when he called anybody, they should appear before him in a fearless military uniform. I so appeared and then he directed me to go to earth. "To command and guide you, all arrangements have been made. Go there and understand your duty from the Supreme Commander who has already reached there." I prostrated and took his blessing, and then left to fulfil my allotted duties.

After completing my puja, I remained there for some time. When I recovered my normal state of mind, I went to the tiger's grave where Baba was sitting. Baba started to say something about *jiivakoti, ishvarkoti* and *mahapurushakoti*. It was not difficult for me to understand that Baba's discussion was related to my puja. He said that among you people a *mahapurushakoti* sadhaka exists. His activities and expressions are like a Mahapurusha but he does not know he is a Mahapurusha, such as Swami Vivekananda. Ramakrisna Paramahamsa Deva knew that he was a Mahapurusha but Swami Vivekananda did not know he was a Mahapurusha. After hearing this, I asked Baba if that was why Ramakrisna Paramahansajii had said, "Naren is not a man of this world; he has come as a human being from a stellar region and when he knows it, not a single moment longer will he stay here." Baba said it was correct.

I prayed to Baba to say something more about *jiivakoti, ishvarkoti* and *mahapurushakoti*. Baba explained that in human society those householders who lead a family life while keeping absolute faith in Parama Purusha come within the periphery of *jiivakoti*. The *ishvarakoti* man leaves his personal life and dedicates himself to the welfare of the society, and with the help of the *jiivakotis* they build a nice society. Society is like a derailed train and together they put the train back on the track. *Jiivakoti* alone does not have the strength to put a derailed train back on the right track. They must cooperate with *ishvarakoti* for this work, while *ishvarakoti* works under the command of the *mahapurushakoti*. Then the society can be set right. The moment the work is finished, the *mahapurushakoti* departs. His work is completed on this planet for ages to come. Just before his departure, he will come to know what his sadhana was for and why he came to this planet. He will get all the answers. Ultimately he will know his true identity and he will be eager to return to the stellar region where he was ensconced in his spiritual practices.

64
Antaratma: An event of 1956

During one darshan, Baba said that Parama Purusha is watching every action and thought of everybody. Nobody can conceal anything from him. The moment any thought arises in the mind, he knows it. That is why he is known as Antaratma, the All-knowing Inner Spirit. Lord Buddha has said:

> *No antarikhsey no samuddamajhey, no pabbatanam bibaram pravisha,*
> *No bijjati so jagatippya desha jattatitha monchajja papakamma*

> While doing any sinful work you cannot hide yourself anywhere in this universe. If you hide in the sky, under the deep ocean, in the mountain cave, or any other place in the universe, two eyes are watching you. That is why Parama Purusha is known as the Witnessing Entity. Sitting within the heart of every living creature he witnesses each and every one of their actions.

If one remains in a secluded place, such as the ocean, a secret cave in the mountains, or in the countryside, still one cannot hide any thought from Parama Purusha. When this discussion was going on, Baba from time to time pointed out the past sins of some of the devotees, giving the time, place, and actions. Many of them thought that no one knew their sins. Now they realized that the past, present, and future could not be hidden from Baba. The smiling face of Kalyanasundaram Baba attracted the devotees and at the same time he observed the inner core of the heart of every individual.

Baba said, "You are all the children of Parama Purusha; therefore it is my duty to clear the dirt from my devotees." He also said, "How can I throw you out? There is no place outside Parama Purusha." After that, he told a sadhaka to see the mental light of one offender. It was polluted but the holy touch of Baba made him pure and fit for spiritual sadhana. The sadhakas felt a heavy load of sin removed from their heads. Kabiguru Rabindranath Tagore has said:

> *Antara glani shansaya bhar paloko felitey holo akakar*
> *Apanar majhey swarupa tomar dekhi barey jena pai.*
>
> When Parama Purusha glances toward a devotee, the devotee's internal mortification and uncertainty of mind are removed and the devotee visualizes the presence of Parama Purusha within himself.

After one or two bhajans, Baba left the ashram for his quarters. As per his habit, he did namaskar to everybody with folded hands, and again at the time of entering his quarters he did namaskar to the devotees that had accompanied him. I could not accept this. Sadguru is our Ista. Why should he do namaskar with folded hands to his disciples? One day, I asked him about it. Baba said, "The same Parama Purusha exists in all the persons as Antaratma, and he is worshipped and saluted by all. Therefore do not give anyone the chance to salute you first. Salute him first." All the guru's actions are lessons.

Whenever I heard anyone talk of spiritual miracles, I would not be satisfied until I experienced it myself. A question arose in my mind: how is Parama Purusha present within me? It was difficult to feel that presence. Age after age, munis and rishis have performed puja to have the darshan of the Lord. But Baba made this so commonplace that with a little effort for Parama Purusha one could have this experience. Baba gave the time, place, and nature of the sins that we had committed. Many of those incidents we had forgotten, but Baba made us remember. Really it surprised me, the mysterious nature of the universe.

Parama Purusha and his creation are inseparable from each other. After hearing Baba's words, my curiosity to know how Parama Purusha lived within me increased, to know how he knew all my actions and thoughts. I could not tell this to Baba and this caused me much pain and mental clash. But Omniscient Baba never disappoints his devotees. My firm determination always resulted in his grace. The same happened this time.

That day after evening puja I felt some spiritual intoxication. I had felt this sort of intoxication many times before, so I was not surprised. On this occasion I felt that my entire existence was controlled by another entity. I had no freedom at all. After completing my puja, I felt a dual existence within me — me and my Ista. After some time, my "I" feeling merged with my Ista and a singular entity from head to foot existed in my physical body. There was no place for the existence of an individual "I" feeling, only the witnessing entity that witnessed that state.

The next day I went to the office as usual but the feeling gradually increased. My co-workers were used to seeing my different spiritual feelings and abnormalities. They told me that I looked a little abnormal and asked if something had happened to me? I did not say anything. The Lord with his smiling face was living within me, filling me with a limitless flow of anandam. I was moving with the feeling of the witnessing entity. Everything was sweet, everybody was good, and all were affectionate, love for all being the state of anandam. There was no expression of propensities. There were no ups and downs. It was a state of balanced, eternal blessedness. I lost my ability to adjust with the world. I had to take the help of a friend to return to my residence. It was not even possible for me to move unaided. For the next three days I could not go to the office. I remembered something Baba had said: "One who by dint of sadhana merges with Parama Purusha becomes Brahma. At that time he feels that the whole creation is his thought projection. Nothing is outside him in that state, and even if he killed someone it would not be a sin. But in this state he cannot kill anybody, since for him everything is his loving creation."

After one week in this state I told Baba that I was indeed fortunate that his unbounded grace was always with me. Baba did not allow me to continue. "You want to say that you have lost your ability to adjust with the world," he said. "This will not be permitted because a lot of worldly work is left for you. Parama Purusha will help you to lead a normal life." The next day I became normal and returned to the office. I realized that sadhana is completely dependent on the guru.

65
Organization

THE PRACHAR ACTIVITIES of Ananda Marga soon spread throughout North India. The number of enthusiastic Margis increased. Many educated young men came to Jamalpur from different parts of India for Baba's darshan, attracted by the philosophy, the scientific spiritual cult, and Ananda Marga's fight against superstition. There were not enough acharyas and tattvikas to meet the demand. On the other hand, the general secretary did not like this rapid expansion because as a railway employee with limited free time it was becoming difficult for him to control the organization's activities.

Seeing the attitude of the general secretary and the condition of the organization, Baba privately told me, "See here, the general secretary is not interested in prachar. He wants to make it a club. The way prachar is going, it will take thousands of years to spread the ideology throughout the world. Taking this into account, I have decided to give you a separate responsibility. I want you to build up an independent organization through which prachar work can be expedited. That way the structural part of the organization can be solidified. Take this responsibility, start your work, and my blessings will be with you."

Up to then I had always told Baba that unless and until I developed firm faith through spiritual realization it would not be possible for me to assume any great responsibility. The moment I developed such faith, then he and he alone would exist for me on this earth — I would be totally his. Baba did everything to develop my faith, and on that day I was fortunate that he chose me as his faithful servant and gave me the responsibility to build up the organization.

That evening, I was alone with Baba on the walk to the field. When we reached the church on Peach Road, Baba stopped and said, "If I die today, how many people will have come to know our ideology?" Baba fell silent and looked at me. I asked Baba what I should do. "Should I take the whole responsibility?" Baba said, "All right, take the responsibility independently. Go ahead and do your work from today. I shall be expressed through you. You will never feel that you are alone."

After that I began using VSS to build up the structural side of the organization and fulfil the mission Baba had given me. I began organizing VSS camps and used them to train young Margis in the philosophy and social service, helping them to develop intense love for Ista, regularity in their sadhana, spiritual discipline, and devotion to duty. In the beginning there was no one to assist me. I used my salary to finance the work. Baba did not give me any instructions. My only resources were his blessings. And within a short period of time these programmes began to have a big influence among the educated young sadhakas.

Due to the pressure of work, I asked Baba to give me permission to leave my railway service. Baba said, "The time has not yet come to leave your service. When the time comes I shall let you know." Thereafter I started my work to educate the devotees, beginning in Jamalpur. Baba taught a higher tattvika class in Jamalpur, which was published as *Idea and Ideology*. I attended that class and obtained some knowledge. Based on Baba's classes, I created a course for the newcomers in the VSS camps. After giving them the proper training, they took responsibility for their concerning areas.

Within a short period of time, we got a tremendous response from the field. Many people wanted to take initiation. As a result, the demand for acharyas increased. Local acharyas were not able to give enough time due to their family responsibilities, so I asked those responsible for the different areas to send me the names of brave sadhakas with sacrificing spirit who were attentive to their sadhana and good looking, so that they could come to Jamalpur for training. Those whom I considered fit for kapalik sadhana, I recommended to Baba for initiation. After kapalik initiation, I gave them responsibility for prachar work in their respective areas.

Once this system was developed, it was not possible for me to oversee everything that was going on, so I distributed the supervisory work among the local acharyas who had attended the training classes. From Krishnagar there was Ac. Sukhenjii, from Birbhum Ac. Sachinandanjii, from Balurghat Ac. Drubanaranyanjii, from Muzaffarpur Ac. Gangasaranjii, from Arah District Ac. Ramashrayjii, from Bhagalpur Ac. Harendrajii, from Ranchi acharyas Kedarjii and Kshitishjii, from Gorakhpur acharyas Pratapadityajii and Raghunathjii, from Saharsa Ac. Natkal Kedarjii, from Chaibansa Ac. Rajmohanjii, from Tata Ac. Chandradevjii, from Bolia Ac. Summangaljii, from Darbhanga Shyamanandalaljii, from Begusarai Ac. Ramtanukjii, etc.

These activities were going on without the knowledge and against the will of the general secretary, therefore he became annoyed. He expressed his anger by rough behaviour, even against the persons who came to

Jamalpur for training. Some of them he sent home without my knowledge. With the help of some householder acharyas who were loyal to him, he started to combat my activities. Amusingly they reported my activities to Baba. Baba told me privately in his office, "The GS and his group are annoyed with your work, but I am happy with it. Your work is going on nicely. Go ahead accordingly; I am with you. But this afternoon come to the jagriti. I will scold you in front of them to make them happy."

After thinking over the matter, I directed the acharyas mentioned above not to send the trainees to Jamalpur. Instead I told them to organize training camps in their areas. I would go and give the classes after approving the dates of the programmes. Accordingly, I fixed a schedule and went to teach classes at the different camps. After the camp was over, I would instruct the new volunteers in their duties and responsibilities. From that time forward they would be known as volunteers and dharma pracharakas, ideal and well-disciplined sadhakas. Now they were prepared to establish our ideology and to fight against all sorts of social superstitions. Earlier Baba had said in his vanii:

> A sadhaka is verily a soldier. The pricks of thorns on the difficult path signify one's progress. The collective welfare of the universe is the crowning glory of one's victory. (Ananda Purnima 1956)

Through everyone's concerted efforts, the demand for initiation continued to increase. I called together the educated youths, those who had no family liabilities, and put each of them in charge of a block or panchayat. The work continued to increase — local acharyas were always giving initiations. At the same time, it was not possible for me to attend each and every training camp. Thus I decided to hold four camps in the four parts of the country and give them the name of central camps. I attended all four central camps and gave different types of classes. I also supervised the programme and conducted the activities as commander-in-chief so that no one would face any inconvenience. The young sadhakas who took part were very enthusiastic. Those who were not able to attend were disappointed. The General Margis were also enthusiastic and cooperative. They were happy to supply yogurt, beaten rice, milk, vegetables, dal, and other materials required for the camp kitchen. In fact, there was competition among the surrounding units to supply those things. Thus we had no expenditure other than train fare. Later on, these camps took the shape of a festival for the General Margis.

Gradually the foundation of a structural organization took shape. Ac. Lalan joined me in this work, but within a short period of time he started to fight for power. Later on, he became the cause of many problems in the organization and he renounced his membership in VSS and eventually left Ananda Marga. Envy is a dangerous foe. Up until then I had an indirect struggle with GS. Now Lalanjii joined forces with him and openly started to challenge me. My difficulties increased and I even became concerned that they might try to liquidate me. "Whom the Lord saves none can kill." I had surrendered unto the feet of the Lord; therefore I knew I was safe by his grace. Baba only said, "You are bearing a great organizational responsibility; therefore you should not take any food offered by anyone."

66
Restoration of Life

*I*N ORDER TO improve the VSS camps, I started to teach the volunteers how to drive. I purchased a motorcycle and two second-hand Jeeps for training purposes. In case of natural calamities, the volunteers would be able to reach the scene without any delay. This became part of the VSS training in the camps.

It was decided that the central camp would be held twice a year. Vehicle training would be given in those central camps under my supervision as the commander-in-chief of the volunteers.

Since it was not possible to teach everyone how to drive during the camp, many of them came to Jamalpur to learn. Once, three volunteers came to Jamalpur to learn to drive the Jeep: Sri Lalan Singh, Sri Om Prakash, and Sri Ramtanukjii. After taking permission from me, they took the two Jeeps and went to the ring road outside the town.

Ramtanukjii was driving one of the Jeeps. Suddenly an old woman stepped in front of the vehicle. In an effort to avoid her he lost control of the Jeep. It slammed into a tree and flipped over, leaving Ramtanukjii unconscious. The volunteers in the other Jeep rushed him to the railway hospital.

Ramtanuk's in-laws lived in Jamalpur. When they heard the news they rushed to the hospital and found him in a coma. They waited for a long time beside his bed but he did not recover consciousness. In the meantime I reached the hospital and found everybody weeping. They requested me to bring Baba to the hospital. After seeing his condition and learning the details of what had happened, I left the hospital and went to see Baba at the office. After hearing the situation, Baba said, "If Ramtanukjii has not recovered consciousness within seventy-two hours, I will go to the hospital to see him." I conveyed Baba's message to his relatives and every day after office hours I went to see him in the hospital. During the next three days there was no change. When I told Baba this, he told me that at 5:00 p.m. the seventy-two hours would be up so we should go to the hospital. Baba sent me to inform his relatives of his visit and then to come back so I could accompany him.

As per Baba's direction, I informed them and then waited at gate number three for Baba. At 5:00 p.m. Baba arrived at the gate and we started walking toward the hospital, a ten-minute walk. When Baba reached the hospital, Ramtanuk's relatives were weeping. They fell down at Baba's feet and begged for Ramtanukjii's life. All his relatives were Margis.

Baba went to Ramtanukjii's bedside. He touched his forehead and called his name in a very sweet voice, "Ramtanuk." Ramtanuk opened his eyes as if he were coming out of a sound sleep. The first sound out of his mouth was, "Baba!" Then Baba embraced him. From that moment his senses returned completely. After seventy-two hours of weeping, his family laughed, seeing the miraculous greatness of Baba.

Ramtanukjii was a lawyer by occupation and was nearing thirty years of age. After this incident, he renounced his personal comforts and dedicated his life to Baba's mission. He became the legal secretary of Ananda Marga, and thereafter he looked after all the legal cases of the organization. When the government of India declared a state of emergency, banned Ananda Marga, and arrested many of us, including Baba, Ramtanukjii, at his own personal risk and with the help of several renowned barristers, conducted the historic legal fight against the cases lodged against Ananda Marga by the CBI. Such a householder devotee is rarely found.

67
Gaonoha and Dumka Central VSS Camps

IN THE MONTH of December, I organized two big central camps at Gaonoha and Dumka. Gaonoha is situated at the extreme north of Bihar, near Nepal Tarai, but the camp was held in a jungle area of Nepal, just over the Bihar border. Dumka is situated in southeast Bihar, near the Bihar–Bengal border. The Dumka camp was held on the bank of the river Mayurakshi, where a large aboriginal fair was held each year at the foot of Hijla hill. That fair is popularly known as the Hijla fair.

In order to reach Gaonoha, one can go by train from Jamalpur to Muzaffarpur, then to Motihari, Bethia, and Narkatiaganj. From Narkatiaganj there is a branch line up to Viknatori, the last railway line in that part of India. From there it was a two-mile walk to reach the camp site in the Tarai jungle of Nepal. It was a remarkable camp. Many royal Bengal tigers lived in that jungle. On the opposite side of the jungle, some Americans had organized a camp to hunt tigers. Our side of the jungle became dangerous, due to the prospect of wild animals fleeing in our direction. Some volunteers brought some guns with them but still the night was terrible. Two days earlier a tiger snatched a buffalo calf from a nearby village and two days before that at a distance of four furlongs from our camp a large buffalo was killed by a tiger. The half-eaten body of the buffalo was still lying there, and each night the tiger came to eat. In this area the inhabitants are neither Nepali nor Hindustani. They are known as the Tharu community. Whenever they went outside their villages they would carry a machete for self defence. Fortunately there were no man-eating tigers in that area. From time to time they would kill domestic animals from the villages.

We pitched our tents in a circle and due to the excessive cold we kept a fire burning at all times in the centre. There were many uprooted and dried trees in the jungle that the volunteers collected for firewood and for cooking.

The Margis from Bethia and Narkatiaganj brought us beaten rice, molasses, yogurt, rice, vegetables, and other necessities. Our devotees in that area were very simple, enthusiastic, and religious-minded. Throughout the Betiah subdivision of Bihar the land is very fertile and crops grow in sufficient quantity. Paddy and sugar cane are the main crops. In every block there was a sugar factory and fruit gardens. The people ate rice both at noon and at night, as in Bengal.

We posted two volunteers with guns as sentries to watch the camp. They were relieved every two hours. If anybody had to go outside the circle of tents in the night to pass urine, a sentry would accompany them. Had they gone alone they could have fallen prey to a tiger. A few volunteers asked me for permission to go hunting in the jungle. This perturbed me. Unbeknownst to me, Ac. Ganga Saran of Muzaffarpur had brought some bullets and flashlights for that purpose.. But how could I give permission to inexperienced people to go hunting in such a dangerous jungle? I was surprised by their audacity. If any untoward incident occurred, it would fall on my head. When I did not give them permission they were offended. A few volunteers grouped together to try to convince me. After making them aware of the seriousness of the situation, I took a personal bond from them and gave them permission to go hunting. If anything happened they would be responsible.

The reason I was against them hunting was because when we arrived there most of the volunteers went to visit a Maha Tantra piitha named Mahayoginsthan about two miles from our camp. Maharishi Vashistha had performed Tantra sadhana there. Most of the volunteers were kapaliks and therefore they expressed their desire to visit that place. I was also eager to go. We went in the afternoon but the visit was not compulsory. In the end everyone wanted to go, so I deputed some local volunteers to remain at the camp and cook. They brought four guns along. Our journey was very pleasurable. When we reached Mahayoginsthan we found that it was encircled by jungle. In the middle was a Shiva temple. After reaching the temple verandah, we entered the inner room. Inside we found a door closed off by bricks. This was a mystery we could not solve.

The atmosphere was well suited for spiritual sadhana. The temple was surrounded by jungle and it was on a small hill with a gentle stream flowing through it. Outside the jungle was a small village. The spiritual vibration of the temple attracted our minds. We sat for sadhana and came to understand the glory of the place where the Mahapurusha Vashistha had performed sadhana.

At a distance of two furlongs from Mahayoginsthan the dense forest started. After visiting the temple, we decided to return by taking a small path through that forest. I had no objection. As we started to proceed along the path, Doctor Bhubaneshwarijii counselled us that it would be better not to pass through the deep jungle at that late hour. He recommended going by the path we had taken to get there. But before I could reply, others suppressed him by making a joke. We continued on the same path but after half an hour it disappeared. The sun was preparing to set and darkness was falling. We were not sure in which direction to proceed. Bhubaneshwarijii commented, "Dadajii, no one gave any importance to my suggestion and now we are facing great difficulty." Several volunteers continued onward and the rest followed but after some time we stopped, stupefied. Everyone was silent. Those who had guns loaded them. Somebody noticed that the left side of the jungle was sparser and suggested we go in that direction. We followed his advice and came upon a hill with a river running past it. By the time we reached the river, it was completely dark. We sat in a circle on the sand and decided to camp there for the night. Four men remained on sentry duty with guns and torches.

After one hour we heard the sound of voices from a long distance. It sounded like a group on their way somewhere. We cried out loudly and they responded, eventually making their way to us. We came to know that they were living in the village near our camp and had gone to the jungle to collect wood. They cordially offered to guide us to our camp. By the grace of Baba we reached there safely.

Due to that experience I was not comfortable with the idea of anyone going hunting. Nevertheless five persons, each having a gun, went to the jungle for hunting around three a.m. Though they had assumed responsibility, I was still anxious for their safe return. If anything happened I would not be totally free from responsibility, so I prayed to Baba for their safe return.

By three p.m. they had still not come back and I became very perturbed. We thought that they might have taken shelter in a tree out of fear, or else were moving aimlessly in the jungle without food. We were very anxious. Finally they straggled back one by one into the camp like storm-lashed crows. I told the others not to disturb them because they were very tired. "Let them eat and rest and in the evening instead of class we will listen to their story."

That evening they told us what had happened. As they entered the deep jungle, thinking to hunt tigers and lions, they reached a place where they were not able to go further due to the tangled brush and huge trees. The jungle there was so dense that no sun rays could reach. Then they heard a sound of a majestic four-footed animal coming toward them. In that thorny jungle it could be nothing other than a tiger. They loaded their guns and took up a position with their backs against a tree as they prepared to face the coming danger. The sound came nearer and nearer, and then with fearful eyes they saw a majestic tigress passing by with two cubs. She wasn't looking around. She was just moving on toward her destination. The gigantic body and free movement gave her a terrible aspect, and all lost their courage. Rather than thinking about killing the tigress, all they could think about was how to save themselves if the tigress looked at them. Gangajii was very humorous. He said, "Dadajii, there are no words to express our mental condition. We were huddled together, knowing that if the tigress looked at us and roared we would drop our guns and soil our pants."

After the tigress passed they agreed that the jungle was not safe and decided to return but to find their way back from the deep jungle was not so easy. They became confused and ended up going around in circles. It had taken them three hours to get there but in six hours they had yet to find the way back. They wandered aimlessly for another two hours until they heard the sound of chopping wood. They reached the woodcutters and with their help they reached our camp.

A week after completing the Gaonoha camp, I started for Dumka. There we held another one-week central camp by the banks of the Mayurakshi River for the volunteers of southern Bihar and West Bengal. After completing both camps I assigned duties to the volunteers and returned to Jamalpur.

68
Piithasthan

*B*ACK IN JAMALPUR, I returned to my job in the railway office and continued to attend to my Ananda Marga work. As usual I would meet Baba in his office at the tiffin hour. I told Baba about our visit to Mahayoginsthan. I also told him that even after thousands of years we could still feel the spiritual vibrations in that place. Baba told me many details about the Mahayoginsthan. He said, "That is why I told you people that after performing your kapalik puja in the burial ground, you should leave the puja piitha alive. As a result the spiritual vibration of that piitha will remain. If you perform sadhana in a particular place regularly, that place becomes spiritually vibrated. The spiritual wave there will help other sadhakas to concentrate their minds."

Baba also said, "In your home district of Birbhum there are still a few Maha Tantra piithas. Among them, Tarapiitha, Baksheshwar, and

Phullara are remarkable. About four thousand years ago Maharishi Vashistha went to China and learned Chinachari Tantra there; then he came to Tarapiitha and established the Panchamundi Asana. From that period on, one Mahapurusha created another Mahapurusha and then left his physical body. This process continued up until the Mahapurusha Bamakhepa who died in 1918. He did not create a Mahapurusha to succeed him. People have been doing sadhana in that piitha for four thousand years and becoming Mahapurusha. That is why this piitha is a Maha Tantra piitha.

"There is a similar piitha in Baksheshwar, established by Ashtavakra Muni. Many spiritualists performed kapalik sadhana on that piitha and attended the supreme goal of life. This piitha also has an attractive hot spring. There are three small springs with hot water at different degrees. The water is alkaline and people who suffer from acidity get relief by drinking that water. For such travellers there was a dharmashala there so that patients who wished to stay for extended periods of time could have accommodations. If a patient suffering from acidity drinks this water over an extended period of time they will be cured of the disease.

"The third Maha Tantra piitha is Phullara. It is situated at Labpur in the district of Birbhum. Sri Chaitanya Mahaprabhu performed Tantra sadhana on that piitha and became a Siddha Purusha."

I told Baba that my family members went to Phullara piitha to shave their children's heads when they reached five years of age and perform the worship of Devi Phullara. Baba said, "Nanur and Sainthia (Nandeshwari Devi) in Birbhum District also had piithas. It is said that there are fifty-one Tantra piithas throughout India. Among those, five are in Birbhum District. This district was once the land of Virachari Tantra, which is why it is known as Birbhum."

After hearing these stories, I had a strong desire to perform kapalik sadhana on those piithas. I asked Baba about my desire. "Yes," he said, "you can do it, but if the piithas are cemented how will you make the Bhairavi Chakra?" He further explained the process how to make a Bhairavi Chakra. He said that before going there to perform puja, if your own Tantra piitha is left alive, then you should withdraw that power as per system; then wherever you go, you will do again everything as the prescribed rules and perform puja there."

69
Phullara Piitha

*A*FTER GETTING PERMISSION from Baba, I did not want to wait. It was the dark fortnight. I took leave from the office, and taking the kapalik puja apparatus, I left Jamalpur for my village home. I stayed there for two days and on the third day in the evening I started for Phullara Piitha. It was a solitary area about five kilometres from my home. There was no habitation within half a mile of it. Near the piitha was a unpaved road that connected Labpur to the village of Bakul, The small Kuya River was one mile to the south of the piitha. There were two or three rooms near the piitha where the priests and other devotees could stay. There was also a small pond on the south side with many trees that give it the appearance of a jungle. Beyond this there was a large field where every year a big two-week fair was held on the full moon of Maghi.

After sunset, the darkness gave the area a grave aspect. In the night no one ventures out except for the occasional sadhu who stays in the dharmashala. The Labpur narrow-gauge railway station lies about one mile from the temple, on the Ahamadpur-Katwa line. Both sides are connected with the broad-gauge line that goes to Calcutta.

As per the rules, kapalik sadhana must be performed between midnight and three a.m. The temple that night was deserted. Being the dark fortnight everything was plunged in deep darkness. In the evening I went to the fair ground to perform my evening puja. Then I returned to the temple area and waited for midnight, relying on my wristwatch and a torch to know the hour. Even without the wristwatch a sadhaka knows when it is time for his midnight puja by the physical symptoms he experiences, such as increased respiration, etc. When it was twelve o'clock I sat for kapalik puja. That night various miracles happened but I am not allowed to reveal them in writing. They might be wrongly interpreted and create some fear complex about kapalik puja.

70
Baksheswar Piitha

THE NEXT MORNING I started for Baksheswar. Baksheshwar is situated to the west of Suri, the district headquarters of Birbhum. From Suri there is bus service up to Tantipara, and from there it is a one-kilometre walk. Baksheswar now has a big thermal plant that it did not have in those days.

I reached there at 5:00 p.m. It was a small village that received many visitors. A dharmashala had been constructed for them. As Baba had told me, it had several hot springs with alkaline water of different temperatures where people would come to cure chronic acidity and skin diseases. The dharmashala had been built by a patient who had been cured from acidity and skin disease by drinking those waters. Since I had not slept the previous night and had journeyed all day, I took rest in a room of the dharmashala after performing my evening puja. The residence of the local priest who took care of the tourists was near the dharmashala. His family came in the night to ask me about my meals. I said that I would stay the following day and night and if they could arrange food for me I would be grateful but that I would not eat that night because I was not feeling well. I informed them that I was a pure vegetarian who did not eat garlic and onion and they said that would not be a problem.

Early in the morning I got up and completed my morning puja, after which the priest's son came to invite me to their home for breakfast. The typical breakfast in Birbhum District is fried rice, fried gram, fried potatoes, and molasses. After taking breakfast, I left to find the Tantra piitha. It was a short distance from the dharmashala. There was a hill and a small river by the side of the piitha. After reaching there, I found some old brick ruins scattered around the hot spring like skeletons. To the left of the entrance was a broken room where Ashtavakra Muni had lived. There were hot springs on both sides at a little distance. I put my hand in the water to test the temperature. One of them was scalding hot. Sometimes visitors would dip rice in it to see if it would cook but it wasn't sufficiently hot for that.

Near one of the fallen brick rooms I saw a big banyan tree standing in a peculiar position. It looked like two trees side by side but it was actually one tree with two trunks. It was not possible to know which was the main trunk. This tree was known as Akshoy Bat. At the bottom of the tree is a stone plate with two footprints. They are reputed to be the footprints of Bhagavan Sri Chaitanya Deva, who once visited this place.

After seeing these things I went to another side where I found a hot spring the size of a small pond. I touched the water and saw that it was not so hot; one could take a bath there. On inquiry I came to know that people who suffered from skin disease would bathe in this hot spring. It has a cement bathing ghat and the excess water flows out to the Brahmani River.

At the opposite end of the hot spring was the Tantra piitha of Ashtavakra Muni. Several human skulls were kept there. After visiting the piitha I returned to the dharmashala and took rest. At noon I ate the meal supplied to me by the priest's family. In the evening we discussed the purpose of my visit and then talked about Ananda Marga. After our discussion the priest became convinced. He took initiation from me and removed his sacred thread. At midnight I performed my kapalik puja on the piitha of Ashtavakra Muni. The mysterious realization I had there cannot be recounted, as per the rule.

The next morning I started for Jamalpur.

71
Sitakunda

WHEN I WAS in Jamalpur I visited a hot spring near Monghyr known as Sitakunda. The priests there were earning money by exploiting religious sentiment in the name of Sita. From Jamalpur it was about nine miles. Between Jamalpur and Monghyr there is a railway station named Purabsarai and from there Sitakunda is about six miles. I went there by cycle. At that time the only vehicles that went to Sitakunda were tongas.

The area is surrounded by a big brick wall. Inside there are four kundas. Each kunda looks like a temple and measures about three hundred square feet. Their names are Ram Kunda, Bharat Kunda, Lakshman Kunda, and Satrughan Kunda (*kunda* means "pond" or "spring"). The water of those kundas is quite dirty. There is an ongoing puja in each kunda overseen by the priests. There was also a dharmashala where outsiders could stay, and on payment priests would supply food for them. Apart from those four kundas, there is the larger Sitakunda, which measures about one thousand square feet. The hot spring was located here, encircled by an iron fence for protection. There was a drain for the excess hot water. Washermen were washing clothes in that drain.

I visited everything not under the influence of priests. I should point out here that Sitakunda was not created by the grace of the Sita deity. That was proved by the British government. They dug a 150-square-foot pit about hundred yards away from Sitakunda and ten feet deep, and boiling water came out from the bowels of the earth, which proves that it is a natural characteristic of that place. To protect the people and animals from falling in, they fenced off this artificial kunda.

After Sitakunda I visited Rajgir in Nalanda District. There are also a few hot springs there and they were also exploited by the priests. But I saw everything with a scientific outlook. I thought that unless and until the people of our country are scientifically educated, this sort of exploitation will continue. Indian people in general are religiously sentimental, whether they are literate or illiterate. It is hereditary. Proper spiritual knowledge can save us from such religious exploitation.

72
Tarapiith

*T*HE DAY BEFORE the new moon I started from Jamalpur for the famous Tantra piitha known as Tarapiith to do kapalik sadhana. It is situated in the district of Birbhum. That year the Tarapiith railway stop had started service. I reached there about 11:00 a.m. under a scorching sun. There was no ticket counter, no tea stall, not even an unpaved road to Tarapiith, which was near the sub-division town of Rampurhat. I set out on foot and after two hours I reached there, making my way through the rice paddies for several kilometres. Since I had never been there before, I had to ask the farmers the way. After reaching there I took rest under a dilapidated tin awning.

I was tired after the night train journey and the long walk through the paddy fields under a scorching sun. I was also hungry. A priest came to inquire about my food. I told him I was a vegetarian and therefore I was not able to take the food of the deity. Some fried rice would be sufficient for me. He told me that one priest family was pure vegetarian and he sent someone to inform them about my requirements. After receiving the message, the vegetarian priest came and cordially invited me to his house where he made arrangements for my bath and meal. They invited me to take my night meal there as well and I reimbursed them for their troubles.

After taking my meal I returned to the shade and rested for an hour or so, dispelling my tiredness. Nearby there was a Tara temple with its four sides open. I found that the idol of Ma Tara Devi looked almost identical to the idol of Kali Devi. Near the temple a young sadhu was sitting silently. I asked him a few questions but he did not reply, so I did not disturb him further.

After that I headed for the cremation ground. Along the way I came across the historic Panchamundi Asana, which was made by Maharishi Vashistha four thousand years ago. Since then it has been known as a siddha Tantra piitha.

The Tarapiith temple and the cremation ground were situated to the west of the nearby village. In between the temple and the village was a jungle and a cremation ground. About two hundred yards from the temple, past the jungle, was a small river called the Dwarka. There was another village by the river.

In between the Panchamundi Asana and the temple ran a narrow path by which I reached the Tantra piitha. From there I could see the smoke of a funeral pyre rising by the river. It is said that since the days of Bamakhepa at least one body daily has been cremated there. I passed the Panchamundi Asana and entered the jungle to verify the fact. I found tombs at every step. The jungle was so dark that even in the daytime the sunlight did not penetrate. Pieces of bones and torn clothes were scattered here and there. Then I returned to the Tantra piitha.

The Tantra piitha was about two feet high and four hundred square feet in area. It was cemented and in the middle of it there was a sixteen-square-foot area resembling a temple. It was written in Bengali inside the wall of that temple that this Panchamundi's seat had been established by Maharishi Vashishta. Some tourists were sitting there, enjoying their holy visit. Some had come with their entire families. I talked with them and came to know that some people had come from Calcutta and some from Barrackpore. A few months earlier a film had been made that showed the glorious spiritual life and history of Bamakhepa. As a result an attraction to this place had developed in the mind of the general public. Unfortunately the place was inaccessible by road, which made it difficult for family people to reach there. There was not a single tea stall, either where the train stopped or at Tarapiith.

After some discussion with the tourists, one of them took my hand and asked me to sit with them. He requested me to say something about the history of Tarapiith and Tantra. They said, "Having met you, our visit to Tarapiith has become a great success." I tried my level best to explain Tantra in a simple way. After a half-hour discussion of Tantra I started to explain about Ananda Marga. They requested me to remain with them for the rest of the day. I told them that I could stay until 10:00 p.m. After that I would need to go somewhere else to perform my new-moon puja. But I would meet them again the next morning. They gave me their addresses and requested that I visit their homes. I told them if I got the time I would surely come, but that day has not yet come.

After my evening puja, a member of the priest's family came to invite me to take my dinner in their house. By then the news of my afternoon "tattvasabha" had spread and they had started to regard me as a spiritual person. They made special food for me, including luchis and sweets. When I tried to reimburse them for the meal they refused to accept any money. "We are householders," they said. "We have our own dharma. Please help us to follow our dharma. You are our guest. We cannot behave like businessman. Your arrival in our poor family is nothing but the grace of God."

I had heard that Birbhum District is the place of devotees. In this district lived the poets Jaidev, Chandidas, and also Nityananda. On the path from the Tara Devi temple to the Tantra piith there is a small room where one old man was living who had known Bamakhepa. Many tourists would visit him and ask questions about the life and history of Bamakhepa. I watched but I did not ask him any questions.

I remained with the tourists until 10:00 p.m. and then I left to prepare for midnight puja. I had gone there to fulfil my long desire to do Tantric puja in the Maha Tantra piitha of Maharishi Vashistha. When it was nearly midnight I went there. The darkness of the new-moon night was enhanced by the atmosphere of the jungle. The sound of jackals and dogs in the cremation ground and the night wind whipping about me created a grave and eerie atmosphere, which gave me much pleasure. When I was alone I found my Ista Devata in Kalyana Sundaram form and within a short period of time I lost myself and merged with Baba Anandamurtijii. Duality ceased to exist. This feeling of his Kalyana Sundaram form had me entranced.

Before reaching the piitha, spiritual vibrations started to flow in my body and mind like the flood tide of the sea, joining me to the spiritual flow of hundreds of Mahapurushas, those who sat in samadhi on that piitha over the past thousands of years. Never before had I felt such mental strength and spiritual effulgence. I felt as if my head were touching the sky and the whole world were cupped in the palm of my hand. At 3:00 a.m., after completing my puja, I collected my puja apparatus and took rest on the same Tantra piitha. Then in the morning, after completing my morning duties, I joined the tourists in the shade of the temple.

The moment I reached them, they did pranam. I sat with them for one hour; then I walked the three kilometres in the cold to the train stop and returned to Jamalpur.

After visiting these piithas I realized that the piitha selected by the guru is the best piitha. At the time of giving Tantra initiation, Baba said, "Your piitha is the greatest piitha in the world. This piitha I selected for your Tantra sadhana — that is the fittest place for you." After visiting these other piithas I could hear the voice of Baba and knew it to be incomparable. During the pre-British period in India the Kali temple area in Jamalpur was a place of Tantra.

73
Panchamakara Sadhana

PANCHAMAKARA SADHANA HAS encouraged so many misguided systems in the name of Tantra sadhana. Due to that, a wrong idea has developed in the mind of the public. I want to remove those ideas by explaining the reality behind the practice. The founder of Tantra sadhana was Lord Sadashiva. Those who are desirous for salvation can adopt the process of Vidya Tantra given by Sadashiva for liberation. This Tantra sadhana is divided into different methods, such as pashyachara, virachara, kulachara, and divyachara. During ancient times, people who were not followers of a religious path were considered to be like animals. Even today a person who does not follow the path of self-realization falls into the same category. Those who base their life on food, sleep, fear, and sex are no better than animals because animals pass their lives in the same way., When one starts spiritual practice in this condition it is called pashyachara in Tantra. In the beginning the sadguru teaches the aspirant how to leave behind the animal state; thus in this stage the guru is known as Pashupati, Lord of the animals. One of the names of Lord Shiva was Pashupati. When the sadhaka leaves behind the state of animality the guru teaches him the process of virachara. When the sadhaka by dint of his sadhana is able to fight against all sorts of weaknesses in family life, social life, and inner life, fighting against all such mental and physical complexes, he is known as a virachari sadhaka or a shakta, and Lord Shiva or the guru is known as Vireshwara. When the sadhaka leaves behind this state, the guru teaches him kulachari sadhana. Kulachari sadhana refers to the raising of the kulakundalini from the nadir point of the spinal cord to the culminating point in the sahasrara chakra, the seat of Paramashiva. He achieves unification with him as a result of sadhana. Here the thought of renunciation dominates the mind. In this stage the sadhaka is known as vaisnava, the process of sadhana is called kulachara, and the guru is known as Mahakaul. Finally the guru teaches the sadhana of divyachara, which leads the sadhaka toward divine knowledge and unification with Paramashiva. Now the sadhaka is known as shaiva and the guru is known as Devadidev Mahadeva. Thus the process of sadhana is from animality to shakta, from shakta to vaisnava, and finally from vaisnava to shaiva. These are the different stages of sadhana according to mental development. The sadhaka who does not attain the state of shakta cannot reach the state of vaisnava, and one who does not reach the state of vaisnava cannot reach the state of shaiva. If a sadhaka cannot reach the state of shaiva, he cannot unify himself with Paramashiva.

Panchamakara (literally, five letters) refers to the first five letters of the five words used in *panchamakara* practice: *madya* (wine), *mansa* (meat), *matsa* (fish), *mudra* (control over the tongue) and *maithuna* (intercourse). These definitions are misleading.

1) Madya: *somadhárá kśared yá tu brahmarandhrát varánane; piitvánandamayastvam sa eva madyasádhakah*

The person who has the knowledge of physical science knows that every gland secretes hormones. Similarly every sadhaka also knows that the pineal plexus (sahasrara chakra or *brahmarandhra*) secretes a particular hormone that in spiritual science is known as *amritarasa* or *somadhara*. When by dint of the sadhaka's mental concentration, the kulakundalini reaches the culminating point of the sahasrara chakra and drinks that nectar, he attains samadhi, the state of unification with Parama Purusha. The sadhaka who performs this process of sadhana is the real *madya* sadhaka. When Thakur Ramakrishna drank the *amritarasa* he became intoxicated and danced in *mahabhava*. Seeing the condition of Ramakrishna, Girish Ghosh thought he was a drunkard like himself. Thakur Ramakrishna perceived his thought and said:

Surápán karine ámi sudhá khái jaya Kálii bale;
Man-mátále mátál kare mad-mátále mátál baley.

I did not drink wine. I drank nectar (secreted from pineal plexus). As a result my mind is overwhelmed with emotion and thus I am dancing. To see me in such condition a drunkard says that I am also a drunkard.

Lord Sadashiva has said that while drinking *amritarasa* the kulakundalini forgets her existence and merges with the ocean of *amrita*. This is the state of samadhi.

Piitva piitva puna piitva patitacha mahitaley
Uthaio punha piitva punar janma no vidyatey.

The kundalini, reaching the *amakala* (storehouse of ambrosia), which is situated at the top of the pineal plexus, drank ambrosia until it was full. It fell down and then after a little while it got up and again drank the nectar. As a result rebirth will not take place.

2) Mansa: *má shabdádrasaná jineyá tadamsán rasaná priye; yastad bhakśayennityam sa eva mámsa sádhakah.*

The philosophical meaning of *mansa* is to control the tongue, to control one's vocal expressions. We know that those who know the art of expression can express a sentence in different ways. We also know that each and every expression, whether good or bad, is known as culture, and the rational control over culture is called civilization. That is why one should always avoid unnecessary talk and should talk in a controlled way. The sadhaka who is always alert about his expressions and follows the rules of rational control over vocal expressions is a *mansa* sadhaka as well as a civilized person. The founder of Tantra, Lord Sadashiva, directed his disciples to follow this *mansa* sadhana. He did not instruct them to eat meat (*mansa*).

3) Matsa: *gaungá yamunayormadhye matsyao dvao caratah sadá; tao matsyao bhakśayet yastu sah bhavenmatsyasádhakah.*

Through the science of yoga we learn that there are three nadis found within the spinal cord, known as the *ida, pingala* and *sushumna*. These three nadis have different names in different scriptures, such as ganga, yamuna, sarsvati, lalana, rasana, avadhutika, etc. They originate in the muladhara chakra. The sushumna nadi connects the muladhara to sahasrara, the seat of Paramashiva. The ida and pingala wind left and right, crossing the five chakras. Ida ends in the left nostril and pingala in the right. Ida and pingala have been compared with the Ganga and Yamuna rivers. We know that the work of our physical body is controlled by the respiration, and this aerial factor works throughout the body with the help of ida and pingala. If the aerial factor in the physical body is disturbed, then the mind is also affected and becomes disturbed. Unless and until one is able to control the aerial factor, one will not be able to concentrate the mind. They are interrelated. This is very important to a yogi, therefore the technique of pranayama was introduced so that a sadhaka could control the aerial factor in the body. *Rechakanta* and *purakanta kumbhak* pranayam is given to the disciples to bring into balance the aerial factor and thus facilitate proper concentration of the mind. The sadhaka who is engaged in controlling the aerial factor through his yogic practices is a *matsa* sadhaka. It has nothing to do with eating fish (*matsa*).

4) Mudra: *satsaungena bhavenmuktirasatsaungeśu bandhanam; asatsaungamudrańam sá mudrá parikiirttitá.*

Mudra sadhana is very easy. The mudra sadhaka knows that good company is helpful for liberation and that bad company is harmful and can cause bondage. Thus one should always avoid bad company and try to maintain the purity of the mind by cultivating good company. The sadhaka who always endeavours to lead a pure and perfect life with the help of good company is a mudra sadhaka. It does not have to do with posture.

*Tyaja durjana sansargang bhaja sadhu samagamam
kuru punyam aharatra smara nityam anityatam.*

Give up the association of wicked people and accept the company of noble persons. Remembering Parama Purusha, engage yourself with virtuous work day and night.

5) Maithuna: *kulakuńdalinii shaktirdehinám dehadhárińii; tayá shivashya samyogah maethunam parikiirttitam.*

Every yogi knows that the nadir point of the spinal cord is the muladhara chakra. The lower part of the tail bone is bent. That bent part is called kula. In this kula the kundalini resides in a dormant state. When the Ista mantra is empowered and strikes the kundalini, she wakes up from sleep and rises up through the hollow passage of the sushumna nadi toward the sahasrara chakra, the seat of Paramashiva. When she unites with Paramashiva, the sadhaka enters the blissful state of anandam. This process is called *maithuna* sadhana. It does not refer to sexual intercourse. A sadhaka overwhelmed with emotion sings a song:

*Jaga ma kulakundalini muladhara nivasinii,
Shirashi sahasra daley Paramashivatey miley,
Krira karo ma kautuhaley nityananda dayinii*

O Mother Kundalini inhabitant of muladhara, the nadir point of the spinal cord, please rise up to the culminating point of sahasrara chakra, the thousand-petaled lotus at the top of the head, the abode of Paramashiva, the supreme reality. Please reach there and mix with Paramashiva; play with him with excited curiosity and give me constant joy.

When a sadhaka by the grace of guru realizes this Paramatattva, he attains the rare Brahma Jinana. He comes to know both the saguna and nirguna states and reaches the supreme goal of life. After his prarabdha karma is exhausted, he will merge with Parama Purusha and will not take rebirth. This is called salvation. In this regard Sadashiva has said:

*Maithunasya parama tattvam sristi sthitanta karanam
Maithunang jayetey seddhi brahma gyana sudurlavam.*

Here *maithuna* means the unification of kundalini with Paramashiva. This unification is the cause of the creation and preservation of the universe. The sadhaka by the grace of the guru come to know the reality of this spiritual science, which is difficult to obtain. After knowing it, the sadhaka obtains divine knowledge.

74
A Mysterious Event

AFTER GETTING PERSONAL contact with Baba in the year 1955, I used to accompany him on evening walk nearly every day. Sometimes I would go to the field and wait for Baba to arrive at the tiger's grave and then accompany him back. Sometimes Baba reached first, sometimes I reached first, and sometimes we both reached at the same time. Sometimes I was the only devotee there with Baba.

When Baba left his residence he would carry a flashlight. Before reaching the tiger's grave he would sometimes walk along Peach Road, which encircles a big field, and then come to the tiger's grave. After reaching there, he would drink water brought by a local devotee named Ravin-da, and then he would talk with us. He used to come to the tiger's grave from a particular direction, so we always looked that way and when we saw the beam of a flashlight approaching we knew it was Baba.

In the summer season many people from town used to come to the field in the evening to walk and sometimes they would sit on the tiger's grave. If the tiger's grave was occupied, we would sit on the grave of the Englishman. It was twenty yards from the tiger's grave. By 9:00 p.m. the local people would invariably return home and then we would move to the tiger's grave. At one time this area was a jungle. Once an Englishman went hunting there and he was attacked by a tiger. Both died in the encounter and were buried at a distance of twenty yards from each other. Baba used to go to the field for his walk every evening in all seasons and would stay up to 10:00 p.m. When we heard the 10:00 p.m. bell from a nearby military camp we would start back.

One evening Baba and I were sitting on the Englishman's grave. No one else was there. Suddenly Baba said to me, "Sit a little further up. You are covering the hole where a cobra lives and he will face some difficulty breathing." Hearing this I became startled. Baba said, "No need to be alarmed. The hole is clear now." I told Baba that we should go somewhere else so as not to sit near a venomous snake. But Baba said, "You are sitting with me, so there is no need to worry, but you should never sit here alone in the dark."

One evening a few days later I went to the field. The previous few days had been excessively hot and I was tired. No one was on the tiger's grave and I soon fell asleep. When I woke up it looked like midnight and still Baba had not yet come. However I didn't have a flashlight or a watch, so I couldn't be sure of the actual time. As on other days I was watching for the beam of Baba's flashlight in the direction from which he normally came. I was thinking that if Baba wasn't going to come to the field, he would have informed me earlier. Since he hadn't said anything I continued to wait.

Half an hour passed. Then I found the beam of a flashlight advancing toward the tiger's grave in the same direction from which Baba usually came. When it got nearer I saw that it was indeed Baba. "Today I thought that I would not go to the field," he said, "but then I changed my mind and came. But today I shall not sit. Let us go back now."

On the way back we talked on different subjects. We didn't pass anyone. When we reached the market area I found that all the shops were closed except for one or two tea stalls. From the market we went in different ways — Baba to Keshavpur and I to Rampur colony. When I reached my quarters I saw that it was one a.m. I could not control my tears.

75
Raja Yoga

*R*AJA YOGA MEANS "kingly yoga." The specialty of this yoga is the inseparable connection between body and mind. This science is explained in detail in raja yoga. All expressions of the mind are expressions of certain propensities known as vrittis. Each and every thought comes within the periphery of these propensities, which are fifty in number. These fifty propensities affect the fifty main glands of the physical body. The vibration of the gland creates a certain sound known as *varna*. The fifty vrittis thus generate the fifty varnas or letters of the Sanskrit alphabet, from *a* to *ksha*, popularly known as the *varnamala* or alphabet. A sadhaka poet has said:

Yata shona karṅapute sabái máyer mantra bate
Kálii paincáshat varṅamayii varṅe varṅe viráj kare.

In meditation a sadhaka hears the sounds of the petals and all are mantras of mother Kali (Parama Prakriti). She is expressed in fifty colours and fifty petals and is present in each and every petal.

As all sadhakas know, the uppermost part of our physical body is the sahasrara chakra and the lowermost part of the spine is the muladhara chakra. In total there are seven chakras: muladhara, svadhisthana, manipura, anahata, vishuddha, agya, and sahasrara. The chakras are shaped liked lotuses with various petals representing the different glands and vrittis. The sahasrara chakra is beyond the scope of the mind; it is the abode of Parama Purusha. The remaining six chakras have fifty petals of different colours, each petal symbolizing a specific vritti, each with its varna. The vrittis are as follows: dharma, artha, kama, moksha, avajina, murchha, prashray, avishash, sarvanash, krurata, lajja, pishunata, irsha, susupti, visad, kashay, trisna, moha, grina, bhay, asha, cinta, cestha, mamata, dambha, viveka, vikalata, ahankar, lolata, kapatata, vitarka, anutap, sadaj, rishab, gandhar, madhyam, paincam, dhaevat, nisad, om, hum, phat, vaoshat, vasat, svaha, nama, visha, amrita, para, apara.

Suppose a particular vritti is creating a disturbance in the mind. The sadhaka who knows this art can easily control it by concentrating his mind on the affected gland.

Inside the spinal cord there are three nadis: sushumna, chitrani, and brahmani, like hollow pipes, one inside the other, connecting the various chakras. Through that hollow passage the kundalini shakti (jivatma) rises up to the sahasrara chakra, the seat of Paramatma, and attains unification, otherwise known as samadhi. Thus the definition of yoga is: *samyogo yoga ityuktah jiivatma paramatmana*, yoga is the union between the unit soul (jivatma) and the Supreme Soul (Paramatma).

Raja yoga consists of both physical and psychological science. It must be learned from the sadguru. Only the sadguru can properly teach and guide the spiritual aspirant toward the supreme goal of human life, unification with Parama Purusha. If a sadhaka systematically and scientifically practices this yoga, he is known as a raja yogi.

To practice all the lessons every day, at least six hours are needed: three hours in the morning and three hours in the evening. By the grace of the guru a sadhaka who practices this yoga will exhaust his samskaras and merge permanently with Parama Purusha. This is called moksha, the goal of human life.

76
Renunciation

*I*BECAME ATTRACTED TO the idea of extreme renunciation, for which detachment from worldly affairs is essential. As I result I started to sleep on a thin blanket using bricks as a pillow and forgoing the use of a mosquito net. I took the minimum amount of food necessary to survive, like a mendicant. My mind was tending toward the unknown world. I became attracted to solitary caves surrounded by hills, mountains, and jungles. In those solitary places the mind wants to meditate on its adorable devata. It wants to merge with him for the attainment of peace and tranquillity. Worldly relatives, employment, money, organization, and so on are obstacles on the path. I wanted to be alone, to be an inseparable part of the Supreme Entity, whom I had been running after life after life. I was unable to control such feelings. Everything else looked like a mirage and running after them, nothing but a waste of time.

Omniscient Baba was watching all my thoughts from the inner core of my heart. After this tendency had been growing in my mind for some time, Baba told me in his railway office, "You should wear good-looking clothes and keep your hair and beard properly styled so that from the outside no one can know that you are a vishesh yogi. Everybody will assume that you are a stylish person."

After hearing Baba's advice I thought that perhaps he was testing me, so I did not change anything. As usual I went to Baba's office every day. After one week, he suddenly started scolding me mildly. "I told you to dress stylishly and groom yourself nicely. Why you are not following my advice?" Then I understood that he was serious. Baba wanted me to look like a dandy.

Accordingly I spent a lot of money to buy better clothes and other such items. I was not happy with this but I obeyed Baba's order and passed my days in this way.

After becoming an avadhuta I again became disinterested. Baba again told me, "You are mixing with people from different sections of society.

You should make sure that you are always presentable so that you will receive invitations from all corners."

77
Omniscient Baba

*H*ERE I WANT to say something about the inner relation between guru and disciple. In the beginning Baba often pointed out my defects in day-to-day life. When he remained silent for some time then I thought that perhaps he was not watching me. Out of reaction I deliberately committed some wrong acts to draw Baba's attention, but I soon learned that I could not hide any thought or action from him.

Whenever he pointed out my faults he did it as if he had been there to witness it. How did he know my every thought and action at all times? I could not suppress my curiosity. Ultimately I told Baba that I was extremely eager to know the mystery and scientific basis of how he knew everyone's thoughts and actions. Baba replied with his glorious smiling face, "I am just a fool. I know nothing about it." Saying this, he looked at me with tremendous affection. I could not control my tears.

After this I decided to renounce my worldly life. I went to my village home to obtain permission from my wife to lead a monk's life. As per the rule at that time, if a married man wanted to become a monk he had to obtain permission from his wife. On the way back to Jamalpur after taking her permission I started thinking back over my experiences since the day I took initiation in 1955 and came in Baba's contact, how gradually I fell under the influence of that great personality and ended up deciding to become monk and dedicate my life to him.

Part Two

1962 – 1966
Prachar

Preface

*A*s of 1962, we had only opened a few branches of Ananda Marga in different parts of North India and at that rate it would take several generations to spread the ideology of Ananda Marga throughout the country, what to speak of the whole world. Seeing this, I remembered the words of Kabiguru Rabindranath Tagore: "to go ahead alone." Leaving behind my personal comforts, spiritual achievements, and desire for liberation, I took an oath to bring the immortal teachings of Ananda Marga to the world. I surrendered unto the feet of Baba Anandamurtijii, and after taking the blessing of Baba I was determined that within a short span of time DMC would be held throughout India, from Kerala to Kashmir, from Dwarka to Assam.

As I started my work, full of missionary zeal, many persons came forward to help — relatives, Margis, and non-Margis also. I did not know what they saw in my character or in my work. Their love, affection and cooperation pushed me from the finite to infinite. That is why, for the all-round success of my mission, I salute ever and again the feet of the divine incarnation of the age, he who gave me the mental strength and energy I needed for this work, he who made me a dignified servant of society.

1
Miracles of Baba

*I*n the year 1959 Baba entrusted me with the responsibility of establishing dharma in society through his great mission of Ananda Marga. I became afraid of so much responsibility. How would I be able to adjust to being away from him during my missionary work? At that time I felt uneasy if I could not see Baba at least once a day.

When I told Baba about my mental condition, he said, "The grace of Parama Purusha always will be showered on you; therefore you will never feel alone, nor will you feel any difficulty in your missionary work. He is all-knowing and omnipresent and he is always with you."

I started doing dharma prachar, forming units, holding seminars, creating dedicated workers, working to establish the Education, Relief and Welfare Section. I toured throughout India, from Jammu-Kashmir to Kanyakumari, from Dwarka to Digboy. Wherever I went, I delivered lectures on the socio-spiritual philosophy of Ananda Marga, especially among intellectuals and colleges students, and I got good response from all corners. Many young men were attracted to our philosophy. I held seminar camps for them in which we explained the different teachings of Ananda Marga. As a result many of them dedicated their lives to the cause of our great mission. Within five years we had dedicated workers throughout India. During this period I was able to create thirty-five avadhutas whom I posted in different parts of India, and Dharma Maha Chakras were held throughout the country.

The moment I left Jamalpur for missionary work I felt that Baba was going with me. Wherever I went the Margis garlanded me. I lost myself and Baba appeared within me. Such a marvellous, mysterious feeling I can't express in words. Margis were attracted to me almost as if Baba were coming for DMC. How the Omnipresent Entity played with his representative! I never felt any separation from him, even for a moment. I felt that he was doing his missionary work through my physical body, like a machine man operating a machine. My body and mind were vibrated with Baba's presence.

From time to time I would be absent from my physical body and in my place Baba would appear. I never imagined this could happen. Though he was in Jamalpur, I felt that he was physically present everywhere. His ever-open eyes were observing every action of the creation. Once one of his American devotees asked him to write his biography. In reply Baba said, "I was a mystery, I am a mystery and I will remain a mystery."

Because the devotees felt Baba's presence within me they requested me to accept their offerings to Baba on his behalf. But I dared not accept them. When I asked Baba about it, he said, "You are my mini-Baba; thus I permit you to accept their offerings on my behalf and make prasad out of any food that is offered." Thus I realized that Baba's physical body was not limited to Jamalpur. He is an omnipresent and omniscient personality.

2
Angle of Vision

*L*EAVING BEHIND THE enchantments of worldly life I surrendered unto the feet of the Lord of the Age and adopted a life of dispassionate selfless service. From then on I had no family, no friends, and no property. The Lord was my only companion, accompanying me from one birth to another in the form of the sadguru, releasing me from all sorts of bondages and graciously accepting me in his service. No longer would I look behind me. Kabiguru Rabindranath has said:

> *Purano abas chheray jai jobey,*
> *Money bhebay mori ki habey na habey,*
> *Nutaner majhey tumi puratan, say katha jey bhuley jai,*
> *Durkey kariley nikat bandhu. parkey kariley bhai.*

Due to stoicism, when a devotee leaves home to dedicate his life for the cause of human welfare, he wonders how he will adjust with the uncertainty of his future life. In this mental condition one forgets that in this new life the ancient controller of the universe, Parama Purusha, lives within him watching each and every action of his mind. Due to his presence the far becomes near and the known person becomes one's brother.

Receiving the love and affection of Parama Purusha and merging with his rhythm, going ahead with his mission, is the start of satya yuga. A rishi has said:

> *Kalao shayáno bhavati sainjihánastu Dvápara;*
> *Uttiśthan Tretá bhavati Kratam sampadyate carań;*
> *Caraeveti caraevetii.*

When a person sleeps, his fate also sleeps; that is kali yuga. When he wakes up, his fate also wakes up; that is dvapar yuga. When a person stands up, his fate also stands up; that is treta yuga. When a person goes ahead, his fate also goes ahead; that is satya yuga. That is why the rishi has said, "O sadhaka go ahead, go ahead."

In this way a day will come when one will establish oneself in satya, in eternal bliss, which is the goal of human life. When one attains that state of anandam, he can say:

> Sei Ánanda carańa páte; śadrtu ye nrtye máte.
> Plávańa bahe yáy dharáte; varań giiti gandhere.

After touching the feet of Parama Purusha, the devotee is overwhelmed with joy. The six cardinal passions start dancing and the mind merges with the universal rhythm. The aspirant becomes abnormal by its influence.

From this time my life's penance has been magnanimity in dharma, dispassionate work, the ideation of *brahmabhava* in yoga, *samyoga* with Ista, surrender to the Lord, the ethics of equality, service to humanity, sacrifice and trying to free myself from all sorts of attachments, and engaging myself in service to the suffering humanity. Seeing the state of worldly affairs, I remembered a few lines of poetry from a Western poet:

> I slept and dreamt that life was beauty,
> I woke and found that life was duty.

When I was going to accept the avadhuta vow, Baba quoted from a shloka about the avadhuta:

> Shmasháne vá grhe, hirańye vá trńe,
> Tanuje vá ripao, hutáshe vá jale.
> Svakiiye vá pare samatvena buddhyá,
> Viráje avadhúto dvitiiyo maheshah.

For him the crematorium and house are the same, gold and grass are the same, son and enemy are equal, fire and water are the same, himself and others are the same. With such an outlook he is like a second Shiva on the earth.

It is not possible to attain this state of mind by practice. Only by the grace of guru can one attain this state. What is the definition of guru?

Shánto dánto kuliinascha viniita shuddhaveshaván
Shuddhácárii supratiśthita shucirdakśah subuddhimán
Áshramii dhyánaniśtashca tantramantra visháradah
Nigrahánugrahe shakto gururityabhidhiiyate.

He is calm and quiet, of good family, modest, and virtuous,
His behaviour is pure; he is well-reputed, highly efficient, and sensible,
While living in a hermitage, he has no need of meditation; he is expert in Tantra and mantra,
When his disciples do any wrong, he is persecuted, but he is gracious to all. These are the formal qualities of the guru.

Only a person who is desirous of salvation can get the proximity of the sadguru. None can identify that person from the outside. That is why Lord Krishna told his disciple Arjuna, "You can know me through yoga. Practice yogic meditation and complete your work."
    A rishi said:

Yogastha kuru karmani sanga tyakta dhananjaya
Siddha siddha sama bhutva samatva yoga uchatey.

Leaving all others, keep your mind attached to Parama Purusha, who is sitting within your heart, and do your work without thinking whether you will get salvation or not. A person with this type of balanced mind, unaffected by any stimuli and attached to Parama Purusha, is a true yogi.

The glorious avadhuta Dattatrayii, in his *Avadhuta Gita*, described the meaning of each letter of the word *avadhuta* as:

A: *asha pasha vinirmukta adi madhyanta nirmal*
anandey bartatey nityam akarastasya lakshanam.

An avadhuta is free from the bondages of hopes and aspirations. His past and present are pure. He always remains in the state of bliss. These are the signs of the letter *A*.

Va: *Vasana barjita jena baktabancha nirarnaya*
bartamanesu bartey bakarastasya lakshanam.

He has given up his all longings, his speech cures others, and he lives in the present—these are the signs of *Va*.

Dhu: *dhuli dhusara gatrani dhutachita niramaya
dharana dhyana nirmukta dhukarastasya lakshanam*

He rubs ash on his body and by this he purifies it. He is free from all ideation and dhyana. These are the signs of *Dhu*.

Ta: *tattva chinta dhrita jeno chinta chestha vibarjita
tamo ahamkara nirmukta takarastasya lakshanam.*

He does no other thinking or effort other than on the fundamental truth. He is free from vanity and vice. These are the signs of *Ta*.

In another scripture there is a description for avadhuta:

*No biro, no dhiro, no ba sadhakandra,
No yogi, no bhoyi, no ba makshakankshi,
No shaiba, no shakta, no ba vaisnabascha,
Birajey avadhuta dvitiiya mahesha.*

An avadhuta is neither a hero nor calm nor a great devotee. He is neither a yogi nor an enjoyer. He is not eager for salvation, nor does he worship Shiva or Shakti. He is free from worldly attachment. He lives on this earth like a second Shiva.

The guru who creates such an avadhuta is not an ordinary personality but the Parama Purusha himself incarnated in a human body to give salvation to deserving candidates. He incarnates himself on this earth in a physical body of five fundamental factors. How can one describe him? If the goddess of learning, Sarasvati, writes in praise of him for an indefinite period of time, she will not succeed. A rishi has said:

*Asitagirisamam syát kajjalam sindhupátre
Suratarubarasháhká lekhanii patramúrvii
Likhati yadi grhiitvá Sárádá sarvakálam
Tadápi tava guńánámiisha páramna yáti.*

If the Himalayan mountains are the ink tablet, the ocean the ink pot, the pen made from the branches of Parijato tree, and the surface of the Earth the writing pad, and if the goddess Sarasvati herself writes for an indefinite period, still the qualities of Parama Purusha cannot be expressed properly.

We human beings, how can we write or express his qualities? From this very moment, O Lord, do your work through me and the people will see that I am doing your work. I have realized that you are my *bandhu, suhrid, mitra* and *sakha*, my only true friend. Knowing this, I am overwhelmed with joy that I have gotten the Lord. The mission of my life must certainly succeed with his most affectionate guidance. A rishi has said:

Atyágasahano bandhu sadaevánumatah suhrd;
Eka kryam bhavenmitram samaprániáh sakhásmrtah.

The definition of *bandhu, suhrd, mitra,* and *sakha*, as expressed in the above shloka, are:

Bandhu: Where separation from each other is unbearable.
Suhrd: Where both are always of the same opinion and there is no difference in any circumstances, only the inseparable relation with one's dharma and not any other worldly relation. Dharma accompanies one after death also.
Mitra: Where both are doing the same work. Suppose both are teachers. In this case both are *mitra*.
Sakha: The rhythm of the *prana* of both persons is identical. This type of relation can be established with Parama Purusha only. Such was the relation between Lord Krishna and Arjuna.

3
Karma Yoga

WHAT IS DISPASSIONATE karma yoga and what is the technique behind it? In the Mahabharata, Yuddhistira says that one should impose the idea of *brahmabhava* on one's work, doing selfless service without any vanity and surrendering the result of one's work to God.

This is dispassionate work or seva. In Ananda Marga, sadhakas practice this through *madhuvidya*. This is the real karma yoga. Work in which there is give and take is business and a cause of bondage.

Sadhakas learn the process of madhuvidya from an acharya. If they practice it properly they will not earn any new samskaras. Only their prarabdha karma, the effects of their past deeds, will be left. When these prarabdha karmas are exhausted they will merge into Parama Purusha. This is called moksha, or salvation.

Many people think that if they do good work they will not take rebirth, but this is not correct. Good work makes for good prarabdha karma and bad work for bad prarabdha karma. Unless and until the techniques of madhuvidya are learnt and applied at the time of work, people will not be free from the bondage of karma. We know that every action creates an equal and opposite reaction and this reaction in its potentiality is called samskara. Good work binds by a golden chain and bad work binds by an iron chain, but both are bondages and a person in bondage cannot be free. Only madhuvidya can free a person from bondages. In this connection a rishi has said:

> *Yávanna kśiiyate karma shubhamcáshubhameva ca*
> *Távanna jáyate mokśa nrńám kalpashataerapi*
> *Yathá laohamayaeh páshaeh páshaer svarńamayaerapi*
> *Tathá baddho bhávejiiva karmábhishcáshubaershubaeh*

> This world is a field of action; therefore everyone will have to work, whether that work is good or bad. Every action has an equal and opposite reaction and reaction in its potentiality is the cause of bondage. Unless and until the techniques of madhuvidya are learnt and applied at time of starting any work one will not be free from bondage and will not be able to attain salvation. Good works bind with a golden chain and bad works binds with an iron chain, but both are bondages.

Regarding karma yoga, Lord Krishna said: *yoga karma sukaushalam*; yoga means to learn the art of karma. We have come from an unknown world and for a certain time we will remain in this objective world where karma is a must. Through yoga we learn the necessary techniques to work efficiently. Again after sometime we will go back to the unknown world. That moment will not wait for us under any circumstances. It is a never-ending process. The infant will be converted into a child, the child into a boy, the boy into a youth, the youth into an adult, the adult into middle age, middle age into old age, old age into infirmity, and infirmity into death. This cannot be stopped; thus we are all travellers. A sadhaka poet has said:

> *Janam maran pa fela are pa tola orey pathik*
> *Smaran jadi rakhis padey padey bhulbi na dik*
> *Naiko suru antur gharey shesh naiko chitar parey*
> *Ageo achhey pareo achhey ai kathata bujhey nay thik*

One should know that birth and death are steps in a journey. Remembering this fact: if one moves forward one will never forget the true path. One should also know that life does not begin in the birthing room and does not end on the funeral pyre. Before taking birth and after the funeral pyre there are many things.

After taking birth in this objective world, one should know what is jiva, jagat and Brahma. That will enable one to understand the goal of one's life. To reach the goal that person must learn the techniques of spiritual practice from a sadguru, the systematic and scientific process of yoga so that one can practice it in one's day-to-day life until the goal is achieved. This practice for attaining self-knowledge is called dharma. As long as one does not understand the science of jiva, jagat and Brahma properly, one can not follow dharma. If one follows dharma on the basis of blind faith, one is no better than a bullock going round and round an oil mill with his eyes covered by a piece of cloth. There is no progress at all. It is a waste of time. Ultimately the man of blind faith will be forced in regret to utter these lines of a sadhaka poet:

> *Vrthá janma goináyaluin hena Prabhu ná bhojaluin*
> *Khoyáyalu soha guńanidhi,*
> *Hamár karama manda na milala eka bunda*
> *Premasindhu rasaka abadhi.*

If a person taking birth on this earth is not able to please his Ista, the summum bonum of life, he is truly unfortunate, since he has not been able to get a single drop from the ocean of love.

The person who, taking birth on this earth by the grace of God, gets a chance to learn the systematic and scientific process of yoga from a sadguru, is truly fortunate. Only the person who always keeps his mind on his Ista while performing work can be free and without bondages.

4
Preparation

IT WAS OCTOBER 30, 1961. As on other days I went to Baba's office. Just after reaching there Baba gave me a piece of paper and asked me to note down the avadhuta rules. He gave dictation and I noted down about forty items. After writing them down, I started to study them and found that some of those rules would be very difficult for people living in the society to follow. I discussed those points with Baba and then and there he eliminated them. I then asked Baba to give me one day's time to think more over the matter and the next day I would tell him if I thought there should be any further alterations. Baba gave me permission and the next day in his office I discussed with Baba some more points that I considered impractical. He also omitted them. Baba was never rigid on any issue. He was always liberal and practical. He always encouraged us to analyse things on the basis of logic and reasoning and to not accept anything blindly.

From this time forward, I read those rules every day and tried to determine how far it would be possible for me to follow those difficult rules for my entire life. Human beings are composed of good and bad. Many weaknesses arise in the mind. In a weak moment one may transgress a certain rule and thus tarnish the image of the avadhuta life as well as the organization, which would be a matter of deep repentance. This sort of conflict was going on in my mind throughout the month of November.

In the avadhuta rules there was a provision that the candidate must follow the avadhuta rules for one year before becoming an avadhuta. I thought that I would be able to test myself during this period to see if it would be possible. If I found that I was not fit, then I would not accept avadhuta initiation. After coming to this conclusion, I started to follow the avadhuta rules on December 10, 1961 and duly informed Baba.

Now in my mind there arose a feeling of great stoicism, the feeling that I had left behind my worldly life to follow these avadhuta rules. A cyclonic storm was raging inside me. I felt a tremendous strength in my body and the mind and a creative faculty of divine power in my heart and soul. At the same time my actions were full of spiritedness. When I sat for puja I felt like a supernatural being. I could not tell anybody about this, knowing that they would laugh or say that these symptoms presaged my going mad.

When the general secretary learned of my decision to follow the avadhuta rules, he became mortified. He applied all his intellectual powers to dissuade me from becoming an avadhuta. He thought that my sacrifice and devotion to the guru would be in conflict with my decision. He even utilized his organizational machinery for the purpose of dissuading me from this path. When all his efforts failed, he stopped cooperating with my activities, thinking that under the pressure of circumstances I would be compelled to give up the idea.

5
Omnipresence

ON DECEMBER 15, 1961, I went to Madhya Pradesh to see to the arrangements of the DMC scheduled to be held at Raipur on December 21 and 22. After the DMC Baba was scheduled to stay for one day in Tatanagar at the residence of Acharya Chandranathjii, who was at that time posted at Tatanagar as deputy superintendent of police. He was a great devotee of Baba and since the beginning of Ananda Marga he and his wife had served Ananda Marga very sincerely as acharyas.

As per Baba's programme I also adjusted mine. After completing the DMC at Raipur we reached Tatanagar at noon on the twenty-third. After leaving Baba with Chandranathjii, I was to start for Jamalpur by the evening train so I could make it in time for the one-week VSS camp that was due to begin the next day in Ranchi. I was to conduct the camp as commander-in-chief. It was decided that some volunteers would wait for me at Jamalpur and from there we would go in our two Jeeps to Ranchi.

After completing my evening puja in Tatanagar I went to Baba's room to prostrate before him and obtain his permission to go to Jamalpur.

A car was ready to take me to the railway station. After coming out from Baba's room, Baba called me back. Baba was lying on his bed in *anantashayanam* mudra. As per my habit, I sat on the floor near his feet. Five minutes passed but Baba said nothing. His eyes were partially closed and the atmosphere in the room was solemn. We were alone in the room. At that time there was a rule that when I was in Baba's room no one should enter without permission. My luggage was in the car and the others were waiting anxiously to take me to the station, since it was nearly time for the train to leave. I was surprised to see Baba adopt such a mudra without talking. Why was Baba in that mood? I wondered. I had never seen him like that and did not dare to ask any question.

In this way half an hour passed. On the one hand I was looking at the time and on the other I was looking at Baba. The expression on Baba's face was serene. Another fifteen minutes passed. His puja time was also going to be over. Having no other alternative, I prostrated and told Baba that I had to leave to catch the train. Baba did not reply. He returned my namaskar in silence, looking at me with piteous eyes. I had no wish to leave but I had no choice. After leaving Baba I could not talk to anybody for some time. The moment I reached the station the train started. While in the train I remembered Baba's mudra for a long time, until I slept.

I reached Jamalpur early in the morning on the twenty-fourth and went to the jagriti where all were waiting for me. After breakfast I told them to check the Jeeps and get ready. We left for Ranchi about 8:00 a.m., sixteen persons in two Jeeps. I was driving one Jeep and Sudhir (the son of the superintendent of police, Mr. Akhorijii) was driving the other. We reached Hazaribagh in the afternoon, where we took some rest and tiffin while Lalan and Sudhir brought the Jeeps to a mechanic for a checkup. The mechanics told them that one Jeep should be repaired before driving it but they ignored his advice and the matter was not reported to me. I was driving that Jeep.

We started again for Ranchi. Eight kilometres from Hazaribagh we reached a hilly area. There was road sign announcing sharp curves ahead and a speed limit of fifteen mph. I applied the brakes and the Jeep flipped over. The other passengers landed on top of me. Due to their weight I could not escape. My left hand was stuck inside the moving Jeep, breaking the ulna bone, and my face was scraped along the pavement. While I was being dragged I saw Baba standing in the road in *abhaya* mudra. The moving Jeep came to a halt just at his feet, and at that moment I became unconscious.

When my senses returned, it was the next morning and I was lying in a bed in Hazaribagh Sadar Hospital. Immediately I remembered being in Baba's room in Tatanagar on the eve of my departure for Jamalpur. Why had Baba been in *anantashayanam* mudra, looking at me in silence with piteous eyes? Now I understood that his mood had been a sign of the harm that was awaiting me. Had I not left Baba's room I would have been saved, but I had to face the consequences of my samskaras. It was my prarabdha karma.

Pita jasya dhananjaya matula jasya basudeva
Abhimanyu raney hato daibang balabato tatha.

Abhimanyu, whose father is Arjuna and maternal uncle is Lord Krishna, died in the battlefield of the Mahabharata; it was destined due to his past deeds.

I have no doubt that Baba had saved my life. *Rakhey hari to marey kay.* No one can kill one whom God protects.

When I came to my senses in the hospital that morning, I learned that my whole body and face had been dragged on the road during the accident. I went to the mirror on the hospital wall and saw that my face was so badly disfigured I could barely recognize myself. My left hand was without feeling. Fortunately the local Margis were taking care of us. Somebody had gone to Ranchi to inform them. At 9:00 a.m. that morning Acharya Kedarjii, Dr. A. N. Chakravarty, a lecturer at Darbhanga Medical College, and Dr. Suresh, the civil surgeon of Chatra Hospital, had reached Hazaribagh. From them I came to know that another four persons were injured: Pranav, Asiim, Vashistha, and Chinmay. I was the only one who had lost consciousness. I told our doctors that I was without feeling in my left hand. They arranged for X-rays and discovered that the ulna bone was broken. My hand was put in a cast and at eleven we all left for Ranchi. Dr. Chakravarty and Dr. Suresh also joined the central VSS camp.

After reaching Ranchi we patients were treated by our two doctors in a room near our jagriti. Vashishta's knee became infected and he was in a lot of pain. The doctors operated and a lot of blood mixed with pus came out. Dr. Suresh was polite and Dr. Chakravarty was very strict. Pranav had lost a tooth and had lacerations on his face and Asiim's leg was in a cast. Though it was hell, our team spirit helped us to forget our sadness. However, my absence from the camp became noticeable. No one was obeying orders properly. After hearing this I was compelled to join the camp on the fifth day. When I arrived the participants were extremely glad. The final two days went smoothly. After the camp was over, all took some organizational responsibility and left Ranchi full of missionary zeal.

When I returned to Jamalpur. Baba was in his room in the jagriti with the devotees. The moment I reached the door to his room, he said, "Nityananda, you might have realized that an invisible power always remains with you and whenever needed he appears in physical form before you. During the accident in Hazaribagh you might have seen him physically."

Hearing this, tears flowed from my eyes.

6
Calamity

EXCEPT FOR ASIIM Kumar, we all returned to the Jamalpur jagriti. There was a small charitable dispensary room in which we patients stayed, even though the work of the dispensary was going on for several hours every day. No Margi came to see us, not even the general secretary. A Margi named Gaya Saha lived near the jagriti with his family. He had started a vegetarian restaurant in his residence to serve the Margis who were coming from outside Jamalpur to have Baba's darshan. Gaya Saha took a lot of trouble to look after our needs. The general secretary thought that now we would be compelled to return to our homes. Some Margis from his team told us to go back home because there was no one to look after us. I replied that he who sent the mother's breast milk before the birth of a child would take care of us.

It was a grave situation and through this Baba tested our patience and endurance. I got inspiration remembering a few lines from a poem of Kabiguru Rabindranath:

Amar jatra holo shuru, ogo karnadhar,
Tomarey kari namaskar,
Tufan chhutuk batas uthuk firbo na ko are.

O Parama Purusha, doing namaskar to you, I am starting my journey to do your work. No matter what adverse situation I might face, I shall not go back again.

These few lines kept my mind strong and my decision firm. But the general secretary did not hesitate to create circumstances so that I would be compelled to abandon the idea of becoming an avadhuta. One day he suddenly appeared and told us that our room was needed for urgent organizational work and that we had to vacate it. I kept silent. The next day Baba came to the jagriti and I told him everything. I also said that we would shift to a government room near the Kali hill that had been lying vacant for a decade. It was a solitary place at the foot of the hill, near a spring cared for by the railway department. In reply Baba said that unless and until he gave us further instructions we were not to shift anywhere. The next day Baba sent us a message that we were to stay in that room as long as required. After that the general secretary no longer bothered us about the room.

At that time parliamentary elections were going on. The election date was fixed for February 1962. I was mostly confined to my bed due to my injuries, and due to this the volunteers were not receiving proper guidance. Lalanjii, who was also against my becoming a dedicated worker, was supervising the workers in his own way, while the general secretary was openly against the organizational work being done by the dedicated wholetime workers. During the previous months he had sent home a number of young workers who had come to work under me. During this time I was meeting the expenditure of those workers from my salary but that was not sufficient and we had no other source of funds. Thus the situation was critical. In Jamalpur the householders were not taking much interest in the development of the organization and this worried me.

After the parliamentary elections were over, Baba arrived at the jagriti one fine morning at about eight. No one else was there. He took me from my sick bed and started to walk with me in the jagriti courtyard. Baba said, "What is the present condition of your organization?" I discussed the situation in detail and informed him that the persons who had come to work for me had all left for their homes. Even the general secretary and his co-workers were not coming to jagriti regularly. When I asked them why they were not coming regularity, they said that they were engaged with their personal affairs and for them the work of the organization was secondary. Under such circumstances the organizational work was being hampered on all sides.

After hearing this, Baba asked me what I was planning on doing about it. I told Baba that when there is a disease a remedy has to be applied. The best remedy was the creation of a cadre of dedicated workers. They will have no personal life and will engage themselves full time in the different activities of the organization. They will bring an all-around revolution by their sadhana, service, and sacrifice. They will do penance through their individual sadhana for spiritual salvation and the rest of the time they will engage themselves in the service of humanity. I further told Baba that I couldn't wait for my hand to heal. If I did, then what little progress we had made would be lost. Thus I was thinking to go back on tour the following week.

After listening to me, Baba said, "Effective immediately, do whatever you think proper and work independently. There is no need to consult with me. The invisible power of Parama Purusha will always remain with you and help you in all respects. Do your work fearlessly." I prostrated before Baba and he blessed me, saying, "I bless you for the all-round success of your mission."

After Baba's departure from the jagriti, I chalked out my tour programme, beginning the very next week. First of all, I would visit North Bihar and Uttar Pradesh, and then East Bihar, West Bengal, and South Bihar, including Muzaffarpur, Darbhanga, Bethia, Hazipur, Gorakhpur, Lucknow, Allahabad, Varanasi, Ghazipur, Buxar, Ara, Patna, and Gaya. I informed the local acharyas ahead of time of my programme and told them that they must be present in their unit with their accompanying workers as per the scheduled time and place of my arrival.

Throughout this time my broken hand was in a sling. I took one attendant with me and met with the acharyas in each local: at Muzaffarpur, Acharya Gangasharan; at Darbhanga, Acharya Shyamananda; at Bethia, acharyas Ananda Kishore and Paramananda; at Gorakshapur, acharyas Pratapaditya and Raghunath; at Lucknow, acharyas Om Prakash and Chamanlal; at Allahabad, Acharya Chandradeo; at Varanasi, Sri Shitalajii; at Ghazipur, acharyas Kashoprosad and Indrajit; at Ara, Acharya Ramashray; at Patna, Acharya Prem Bahadur; and at Gaya, Acharya Satyanarayan.

After completing this programme, I took one week rest and then visited Bhagalpur, Saharsa, Purnia, Birbhum, Nadia, Calcutta, Howrah, Bardhaman, Midnapore, Tata, and Ranchi, and then returned to

Jamalpur. The main workers of those places were Acharya Harendra at Bhagalpur, Acharya Nat Khat Kedar at Saharsa, Acharya Indrajit at Katihar, Acharya Sachinandan at Birbhum, acharyas Sukhen and Monorainjan at Krishnagar, Shrii Vishwanath at Calcutta, Shrii Sailen Ghosh at Howrah, Shrii Kinkar at Bardhaman, Shrii Subol at Midnapore, Acharya Chandradeo at Tata, and acharyas Kshitish and Kedar at Ranchi.

Seeing my various injuries and my hand in a sling, all felt the importance of the work and promised me that in the future such laziness would not be repeated. After that, they started to work with missionary zeal.

At this time Acharya Ramtanukjii, our legal secretary, came forward to help me in my work. After the new programme was started, information reached me from different parts that many educated young men wanted to join the organization as wholetime workers. After getting this news I directed the organizers to come to Jamalpur on a specific date with a list of the wholetimer candidates. In that meeting I introduced Ramtanukjii to the field organizers. We discussed how the expenditure of the wholetime workers would be met, what would be their source of income in the present as well as in the future. I told them that up until then I had borne their expenditure from my salary but that little expenditure had exhausted my funds. For large-scale activities one individual could not bear such an expenditure. A concerted collective effort was needed. It was decided that each person with a regular job or business would contribute one month's income each year to meet the expenditure of incoming wholetime workers. Those who had outstanding loans would be exempted until they repaid their loans. Also persons whose earnings were not sufficient to maintain their family would be exempted.

They drew up a list of subscribers and handed it to Acharya Ramtanukjii. Since he would not be able to collect the money, it was decided that it would be sent directly to me. Acharya Ramtanukjii was the lone earning member in his family. His wife was studying in college so he had to look after his family, but in his free time he was helping me very sincerely. Now that the financial difficulties had been solved to some extent, I started inviting the wholetimer candidates to join. The first was Sudhir Kumar, then Asiim Kumar. The third was Ramesh Kumar and the fourth was Ramswarth. Through this concerted effort and active cooperation we started a new chapter in the organization.

After some time I had my cast removed but my hand still wasn't regaining its strength. I had an X-ray done at Monghyr and found that the bone had not joined. I consulted with the doctors and collected different opinions. Ultimately I went to Ranchi and Acharya Kshitishjii and Acharya Kedarjii accompanied me to the American missionary hospital at Mander, some sixteen kilometres distant. The head of the department was an American nun and surgeon about thirty-five years old.

After entering the gate of the hospital-cum-tribal-girls high school, I went to the hospital side. There were two counters, one for the expensive doctor and another for the inexpensive. In reality there was no difference between the expensive and inexpensive doctors. If the disease was complicated both doctors attended the patient, but because this was a poor tribal area they had made this system. The fee for the inexpensive doctor was one rupee and the expensive doctor's fee was ten rupees. I took the ticket of the expensive doctor and entered. A nurse took me to a small room with a bed where she did the initial examination. Then she took me to the doctor, who turned out to be the American head of the department. She checked me and said that the hand to be reset and put in a splint. The bone had not been set properly. She gave me a date to return and have the bone reset.

I returned on the scheduled date but after reaching there I found that they were not accepting outpatients. On inquiry I learned that it was operation day and outpatients were not admitted. A caretaker told me that the following day was for outpatients. I showed him the slip the surgeon had given me and asked him to show it to her. After some time he returned and said that the doctor had made a mistake but she would take care of me today.

After two hours she called me inside the operation room. Many different patients were there undergoing or recovering from operations and the room was filled with surgical apparatuses. The surgeon was very cordial. She examined my hand and directed the nurses to bring the necessary equipment — wood, saw, hammer, etc. She did all the work herself while the others watched — cutting the wood, mixing the plaster, applying the bandages, etc. I was surprised to see that she had no vanity of post and position. She was doing everything in the service of God. Previously I had seen many Indian doctors and they all had a fair amount of vanity. She told me that she had to cause me some discomfort. I replied that to remove my discomfort some discomfort must be faced. "Sister," I said, "I am charmed by your motherly treatment." She was moved by my words.

She told me to catch hold of a hanging ring and directed four nurses to hold on to my arm while she reset the bone and tied the splint. Then she took me to the X-ray room to see if the bone had been set properly or not. Thrice she took X-rays until she was satisfied that it had been properly set. Then she very carefully plastered my hand and prescribed some medicines for a period of six weeks. At the time of departure she emphasized several times that I must inform her after six weeks how I was responding, or if possible, come personally to show her.

After six weeks I had an X-ray taken at Monghyr and send it to Mander Hospital through Acharya Kshitishjii. When she saw my X-Ray, the doctor danced around my table and said that by the grace of God my patient was now OK. I was much moved by her service and by the work of the Mander Hospital. I told this to Baba. He said that by their service hundreds of helpless people were benefited and that we should also build up our mission in the same way.

7
Dejected State

SOME WHOLETIME WORKERS had started to work for the organization but they still had difficulties arranging food and shelter. The whole day they worked in the field and in the night they stayed in the railway station. From their place of work they would correspond with me care of the stationmaster or the postmaster of their respective areas. From Jamalpur I would send them the minimum amount required each month for their food by telegraphic money order. I was always alert to meet their needs, but one day I had no money even for my own food. I knew that I was not alone and thinking thus I was prepared to face the situation. That night I could not sleep. I kept thinking that I had started this work depending on Baba and I had told others that Parama Purusha would do his work, we were simply his medium. Would my statement be proved false? I passed the entire day brooding on the matter. I did not go to the post office to see if there were any letters because if anybody was in need I had no money to send them and thus my mental trouble would be increased. I did not even eat. In the evening when I was performing puja somebody called my name. I got up from my puja and went to open the gate. A person was waiting there with an envelope. He said that Sripatijii had sent it for me. After he left I opened the envelope and found that Sripatijii had sent five hundred rupees for the wholetime workers.

8
Avadhutaship

*I*T WAS MAY 1, 1962. At about 8:00 a.m. Baba arrived unexpectedly at the Jamalpur jagriti. I met him at the entrance of jagriti and he asked, "Are you ready now?" I could not understand what he meant so I didn't reply. After a short silence I asked Baba why he had asked me such a question. Baba replied, "If I make you avadhuta right now, are you ready?" I was astonished. One was supposed to follow the avadhuta rules for one year, but I had only been following them for six months. Then Baba asked, "What do you think about it?" I told Baba that I had some difficulty. "What is your difficulty?" he asked. Several other persons were there at the time so I told Baba that I could only tell him in private. Baba took me to his room and directed me to tell him about my difficulty. I told Baba that one rule in particular was very difficult for me, the rule that enjoined avadhutas to treat all women of the world, including one's wife, as mother. My mind was not yet able to think always in that way. I said that as long as I was not habituated in such thinking then I would like to wait for some more time. Baba said, "Don't worry, it will be gradually set right in your mind." I told Baba that if he took the responsibility to remove that weakness from my mind then I was ready to accept avadhuta initiation. "I shall take that responsibility," Baba said.

Immediately thereafter I touched Baba's feet and took the avadhuta oath, repeating the words after Baba. Baba sad that from that auspicious moment the physical body of Acharya Nityananda would thenceforth be known as Acharya Satyananda Avadhuta.

After administering the oath and completing the initiation, Baba said, "You are my first avadhuta of Ananda Marga. You will don the saffron dress on May 17, on the occasion of Ananda Purnima. Traditionally the guru gives the disciple the saffron dress, so in the meantime think over the matter and purchase the appropriate dress."

On May 17, on the occasion of Baba's birthday, a great number of devotees assembled in the jagriti. Baba arrived about 9:30 in the morning. I went to his room and told him that my saffron dress was ready, as per his instructions, and asked him if I should bring him the dress so that he could complete the formalities. "My blessings are always with you," Baba said. "Go to your room and put on your dress there in front of my picture. But first bring a lungota and I shall give it to you according to the tradition." I brought Baba a lungota and he dropped it and I caught it. In this way the work was done.

After this I returned to my small room in a corner of the jagriti, took out a picture of Baba in varabhaya mudra, and after doing sastaunga pranam in front of the photo I put on the saffron dress. My whole body became horripilated as my mind was overwhelmed with emotion. In front of my eyes I saw a vast celestial realm. I remained in that state for some time, looking toward the sky through the window. I lost my self-existence and felt that Parama Purusha existed within me in the form of Baba Anandamurtijii. It is impossible to express that feeling in language. After a few minutes, when I became to some extent normal, I left the room, but even then I could feel the smiling Kalyana Sundaram face of Baba inside me.

I came out from the room wearing the avadhuta uniform: saffron lungi and gown, waist band, and turban. I had a necklace of rudraksha beads, vermilion paste smeared on my forehead, and a pair of wooden sandals. I carried a one-inch diameter wooden staff that reached to my chest and a dagger. I already had the required long hair and beard. Baba had only told me to wear saffron-coloured dress. He had not specified the design so I chose the apparel as I thought best. Later on Baba told me not to use the rudraksha beads or the vermilion mark on the forehead because they might frighten the public. While designing the avadhuta dress I experimented with a number of different combinations, including dhoti, pajama, kurta, etc., before deciding on the uniform that is in use today.

Since it was Baba's birthday, Margis had come from different parts of the country and they were engaged in bhajan-kirtan, creating a heavenly atmosphere in the jagriti. When they saw me in the avadhuta uniform, some of the devotees began weeping. Others were confounded. Some elders and some younger devotees did pranam and took the dust of my feet and touched it to their foreheads. Others embraced me. I was unaffected as I mixed with them. I still felt Anandamurtijii within me and was absorbed in that blissful state.

The Ananda Purnima DMC was held in the Goenka Dharmasala in Monghyr and it was there that the avadhuta system was introduced in Ananda Marga. Baba arrived at noon for General Darshan. I sat on the dais beside him in full avadhuta dress, just by the side of his cot and near his feet. The Margis were curious to see me but their curiosity could not last before the physical presence of Baba, which carried everyone away.

After Baba's departure, I joined the Margis for bhajan and kirtan as they filled the hall with spiritual vibration. But after some time I called the workers and held meetings with different groups, discussing the future course of our organizational activities. It was a matter of great regret that the cast on my hand had not yet been removed. It made it difficult for me to mix freely with the others but my mind remained blissful.

After becoming avadhuta, Baba told me, "If anybody by mistake or unknowingly calls you by your old name, then and there you will tell them that now you are Acharya Satyananda Avadhuta."

9
Panic

THE NEWS THAT I had become an avadhuta spread quickly in the organization. Some were thrilled but others became afraid of the new system. Margis who had adult sons were afraid to lose them. They wanted to protect their sons from such a life and thus kept them away from the organization. But they themselves came to the jagriti as usual. The parents of the young educated workers who were helping me with the work now made efforts to bring them back home. Many of them came to me directly and requested me not to take their sons for organizational work. As a general rule, I never accepted anyone as a wholetime worker without the permission of their parents.

Amusingly, many young housewives came to me in tears and requested me with folded hand not to take their husbands as wholetime workers. Later on it came to my notice that when the wife of a devotee did not cooperate with her husband in the work of the Marga, the workers would frighten her by telling her that if she did not cooperate with the work of Baba's mission then they would call Acharya Satyanandajii to make her husband an avadhuta. I enjoyed the workers' sense of humour but to remove the fear complex from the families I made it a rule and sent out a circular it that if anybody wanted to become a wholetime worker they required the permission of their parents or wife. After this news was circulated among the Margis, people were no longer afraid of losing their sons or husbands. Everyone started cooperating with me wholeheartedly, assuring me that they would help me by all possible means to fulfil the duties and responsibilities given to me by Baba Anandamurtijii. From thenceforth the work proceeded with tremendous speed.

10
Will Power

IN THE MEANTIME three young unmarried educated boys — Sri Sudhir Kumar from North Bihar, Sri Asiim Kumar from Maldah, and Sri Ramesh Kumar from Kalpi — came to me to join as wholetime workers. Later I came to know that they had come without the permission of their parents. Shortly thereafter their parents and relatives came to the Jamalpur jagriti to meet them and ask them to return home. I did not interfere with their personal affairs. I simply directed them to meet with their relatives, pointing out that unmarried persons needed the permission of their parents and married persons the permission of their wife. Without that permission they would have to work as General Margis.

All three left for their homes with their relatives but after a few days they came back, saying that they felt uneasy at home. For some time they went back and forth, staying a few days in the jagriti and a few days at home. Then one day Asiim Kumar came to me and said, "Dadajii, my parents have permitted me to work as a wholetime worker!" I told him that verbal permission was not sufficient; I needed written permission. His father was Dr. Sudhir Kumar Pathak, a civil surgeon in the Government District Hospital of Bihar. He was a pious man and within a week Asiim Kumar returned with written permission. Shortly thereafter Dr. Sudhir took initiation in Ananda Marga along with his wife and other children. They became good devotees of Baba Anandamurtijii.

Ramesh Kumar was the next to get written permission from his parents. Sudhir Kumar, however, was unable to get permission. His father was a police officer in Bihar and was dead set against Ananda Marga. Sudhir, however, told his father that since he took bribes he could not take food from his income. A conflict ensued and ultimately Sudhir Kumar won out. Seeing his son's firm faith in the ideology of Ananda Marga, his father expressed a desire to know more about Ananda Marga. Later on the entire family took initiation. After getting personal contact with Baba, Sudhir's father began to lead a pious life, and he gave permission to Sudhir Kumar to work as a wholetime worker. In this way, one by one, a number of wholetime workers joined and the structural side of Ananda Marga started to develop.

11
Navagraha Yoga

*I*N THE MIDDLE of the 1962, due to a change the position of the planets, there was much propaganda about the possibility of a universal cataclysm and this caused widespread panic. Many people were performing pujas, oblations, kirtan, and worshipping different deities to save them from that destruction. Everyone was worried about what would happen from one day to the next. For those few days almost everyone forgot their envy, malice, and rivalries and instead started to treat each other with love, thinking that only a few days on this earth remained to them. Most people went to stay with their nearest relatives, wanting to spend their last few days with those who were nearest and dearest to them. To save themselves from the impending calamity they all surrendered unto the feet of the Lord and Controller of the Universe, Sri Hari.

At the same time, the so-called pundits and priests unitedly started to make preparations for great Vedic sacrifices in which a huge quantity of ghee would be burnt. The atmosphere was full of fear and no one was able to laugh with an open heart. Everyone's face was cheerless. All were terrified that they were about to leave this attractive world and all they were attached to. How terrible it was! I visited some families and found that they were huddled together with their nearest and dearest ones as well as their prized possessions, waiting for the fatal hour of three p.m., praying for the grace of the Almighty as they suppressed the screams of their heart. It was a heart-rending scene.

During the month leading up to the predicted end, Baba Anandamurtijii's heart melted, seeing the pathetic state of affairs. He went to the blackboard in the jagriti and made a diagram, showing the position of the different planets, especially the position of Saturn, which was reputed to be the cause of the great cataclysm, due to a change in its position. He showed that on that specific day Saturn would remain in a safe place and thus there would be no cataclysm. He then instructed the devotees to print up handbills explaining why there would be no cataclysm and to distribute them in everyone's respective areas.

Baba further said that the so-called pundits were burning lots of ghee in their Vedic sacrifices but that ghee was a nutritious food and should not be wasted needlessly. Instead they should stop these sacrifices and distribute that ghee among the students, which will help them to develop their intellect, seeing as how they are the future generation of the country. The distribution of ghee among the students will be an actual service to society, he said, unlike these sacrifices.

There was so much fear and so many rumours in the air that we were also to some extent affected. As a result we were passing as much time as possible with Baba. On the day of the cataclysm Baba came to the jagriti both in the morning and the afternoon. In the morning almost all the local Margis came to get his blessing, knowing that the great destruction was due to begin at 3:00 pm. When Baba returned to the jagriti in the afternoon there were only a few of us with him in his room. All were cheerless. Baba addressed Acharya Dasarathjii and said, "Dasarath, are you afraid?" Baba's mood became grave. "Don't you know that I have come to this earth with a mission? As long as my physical body remains on this earth no untoward incident can take place. Remain fearless. You have Parama Purusha's blessing."

Then Baba started different spiritual talks. The three o'clock hour came and went. All of a sudden, Baba stopped his spiritual conversation and addressing Acharya Dasarathjii, he said, "Dasarath! Three p.m. has passed and nothing has happened!" In reply Dasarathjii said, "Against your will Prakriti cannot do anything because she is your very own power — *shaktih sa shivasya shaktih.*"

12
Baglata

IN PURULIA DISTRICT of West Bengal, Garh Jaipur block, the local raja, Raghunandan Singhdeo, donated five hundred acres of land near the village of Baglata to Ananda Marga Pracharaka Samgha. On the railway line that runs between Gomo and Ranchi there is a station named Pundag. From Pundag Station, Baglata was about a fifteen-minute walk. Baglata is a small tribal village. Once it belonged to the kingdom of Raja Raghunandan Singhdeo of Garh Jaipur but at this time that particular area was in the name of his wife, Rani Ma. Officially she donated this land to Ananda Marga Pracharaka Samgha for social welfare work.

In August of that year Baba told me that we have gotten some land in Purulia District and that I should go there and arrange to measure the land and make a small hut where one could stay for a few days if required. Later on, he told me that this place would be the headquarters of Ananda Marga.

As per Baba's direction, I started for Ranchi to take the help of some local Margis. After reaching Ranchi on the third Sunday in August, I took the following acharyas from Ranchi with me to Baglata: Ac. Kedarjii, Ac. Kshitishjii, Ac. Amulyajii, Ac. Brahmadeo, Ac. Devichandjii, Ac. Shambhujii, Ac. Balendujii, and two more persons. We travelled in two cars to the residence of Raja Raghunandanjii in Garh Jaipur. He travelled with us from there to the Kotshila railway station, where we left the cars, proceeding to Pundag by train and from there to Baglata on foot. We reached Baglata in the afternoon and made a tour of the area. Then we unanimously selected a hillock near the village of Baglata on which to construct the hut that Baba had requested. Raja Raghunandanjii broke the ground with a spade and one by one we took up the spade and began digging the foundation as part of our auspicious opening ceremony. Afterward we returned to Ranchi in the evening by the same cars, after saying goodbye to Raja Raghunandanjii.

At Ranchi it was decided that Ac. Brahmadeojii was the fittest person to return to Baglata and construct the hut in that solitary place. He gladly accepted the responsibility. The hut was to be a temporary construction. I directed him to build up earthen walls and make a roof with tiles. Ac. Brahmadeojii was physically and mentally very strong at the time. He was able to work under any kind of adverse conditions. We knew we could depend on him. Once he had been an inveterate materialist but by the grace of Baba he had since become a good devotee.

After Ac. Brahmadeojii reached Baglata, he started mixing with the local people and soon won their sympathy. Initially he made a hut thatched with tree leaves and acquired an urn-shaped pot for cooking rice and vegetables. He was able to adjust very nicely in that difficult environment, surrounded by hills and jungle. To see him, I was reminded of the story of Hanuman who faced many adverse situations with a smiling face in the service of his venerable Ram. I also stayed with him in that hut and made an estimate to complete the construction. I gave him the necessary amount and the next day I started for Assam, where a programme had been organized for me by the workers of that area.

13
Assam Tour

*A*c. Asiim Kumar had been posted to the northeastern areas of Assam, Manipur, Nagaland, Arunachal, and Tripura. By this time at least one wholetime worker had been posted in every province or state of India. In Bihar and West Bengal, zone-level workers were posted. Prachar work was in full swing even though the wholetimers had no place to stay, taking on great troubles in order to preach the ideology. During the day they would remain engaged in prachar work and at night they would sleep in either the railway station or a dharmasala. On alternate days they would go to the postmaster to see if any mail had arrived for them.

Apart from raising the money for their monthly expenses, a difficult task that often cost me a night's sleep, I was also engaged in giving them proper training. To teach them how to do prachar, I used to go their respective areas and take them with me as I organized meetings, delivered speeches, formed unit committees, and looked to the arrangements for our meals and lodging. When I would return to Jamalpur I would bring some new Margis with me from that area for Baba's darshan. Once a group of people was prepared in that area, I would organize a training camp and give classes on Baba's ideology and mission. And when that place was ready I would recommend it for Dharma Maha Chakra. Rarely did I get time to rest, often sleeping no more than three hours a night, but today I am happy to see the successful development of the mission for which I laboured day and night.

I had informed Ac. Asiim Kumar of my tour programme for Assam but then China attacked India at the Nafa border. My well-wishers requested me not to go to Assam at that time due to the danger. I asked Baba whether or not I should continue with my tour programme for Assam and he told me that I should go there without any fear. Taking his blessing, I started for Assam. At Barouni Station I found the trains packed with military men. It was a direct train to Assam but it looked like it would be very difficult to get a seat. In the meantime some military men, seeing my saffron dress, invited me to join them in their compartment and gave me a seat. It was a long journey and at every station groups of military personal came to meet me for the sole purpose of asking one question: "What will be our fate?" Their fear showed in their faces. But

Baba had told me that I should go there without any fear and so I told the military personal that they would remain unharmed and that Assam would remain with India.

As per my programme, I stopped at Alipurduar for one day. Ranjit Rudra and Ac. Subrata (both were my initiates) came to receive me at Alipurduar Junction and I accompanied them to their railway quarters. The next evening they organized a tattvasabha at the Alipurduar railway colony. I addressed the tattvasabha and that same night I started for Pandu. After reaching Pandu Station, I found that Ac. Asiim Kumar and a group of Margis had come to receive me. For two days we conducted different organizational programmes there.

During those two days I went to visit Kamakhya Temple. In colloquial language it is known as Kamrup Kamakhya and the local people tell many supernatural stories about the place. This temple is situated in the Kamrup district of Assam on the top of a small hill, about two kilometres from Gouhati, the capital of Assam. A large Himalayan river, the Brahmaputra, passes by the foot of that hill.

While Ac. Asiim Kumar and myself were going up the steps to the temple, we found a number of priests waiting at the top of the steps to greet the visitors. We entered the temple, going down a short flight of steps to the main room. In the middle of that dark room was a five-foot square surrounded by a one-foot boundary wall covered with pieces of cloth. This was the Kamakhya piitha. It was Saturday and there was a heavy rush of visitors coming to offer their puja so we only remained there for a few moments. After coming out we entered the next room where we found a row of young girls, perhaps eight or nine years old, sitting with their bare feet extended. The priests were directing to the visitors to worship their feet. I asked one of the priests about the meaning of this puja. He replied it was known as Kumari puja, the worship of young virginal women. Then we proceeded to the next room where helpless pigeons were being immolated. I could not adjust to that environment, so much superstition in the name of the dharma. This is how the priests were maintaining their livelihood. A village of priests had grown up around the temple and their only source of income was the visitors who came there. The environment became unbearable for me and I asked Ac. Asiim if there were any nearby ashram where we could go to remove this mental pollution. He took me to the ashram of Vijaya Krishna Goswami on the bank of the Brahmaputra River. It was a most sentient environment. On my request the monks of that ashram began doing bhajan and kirtan and that created a divine atmosphere. I stayed with them for one hour and the adverse reactions of my mind were removed.

From there we visited the Shivananda ashram and after that we went to the ashram of Bhumanandajii. He had been a lecturer in an East Bengal college. Thirty-two years earlier he had accepted a monk's life. He was a Brahma sadhaka. We talked with him for some time and found the environment very pleasant.

After returning from these visits we went to Gouhati where a tattvasabha had been organized. In the evening I addressed the tattvasabha and then took a night train for Lumding. The day after reaching Lumding we heard the news of the fall of Bomdila. Indian soldiers had retreated with many wounded but few fatalities. At Lumding I addressed a tattvasabha and the next day we went to Karimganj and from there to a village named Sadarasi. The village had an Ananda Marga unit and the Margis there performed regular sadhana. The village was different from those of West Bengal. Every residence had a garden with fruit trees, such as betel nut, coconut, mango, jackfruit, and also bamboo and a small pond. From a distance the village looked like a jungle. Though the language was Bengali it was a dialect I couldn't understand properly. For honoured guests they cooked a kind of rice that became very sticky when boiled and we found it very difficult to eat. Fortunately they had also prepared some of the foods we normally ate in West Bengal, just in case. I talked to the Margis about the importance of sadhana and advised them to follow strictly the principles of yama and niyama.

From there we started for Shilchar by train, passing through a solitary terrain of hilly jungles and rivers. It was a fearful journey. The train was zigzagging constantly and almost all the compartments were vacant. The jungle was filled with bamboo and bananas and at times we were afraid of being attacked by wild animals. In the jungle I saw many monkeys eating bananas. There was a lot of dry bamboo and nobody was there to remove them. The few train stops were for one minute only and no food was available. The climate was humid due to the many rivers flowing by the railway line. Once I had heard that Assam was full of malaria and black fever and now I knew why.

We reached Shilchar the next evening and stayed at the airport guesthouse. A Margi family who worked at the airport took care of our food. It was similar to that of West Bengal but the system of serving was different. A Margi sister first served us a little rice and one curry. She waited nearby until we were nearly done with that item and then she brought more rice and a new curry. In this way she served us five times, each time with a different curry. When I was full and started to get up, she asked me not to leave. There were still four more vegetables and sweet rice waiting to be served. When I said that I had no room in my stomach, she asked me to at least taste them since they had been prepared especially for us. I agreed to taste everything on the condition that I would not take anything that night. Afterward that I told Ac. Asiim Kumar to warn me about the customs of the area before we went anywhere, so that I would not have to face such difficulties in the future. Later that same day we heard the news of a ceasefire between China and India.

From Shilchar we went to Jarhat. There we were guests of an Assami Margi family. In the evening I addressed a tattvasabha. Here the public's mind was on the war; therefore the atmosphere was not like other spiritual talks. Thus without wasting any time we returned to Lumding and then to Siliguri.

When I reached Siliguri Station, Ac. Sripatijii (later on Ac. Shraddananda Avt.), Ac. Amulya Ratan, and the local wholetime worker of that area, Ac. Anadinath, were there to receive me. Ac. Sripatijii was living in Galgalia and working as an inspector of central excise. Ac. Amulya Ratanjii was the civil SDO of Kishanganj subdivision of Bihar. From there we travelled together to Jalpaiguri. Ac. Anadinath had made arrangements for us to stay in a dharmashala and he had organized a tattvasabha. Many college students attended. Among them was a student named Bidhu who tried to convince the others in favour of Ananda Marga. Later on he became Ac. Jagadishvarananda Avt.

The next day we returned to Siliguri. Ac. Amulyajii went back to Kishanganj to organize my programme there. Ac. Sripatijii and I went to Darjeeling where we stayed with a local businessman. The next morning we went to see the rising sun falling on the snow-covered peak of Kangchenjunga. Tourists would sometimes wait for up to a month for a cloudless sky to see that scene but we were able to see it on the morning of our arrival. Darjeeling District is part of West Bengal but it bears no similarity to the rest of the state. The inhabitants are Mongolian in origin, their language is not Bengali, and their customs are quite different. It looks and feels like a foreign country.

The next day we started for Kishanganj. Ac. Sripatijii got down at Galgalia while I proceeded on to the residence of Ac. Amulyajii. That evening I addressed a tattvasabha and at ten I caught the night train for Jamalpur.

14
Revenge

*N*ow that I had become an avadhuta, certain householder disciples were reacted, fearing a loss of prestige. Under the leadership of the general secretary, Ac. P. K. Chatterjee, they organized a meeting at his residence to discuss their objections to the avadhuta system. Lalan Singh, Naval Kishore, Raghunath, and Harisadhan were among those who attended the meeting. Lalan was especially hostile, Raghunathjii was neutral, while Harisadhanjii was in favour of avadhuta system. In the meeting it was decided to take certain actions to discourage the formation of avadhutas. The general secretary sent Lalan on tour to tell the Margis not to cooperate with the activities of the wholetimers and avadhutas. He also told him to make me appear despicable before the eyes of the Margis so that I would be compelled to leave my avadhutaship under the pressure of the circumstances.

Harisadhan had always said that a spiritual organization should be run by monks but in the meeting they did not know that he was a supporter of the avadhuta system. Harisadhanjii did not made any comment during the meeting but that same afternoon he told me about the conspiracy they had hatched and what they planned to do in the future to foil the creation of avadhutas. I told Baba about it and Baba said, "All right, let them do what they will to the best of their capacity. But continue working as you are doing now." After talking with Baba I remembered a shloka from the Gita:

Yatra yogeshvara krishna yatra partha dhanurdhara
Tatra shrii vijaya bhuti drubha nitirmati mama.

Where Yogeshvara Krishna and his ardent devotee-warrior Arjuna are present, victory is assured. This is my opinion and faith.

Remembering Almighty Baba with firm determination, I went ahead with my work. It went on with tremendous speed and soon all their anger became concentrated on me. They brought allegations against me that my activities were hampering the organization and creating undue disturbance. P. K. Chatterjee brought the matter to Baba through Ac.

Dasarathjii. Baba called me and said, "The GS and Ac. Dasarathjii have reported to me that your activities have made it difficult for them to work in the organization. I want you to come to the jagriti this afternoon. I will also call them to the jagriti at the same time and I shall scold you in front of them, so come mentally prepared for that." I understood that the drama that afternoon would be an interesting one. As forewarned, Baba scolded me severely in front of them. When it was over he called me to his room and told me privately that my work was going on nicely. "Go ahead with your work," he said, "and don't look back."

A few days later Baba directed Acharya Chandranathjii and Ac. Ramtanukjii to cooperate with me. Later a committee was formed consisting of three members: Ac. Chandranathjii, Ac. Ramtanukjii, and myself. I was the secretary and the committee was known as the High Command. My work was to be done in consultation with the other members of the committee.

Ac. Chandranathjii at that time was a deputy superintendent of police in Bihar and a very sentient man. His sweet voice, love, and affection were unparalleled. He was one of the most senior acharyas and was initiated before the birth of the organization. I was delighted to have such a pious man like him in the High Command.

Soon after this P. K. Chatterjee got married. Ultimately his married life put an end to his organizational life.

15
Removal of Crucial Danger

*A*FTER MR. P. K. Chatterjee realized that he could not influence my work, he and Lalan Singh started to treat me like an enemy. I always respected Pranay-da as an elder brother, though his mind was reacted against me. The conflict burst into flame on December 3. That evening in the Jamalpur jagriti I asked Pranay-da about a letter and he burst into anger, scolding me right and left with objectionable language. I became confounded and silently digested his piercing words. When it became unbearable, I left the jagriti for the field to be alone. To remove my mental tension I sought the solitudes of my Tantra piitha. The moment I sat down I burst into tears. I lost my senses and continued weeping while lying on the ground. Suddenly a few feet away I heard a thunderous voice: "Satyananda be silent, be silent. Anandamurtijii is telling you to be silent. I could hear your weeping from a long ways away." When Baba told me to be silent a third time my consciousness returned. Then again he said, "It is my order that you remain silent." I remained silent but the anguish was visible in my body. Baba said, "Get up and accompany me." He repeated his words but I was unable to get up. My body was unresponsive. Again Baba told me to stand up and go with him. Very slowly, like a machine, I got up and followed Baba to the tiger's grave.

We sat on the tiger's grave for an hour but I could not utter a single word. Finally I followed Baba to the jagriti like an automaton.

After returning from the field I sent a telegram to Ac. Chandranathjii and Ac. Ramtanukjii, requesting them to come to Jamalpur immediately. I did not take my meals until they got there. Whenever I was mentally disturbed I would not eat until my normal mental condition returned. Nor could I sleep that night. I recollected that Baba was almighty, omnipresent, and omniscient. I knew that wherever I was he would always remain with me. That night, when I had fallen to the ground on my Tantra piitha, like a tree felled in a storm, losing my senses and weeping most loudly, addressing my most venerable Baba, the Lord had physically appeared before me to soothe my great mental affliction.

Why did Baba come to me at the Maha Tantra piitha, taking trouble in the night for my sake? I was thinking that I was a monk and if my physical presence was unbearable for anyone why should I not remove that obstacle from their path? If my absence would give them pleasure, then let them enjoy it. I was an avadhuta of Anandamurtijii, not of any particular organization. Wherever I went his gracious blessings would shower upon me. I decided to hand over my responsibility to the other members of the High Command and then proceed to the Himalayas to seek unification with the Lord, where there would be no envy, no grudges, no jealousy, fighting, or hostility. As a monk I would always utter the name of the Lord, drink water from the river, eat the fruits of nature, take shelter under a tree with one lungota, one blanket, one water pot, and a stick, the only possessions of a monk. I had no need of vehicles or gaudy dress for outward show, or honour, prestige, and organizational dignity, which only caused others to become jealous. They did not understand that it was all just a drama. Thinking in this way the whole night passed.

In the morning I told Baba about the telegram I had sent to Ac. Chandranathjii and Ac. Ramtanukjii, but I didn't disclose that I intended to hand over my duties and responsibilities to them and then physically leave Jamalpur forever after taking his permission, knowing that wherever I went he would always be with me.

In the afternoon Ramtanukjii and Chandranathjii arrived and met me. I told them what had happened and about my decision. After meeting me they left the jagriti to meet with Baba. In the meantime Ac. Asiim Kumar came to the jagriti. He had come to know about the episode. Then he hurriedly went to the field to tell Baba. He found Baba in a grave mood. After hearing what Asiim had to say, Baba said, "Do not talk to me now. Go back to the jagriti and let me sit in silence."

That evening Chandranathjii and Ramtanukjii came to the jagriti with the general secretary and the three of them tried their level best to make me change my decision. Pranay-da expressed repentance for his misbehaviour and admitted his fault. It was a complicated situation, since no one was ready to take over the charge. I told them that they should take over my charge, and only then would I take a decision about the future course of my life. At last they requested me to give them one day's time and I agreed.

The next morning at eight Baba came to the jagriti. It was a holiday and on holidays Baba would come to the jagriti both morning and evening. After entering the jagriti, Baba came directly to my room. Catching my hand, he took me to his sitting room and told me to lock the door. He tried to make me understand, but I stood firm on my decision. Then Baba said that certain vrittis were being expressed within me. "Control them," he said, "and think over my advice." In this way two and a half hours passed with no result. Then I looked at Baba's face and found that tears were streaming from his eyes. He wiped them with a handkerchief. Seeing this I was much affected. I began to censor myself for having brought tears to the eyes of my guru. It was matter of great shame. I am such a sinner, I thought, that due to my acts Baba has suffered. Unable to bear it any longer, I embraced Baba and asked him not to be angry with me, to excuse me for my behaviour. Baba said, "It is for me that you are oppressed; that is my pain."

"Baba," I said, "from now on, utilize me as you like." Baba had me take an oath that from thence forward I would look upon him and his mission as the same. "Yes, Baba," I replied, "I shall do my level best to fulfil your desire."

16
Hari

*I*T WAS ELEVEN o'clock when I came out of Baba's room. Hundreds of devotees were waiting outside for Baba's General Darshan. Their bhajans and kirtan created a spiritual vibration in the jagriti. I made arrangements for General Darshan and directed the disciples where to sit. Then Baba came and sat on the dais while I went to take bath and sit for puja. For three days I had not eaten anything due to my mental disturbance. At 12:30 Baba left the jagriti and I took my meal from Gaya Saha's small restaurant. I went back to my room for rest but after some time I started experiencing severe chest pains. I became restless and thought that perhaps I would not survive. At 3:00 p.m. Baba returned to the jagriti and started to give personal contact to the devotees. Ac. Dasarathjii was conducting the personal contact. I requested him to allow me to meet with Baba alone for one minute. After taking permission from Baba he allowed me to go inside the room. I told Baba about my chest pains, which had become practically unbearable. Baba said, "You have many samskaras from your past deeds that are being expressed now. You will be all right. Go now." I came out of Baba's room and the pain started to lessen.

After evening puja my chest pain completely disappeared. I became cheerful again. While I was walking in the jagriti compound Baba arrived. I was surprised to see him since it was his time to go to the field for evening walk. I wondered why he had come to the jagriti. Baba went directly to his room and lay down on his bed. He said, "Satyananda, please bring me a glass of hot lemon water. I am feeling ill this evening and for that reason I was unable to go for field walk. That is why I have come to the jagriti."

I was mortified to hear this. Why had I told Baba about my chest pain, I thought. It is because of this that he has become ill. In the future I shall not tell him such things. I told Baba what I was thinking. "Why have you welcomed this sort of suffering on my behalf?" I said. "Your physical body is the most important physical body in this world. If you so desire, you can create hundreds of Satyanandas. Why take on this sort of sufferings due to the past vices of a wretched person like me?"

"You know," Baba said, "another name for Parama Purusha is Hari. Hari means *harati pápánii ityarthe hari* — Hari is he who takes the sins of his devotees without their knowledge. The duty of the guru is to grace his devotees as well as to punish them. Do not worry about this."

Baba remained in the jagriti up until 11:00. When he was leaving, he said, "Tomorrow I shall fast with hot lemon water and take rest. Then I will be all right." The next day Baba did not go to the railway office. He came to the jagriti at 9:00 a.m. and remained with us up until 10:00 p.m., except for evening puja when he went to his quarters for an hour and then came back. Ac. Chandranathjii and Ac. Ramtanukjii were there the entire day as well. When Baba was leaving for the night, he said, "From tomorrow I will resume my normal duties." I told Baba:

Shantaya byakta rupaya maya dharaya vaisnabey
Svaprakashaya satyaya namahastu vishwa sakshiney.

O Lord Vishnu, sheltering Maya within yourself, you have expressed yourself in a peaceful form. I salute that witnessing entity of the universe.

17
Compromise

*A*FTER THIS P. K. Chatterjee joined the High Command. He expressed his desire that all the organizational work should be done with his knowledge and we had no objection. It was our wish that the work be done unitedly and that all misunderstandings be removed. As the general secretary of the organization, it was his duty is to supervise all the unit and district committees of Ananda Marga, to inspire the Margis to follow *Caryacarya*, to inform the Margis about the DMC programmes, to oversee the construction of jagritis in different units, to publish books and magazines, and to maintain the office records. My duty was to organize and conduct volunteer social service camps, to give training for social work, to give recommendations as to which devotees should become acharyas, tattvikas, kapalikas, and avadhutas, to build up and supervise the structural organization composed of wholetime workers, to see to the maintenance and financial security of those wholetimers, to give them practical training in dharma prachar by going with them to the field, and to arrange DMCs and see that they were properly organized.

Whenever Baba went outside Jamalpur, his security arrangements were also an important duty for me.

In this way both sides would work concertedly, fulfilling their own responsibilities and seeing that the work was done in a spirit of coordinated cooperation.

18
Inspiration

*A*T THIS TIME Ac. Ramswarthjii left his family and his government service to become an avadhuta. He became known as Ac. Shivananda Avadhuta and was the second avadhuta of Ananda Marga. When he left his worldly attachments and dedicated his life as an avadhuta, it created a stir among the General Margis, stimulating their sense of sacrifice. After that, many sadhakas individually and many units collectively expressed their desire to bear the expenditure for at least one wholetime worker, so that their numbers could increase. At that time I was anxious as to how I would meet the expenditure of the wholetime workers. Many educated young boys had joined as wholetimers and many more were on waiting list, but due to financial difficulties I could not accept them. With this increased cooperation from the Margis, I gradually allowed them to join as wholetime workers.

In a growing organization financial problems are never-ending, since no one can be victorious over nature. When one problem is solved, another problem takes its place. Take the example of medicines: many medicines have been invented for existing diseases, but each time a new disease appears for which there are no medicines available. There is no permanent solution to this. As long as the creation exists, problems will continue to come, one after the other. We should not let them worry us.

19
New Year's Day

*I*T WAS JANUARY 1, 1963. All day long the in-charges were busy to make the evening programme a grand success. In the afternoon a Margi brother from Baba's office came to me with a message from Baba. Baba wanted me to proceed to gate number three with the car to bring him from his office. I picked him up at gate number three and as per his direction we went directly to the tiger's grave. Sri Ram Swarupjii snapped Baba's photo there and then we started for jagriti. The moment we reached the jagriti compound, the hundreds of devotees who had come for the programme rushed to Baba's car shouting the slogan *Parama Pita Baba ki Jai* and encircling his car. Baba got down from the car and went to his sitting room where he sat on the cot and delivered a speech about knowledge, action, and devotion. After Baba's speech, the devotees started singing bhajans and kirtan. Half an hour later Baba expressed his desire to go and I took him by car to his Rampur colony quarters. Leaving him in his quarters, I went to Rampur Colony field where children's games were going on as part of our New Year's Day celebration. After the distribution of prizes and a speech, the programme ended.

20
Renaissance Universal Club in Delhi.

THAT EVENING, WHILE Baba was at the jagriti, he called me to his room and said, "Satyananda, the work of RU (Renaissance Universal) is not progressing like the other wings of the organization. It should develop parallel to the other wings so that the structural side and the organizational side can maintain harmony between each other. Therefore I have decided that one learned wholetimer should be posted to RU, and that he should open an office in New Delhi. See to it that it is done. That worker will take over the charge of RU from Dr. Nagendra Srivastav and tomorrow he should proceed to New Delhi. Because Dr. Nagendra is a householder as well as a lecturer of Muzaffarpur Medical College, he is not getting sufficient time to travel for this work. He also feels that he is not able to discharge his duty properly and is thus hampering the progress of RU."

I proposed the name of Ac. Lalan and then and there Baba agreed. Then I brought Lalanjii to Baba. Baba instructed him about his duties and directed him to take over the charge from Ac. Nagendra and then proceed to Delhi. Lalanjii left the next day.

On the morning of January 2, Baba came to the jagriti and called me to his room. He asked me about the persons that wanted to become avadhutas. I told him Ac. Asiim Kumar and Ac. Ramesh were ready and willing. Later that day Baba gave permission for Ac. Asiim Kumar to become avadhuta. After taking avadhuta initiation, he became known as Ac. Sambuddhananda Avadhuta. He was nineteen and was the third avadhuta of Ananda Marga. On January 4 Baba again came to jagriti in the morning and gave permission for Ac. Ramesh Kumar to become avadhuta. After receiving avadhuta initiation he became known as Ac. Pranavananda Avadhuta. After this there was a VSS camp scheduled at Ranchi. We all attended and while we were there they received their avadhuta dress. I conducted the camp as commander-in-chief and it lasted a total of fifteen days.

21
Central Volunteer Social Service Camp

ON THE WAY to the Ranchi camp, we stopped at Gaya where Ac. Satyanarainjii, the district executive engineer, and a professor of Gaya College, Ac. Ram Krishnajii, received us and brought us by Jeep to Ac. Satyanarainjii's residence. We spent the night there and the next day Ac. Ram Krishnajii arranged a tattvasabha among the professors of his college, where I delivered a lecture on the philosophy of Ananda Marga. After lunch we started for Ranchi by bus.

Ac. Kedarjii and Ac. Kshitishjii were waiting at the Ranchi bus stand with a car to receive us. They took us to our jagriti at Ratu Road. At that time the area was quite solitary and our jagriti was surrounded by open fields. Two furlongs away there was a big lake. For a spiritual aspirant it was a very congenial environment. We had selected this place for holding the central volunteers social service camp, which was attended by volunteers from different parts of the country.

At that time the whole country was in a state of agitation due to Chinese aggression. The Government of India had given a clarion call to the youth of the country to take self-defence training. Accordingly we included such training in the programme. I called a meeting of senior Margis and workers in which it was decided that besides philosophy classes and self-defence training, we would also include training for facing natural calamities, car and motorcycle driving, first aid, air-raid instruction, etc. The self-defence training was given by the government.

For the self-defence training arrangements, I took acharyas Kedarjii and Kshitishjii with me to meet the Ranchi Deputy Commissioner and the Deputy Inspector General of the Bihar police. The DIG, Sri T. N. Ghosh, was an Ananda Margi and a close personal friend. After the meeting, he gave an order to the Ranchi police major that as per the government circular, all sorts of self-defence training should be given to the Ananda Margis during the next fifteen days, especially since they had come from different parts of India. The DIG took us to meet the police major and together we chalked out a programme. Thereafter I sent different groups of campers at different times to the police for their training.

About 250 volunteers attended the camp. Among them some fifty or so were aged. They were not physically fit enough to attend the self-defence training so we kept them engaged in different light works and theoretical classes. The other two hundred volunteers were divided into different groups and given all the different trainings mentioned above. The volunteers were engaged from 4:00 a.m. to 9:00 p.m. in the different programmes and so for their relaxation we arranged for some form of recreation from 9:00 p.m. to 10:00 p.m., including a humorous talk by Ac. Sripatijii.

Our country has 323 different languages. During the freedom movement, the English language was used so that people from different parts of the country could exchange their thoughts, and so we conducted this camp, which included volunteers from all over India, in English. I gave an order that the volunteers should speak only English during the camp, and it was decided this system would remain in effect in the future for central camps. From then on Ananda Marga accepted English as the official language of the organization.

The camp ended on January 18 and on that day I gave the new avadhutas their saffron dress and presented them before the volunteers as Ac. Sambuddhananda Avt. and Ac. Pranavananda Avt. When Ac. Kshitishjii remarked that we were now four, I told him that once Maharaja Ranjit Singh of Bharatpur asked why there were four red marks in the map of India for Calcutta, Delhi, Bombay, and Madras. His followers replied that those red marks indicated the areas occupied by the British. After a short pause he said gravely that the day will come when all of India will be red. "Today we are four," I told Kshitij, "but a day will come when the entire organization will be run by the avadhutas."

22
More Wholetimers

*A*T THE END of the Central VSS Camp, Sri Someshwar, Dhanalal, Ramtabakya and Amit (later on Amitananda Avt.) submitted applications to become wholetime workers. After giving the necessary exam, I accepted their applications.

The next day Ac. Kedarjii took me in his car to see the Hantru waterfall near Ranchi. It was a scenic spot surrounded by hills and jungle. The water flows down from the hills and ends in a twenty-foot waterfall that falls onto stone, making the place foggy and cool. From there he took me to see the Kankey mental hospital. We did not go inside but walked around the grounds and then had a discussion with the director of the hospital about different aspects of the treatment of their patients.

After returning to the jagriti, I distributed the monthly allowance to the wholetime workers and directed them to reach their respective areas as early as possible. A few workers of South India were detained due to a shortage of funds. The next morning, I left Ranchi for Baglata along with Ram Kishore Gupta, reaching there in the afternoon. A tribal student named Rupa Bhagat was staying there alone at the time because Brahmadeojii had gone to Ranchi for the VSS camp. Once we arrived, I sent Rupa Bhagat back to Ranchi.

Ram Kishore had brought supplies for opening a charitable homeopathic dispensary. He started his work in the little hut that Brahmadeojii had constructed. The next day we went to the surrounding villages to inform them that a dispensary had opened in Baglata. There were no doctors in the surrounding villages so patients started coming for treatment right away. Once Ram Kishore was established, I returned to Ranchi. By that time the local Margis had arranged enough money to send the rest of the workers to their respective fields. After sending them I felt more relaxed.

On January 23 Rajesh and I left for Jamalpur by bus. At the request of Ananga Mukherjii, we stopped at his residence in Nowada for a few minutes and then continued on to Jamalpur by train, reaching at the dead of night. For the past nine months, Ac. Arun Kumar (later Ac. Svarupananda Avt.) had been working as my personal secretary and living in the Jamalpur jagriti. After graduating with an MA in philosophy from Muzaffarpur University, he had joined as a wholetime worker.

He had learned a lot about the organization in these nine months and since we needed a well-educated, Hindi-speaking worker for West Uttar Pradesh, I sent him there and temporarily posted Ac. Anadinath (later Ac. Lokeshvarananda Avt.) as my personal secretary. After some time I sent him to North Bengal and Ac. Rajesh became my personal secretary. Later he became Ac. Ajayananda Avt.

In the meantime Pranay-da appointed an ashram manager, Sri Madhav Jha, to look after the jagriti. He had an MA in political science and was from an orthodox Maithili Brahmin family. Another Nepali boy by the name of Bahadur also lived in the ashram as a caretaker.

23
Sympathy Becomes Enmity

On January 30 the parents of Amit showed up at the Jamalpur jagriti to take him back home, after having first gone to Baba's quarters. Baba had given him the name Amit in place of his family name, Amar. A few months earlier Amit had graduated in engineering from BIT Ranchi and had taken a job in a private firm in Calcutta through a contact of his father's, who was at that time the income tax commissioner in Calcutta. He was also the owner of one hundred hectares of cultivated land in the Gaya district of Bihar, as well as the owner of several buildings in both Patna and Bombay. In short, he was a rich man.

After Amit left his job to become a wholetime worker, his parents were mortified. They came to convince him to return to his job, telling him that he could use the money he earned to help Ananda Marga. I arranged for Amit to meet with his parents and told them that they were welcome to take him back home with them if he agreed. But Amit did not agree. In order to placate them I posted him in the Jamalpur area and told his parents that they could visit him whenever they wanted and thus continue their efforts to convince him. After this, his parents came several times and tried to convince him to return, but ultimately they failed. Finally his father, Sri Shiv Dhyan Singh, filed a kidnapping case in the Monghyr court on behalf of his minor son against me, Baba, and the GS, Pranay Kumar. The magistrate of the court was an acharya of Ananda Marga, Sri Bal Mukunda Rastogir. He arranged for Baba to be released on bail without having to appear in court.

We had behaved very cordially with Amit's parents, extending them every opportunity to convince him to go back home with them but in the end they filed a false case against us. According to Amit's school certificate he was an adult.

24
My individual Prachar Programme

WE NOW HAD a number of highly qualified young men working enthusiastically throughout India, doing the prachar of Ananda Marga. They were very sincere but they had no experience. For that reason I would travel to their area and take them with me as I did prachar, teaching them how to give lectures, how to talk to different individuals, what kinds of answers they should give to the questions they would be asked, and how to work in a psychological way without offending anyone's sentiments.

Now I chalked out a prachar tour for West Bengal and informed the concerning workers to arrange public programmes in their respective areas. The tour was due to begin on February 9 and would take me to Suri, Bardhaman, Krishnagar, Bongaon, Baharampur, Ziaganj, and several other places. I asked them to schedule as many tattvasabhas as possible in different colleges, college hostels, and other public venues. This would give the local workers a chance to learn prachar techniques.

I completed my office work on February 8 and that night we had a meeting of the High Command. Ac. Chandranathjii and Ac. Ramtanukjii came to Jamalpur to attend. The next day I spent some time explaining the office work to my personal secretary, Rajesh Kumar. Then I left for my tour. My first stop was Sabore, where I went to the residence of Ac. Devichandjii, who was the director of Sabore Agriculture College. He had a arranged a meeting for me there. After giving my talk I gave instructions and advice to the local workers of that area and then took a night train for Suri, the district headquarters of Birbhum in West Bengal.

No one had done prachar in Suri before. I stayed at the Suri dharmashala and met with the secretary of Jubilee Library, Sri Nandi Babu. He advised me to contact Dr. Kaligati Babu, saying that without his help it would be difficult to organize a meeting in Suri.

In the afternoon I sought out Dr. Kaligati Babu. I found him surrounded by many patients. I waited until all the patients had left and then we talked. He asked me to come back in two days time and in the meantime he would try to arrange a few meetings for me in different parts of the town.

From there I went to meet professor Dev Rainjan Babu to see if I could hold a meeting in his Kalibari college hostel, which was next to his residence. He agreed and we held a tattvasabha there in which I explained about ashtanga yoga sadhana and the ideology of Ananda Marga. After the meeting many students wanted to take initiation but I only had time to initiate two or three of them before heading back to the dharmashala.

The next morning a Margi named Monaj Chakravarty came to meet me. I asked him to inform Acharya Sachinandan of Indas about my arrival in Suri. By this time some more students had come to the dharmasala to take initiation. In the afternoon I addressed a meeting of the teachers of Ram Krishna Vidyapitha. When I returned to the dharmasala I found some students from the Kalibari college hostel waiting for me. They requested me to go to the hostel for further discussion about Ananda Marga. Most of them were second- and third-year students of Suri Vidyasagar College. I accompanied them and we had a good discussion. Professor Dev Rainjanjii took part and was very interested. He also wanted to take initiation but there was a problem: in order to take initiation he would have to give up the sacred thread and idol worship and this gave him a lot of mental clash. I told him to meet me alone so we could discuss it further.

The next morning a few students came to the dharmasala and took initiation. At noon Dev Rainjan Babu invited me to his residence. When I arrived there he requested me to find a way for him to take initiation without having to give up the sacred thread and idol worship. I told him that I would have to put the matter to our central authority, and if any alternative arrangement was possible I would inform him.

In the afternoon I went to meet Dr. Kaligati Babu. He took me to the residence of the Suri College principal and told him about my mission. After talking to me, he said he would arrange a meeting with the students from his college the next day at 1:00 p.m. From there we went to meet the secretary of the district library, Sri Gouranga Chatterjee. Kaligati Babu requested him to organize a meeting for me at his library and he scheduled a tattvasabha for the next evening. After that I returned to the dharmasala. Some initiated students from the Kalibari hostel came to meet me and I talked with them for some time.

The next morning, I was on the way to a shop to get some breakfast when I met Ac. Sachinandanjii and Ac. Gopinath from Indas. It had been some time since I had seen them. An initiated student, Sri Bashari Mohan Dutta, happened by and I introduced him to Ac. Sachinandan and requested Sachinandan to guide the boy in his sadhana. He had the makings of a good devotee — at the time of initiation he was weeping.

When I arrived at Suri College for the tattvasabha I found the students filled with curiosity. We held a one-hour meeting in which I explained about the aim of life. There was no scope to give initiations so I introduced them to Ac. Sachinandanjii so they could approach him at their convenience for initiation. Then we returned to dharmasala.

After reaching the dharmasala, Dr. Sachinandanjii told me about Suri's famous sweet, *morabba*. He invited me to try it and I found it quite tasty. In the evening I addressed a tattvasabha in the district library to a highly educated audience. After the meeting, Ac. Sachinandanjii and I left for Bardhaman.

Sachinandanjii's brother-in-law, Kinkar Mandal, was a BSC Honours student in Bardhaman. We stayed with him in his student mess. Hearing about our arrival, an Ananda Margi postgraduate student named Satya Rainjan came to meet us. After some time he took me with him to his hostel and introduced me to the other Ananda Margi students living in the same hostel. I told them about my programme and asked them arrange some meetings with the students.

The next morning I discussed Ananda Marga philosophy and yoga sadhana with the students from his hostel. On the way there I had some badinage with a group of students who were amused to see my avadhuta dress. Later on I addressed a student meeting and they came to beg apology for their actions. In reply I told them that it was natural for young people in groups to do such things, that it was an excusable offense.

From there Satya Rainjan and a Margi student named Kanhai met with the hostel superintendent to get permission for holding a tattvasabha in the hostel that evening. He agreed to their proposal. After returning to Kinkar's, a Margi named Yeadramji came to meet me. He was a high-ranking government officer in Bardhaman. His elder brother, Sri Monoharlal Agarwal, was the principal of Jaipur Agarwal College in Rajasthan. Yeadram organized a tattvasabha in his officers' circle. They were Hindi-speaking so I addressed the meeting in Hindi. In the meantime Kinkar organized a meeting the next evening for the students of two Raj College hostels.

That evening we went to the postgraduate hostel for the tattvasabha. I delivered a lecture for one hour on different aspects of Ananda Marga. I was surprised that there were no questions afterward, but some students wanted to take initiation in the morning.

The next morning we initiated some students from the postgraduate hostel. Leaving them with Ac. Sachinandanjii, I accompanied Yeadramjii to address the tattvasabha among his colleagues. Afterward I initiated some of them and at Yeadramjii's request I took dinner and rest in his residence. When I returned to the mess, I found that some persons from the community had come to visit and hear about my mission. I talked with them for an hour and then in the evening I went to the Raj College hostel where 150 students had assembled to hear me talk about Ananda Marga. After the meeting, many students wanted to take initiation. We initiated as many as we could that same night. Since it was not possible to initiate them all, I wrote down their names and requested Ac. Sachinandanjii to make arrangements for their initiation. Then I entrained for Krishnagar.

I reached Krishnagar in the evening. Ac. Sukhenjii was waiting in the station to receive me. He told me that a tattvasabha had been organized that evening at Shantipur so we ran to catch the train for Shantipur, which was about to leave. Shantipur was a half-hour journey from Krishnagar. After reaching there, I gave a talk on the spiritual way of life. Afterward I told those who were interested in taking initiation to kindly contact Ac. Sukhenjii at Krishnagar. We returned to Krishnagar by tempo. Ac. Dhiren and Nimai (later on Japananda Avt.) had come to help me with my prachar work and in the meantime Sukhenjii and Manorainjanjii (Balai-da) had fixed a programme in Krishnagar College for professors and students.

On February 17 a large public meeting was held in the evening at the Krishnagar town hall. Leaflets had been distributed announcing the programme and it had also been announced by mike. The local workers and Margis invited people from all walks of life to attend. When I completed my puja, fifteen minutes before the scheduled start time, I learned that two thousand people had packed the town hall, spilling out into the adjoining field. I reached the dais at 7:00 p.m. and after one song I started my speech. In my lecture I explained about life, death, and samskara. When I was leaving the dais someone from the audience approached me to say that some persons had requested a personal talk with me. I asked them to meet me in the Ananda Marga ashram after half an hour.

It was a half-hour walk to the ashram. By the time I reached there, Ac. Dhiren and Nimai and the other acharyas of Krishnagar had made a line in front of the ashram for those who wanted to meet me. There were about two hundred people in the line. I started to talk to them one by one. I asked each of them what they wanted to know, if they had any questions. Everybody replied that they had come to do pranam and take the dust of my feet. No one had any questions. Some persons said, "Mahaprabhu, have you come again to Nadia?" They embraced me and started weeping. I remembered Baba Anandamurtijii and said internally, "Oh Lord, I am nothing but an instrument in your hands. Let your desire be fulfilled through me." Once I discovered that they had no philosophical questions, I met them all in a group.

From that afternoon an invisible spiritual power dominated my mind. I felt a constant spiritual intoxication. I could feel a spiritual effulgence coming from my forehead while I was delivering the lecture in the town hall and realized that an occult power controlled everything, that it had created a magic spell in that area. That is why people were held spellbound by my lecture. At the ashram, when I started to meet people, I felt that Anandamurtijii himself was playing with his creation through my physical structure. This was the first time I realized such an unprecedented mysterious play.

After that, an ecstatic state flourished within my mind. Wherever I went, that power appeared within me. Wherever any devotee garlanded me, then and there I lost my normal senses and instead of me, Anandamurtijii appeared in my physical structure and gave pleasure to the persons present. Wherever I entered such a state, I behaved like a child and lost my usual balance. I lost the strength to control myself. After this, I began taking my personal secretary with me when I attended programmes, so that he could control me when I entered that ecstatic state. It would come on during organizational programmes and during my puja. The rest of the time I lived as an ordinary devotee of Baba.

When I became a wholetime worker I sometimes wondered if I would be able to bear the pain of being physically distant from Baba when I went for organizational work, wondering if I would tempted to break organizational discipline and return to Jamalpur to have Baba's darshan. But the ecstasy I experienced in Krishnagar greatly influenced me. I realized that Baba was not confined to Jamalpur. He was omnipresent. I don't know if a sadhaka can obtain that feeling by dint of his sadhana, even if he meditates for *crores* of years. But I can say that by the ceaseless grace of Baba one can experience such an ecstatic state within no time.

After the Krishnagar programme, those who attended my programmes were greatly affected to see how I would lose myself when the devotees garlanded me, or when I sat on the dais or went among the masses. Anandamurtijii would express himself through me and create a powerful spiritual atmosphere. These feelings fulfilled the aim of my life. Having gotten this unexpected grace of the sadguru, I knew how fortunate I was.

Jara jar jar sakali vishey tumi achho shudhu nitya nava.
Pratham jedin jegachhiley tumi ujal karia adim nava.
Sai rupee tumi kemaney rakhiley yugey yugey tar kuruna chhara.
Pratham manabey harsha jey dilo purano'ki hai tahar dhara?

For those who think that the Supreme Father is distant from them, he remains far away. For those who think that he is subtle, he is the subtlest. For those who think he is vast, he is vaster than they can imagine. For those who think he near, he is the nearest, living in their heart. That is why one can only know him by his grace. The life of a devotee who has gotten a microscopic fraction of his grace becomes successful. He is truly fortunate.

Mukam karoti vacalam paungam launghayate girim,
Jat kripa tvamaham bondey paramananda madhavam.

O greatly delighted Madhava, by your grace a mute person can give a lecture and a lame man can cross a mountain.

On Monday there was a programme at Krishnagar College at 2:00 p.m. for students and professors. The subject matter was "Physico-Psycho-Spiritual Parallelism." After the programme, a Margi student of Krishnagar Polytechnic College named Pradeep Kumar Guha requested me to go to his college to deliver a lecture. He had attended my lecture at Krishnagar College. In the middle of the lecture he had left to request his college principal to arrange a meeting in his college. I told him that if anybody organized a programme without taking my permission I was not bound to go there. Why had he not asked me beforehand? He repeatedly told me that since he had already committed such a mistake, kindly save him this time, and in the future he would not do it again. There was time, so I went with him and his friends to the polytechnic college. I delivered a talk on "Creation of Unit Mind and its Ultimate Goal." At the end of my speech they requested me to elaborate the matter in further details but I told them that it was not possible in such a short time. "Please ask me some question from the portion that you did not understand properly," I said, "and I will explain it." Accordingly they asked me some questions and after I had answered them to their satisfaction I left to catch the train for Bongaon. I reached Bongaon at night and went to the residence of Chandra Babu at Sripalli.

The next day I addressed a meeting for the magistrates, advocates, and officers of the Bongaon court in the court compound, organized by the Bongaon civil SDO. The subject matter was "Spirituality is Nothing but a Way of Life." After the meeting I introduced Ac. Dhiren and Nimai to them and then we went to the residence of Ac. Amulya Babu at Gopalnagar. From there we returned to Sripalli where we attended the weekly dharmachakra at the residence of Chandra Babu. The next day I delivered a lecture at Bongaon College and then caught the train for Baharampur.

Ac. Dhiren and Nimai accompanied me up to Krishnagar and from there Amit accompanied me. That evening I addressed a tattvasabha in a Krishnath College hostel, attended by some one hundred students. Many of them took initiation. The next day I delivered a noon lecture at Jiagang College and then came back to Baharampur and gave an evening lecture for the public at the Baharampur Grand Hall. By then the general public had come to know about our mission and some of them came to us with presents of sweets, milk, and fruits. They came with their families to do pranam. I discussed some religious matters with them.

On the twenty-first, Amit and I returned to Krishnagar where we held a meeting about publishing a newspaper. We formed a committee and it was decided that the name of the newspaper would be *Notun Prithivi* (The New World) and the first issue would come out that very week, even if it had to be published in bulletin form. It was also decided that Sri Manorainjan (Balai-da) would be the editor and overall in-charge.

25
Return to Jamalpur

*I*N THE EVENING Ac. Sukhenjii and Ac. Manas came to meet me at the ashram, where we discussed the different programmes of the organization. In the meantime a Margi student named Prandip Guha from Madanpur came to meet me with a young boy named Prandip Dass. He requested me to make some time to tell him about Ananda Marga. I took one look at him and told Sukhenjii that there was no need for any discussion, please give him initiation. Later on he became an avadhuta and was known as Ac. Sarvatmananda Avt.

The next morning I started for Tatanagar. Ac. Dhiren and Nimai came with me up to Howrah Station, where Sri Vishvanathjii came to meet me. I often used to stay in his residence. Then I caught the Howrah-Bombay Mail for Tatanagar.

Ac. Chandranathjii and Suresh came to receive me at Tatanagar Station. I accompanied them to the residence of Ac. Chandranathjii, and that night I went to the cremation ground to perform my kapalik sadhana.

Baba was scheduled to hold a DMC in Chaibasa, for which he would first come to Tatanagar. I and the other Margis of Tatanagar went to receive him at the railway station. We took him to the residence of Ac. Chandranathjii, where he had his dinner and a little rest, and then we started for Chaibasa by car. P. K. Chatterjee accompanied Baba as his attending secretary. I was also in the same car. In Chaibasa, Baba stayed at the residence of Ac. Rajmohan, who at that time was an SDO of the Public Works Department in Bihar.

After the evening DMC, I held a meeting with students and workers to inform them about the new programmes and alert them to their responsibilities. The next day after General Darshan I again conducted a meeting with workers. Then Baba started for Jamalpur via Ranchi by car. I accompanied him.

We had already informed the local Margis of Baba's programme, so a crowd of Margis was there to receive Baba when we reached the Ranchi jagriti. They started dancing around Baba, singing bhajans and kirtan, vibrating the entire ashram with spiritual rhythms. Many of them were weeping. Baba remained there for forty-five minutes and then started for Jamalpur. I stayed behind at Ranchi.

The next day I left to supervise the work at Anandanagar, Bardhaman, Krishnagar, and then Calcutta. In Calcutta I stayed at the residence of Vishvanath Sorabjii, where I usually stayed, and while I was there I went to meet Mr. Raghuvir Prasad at his Strand Road office. Sri Raghuvir Prasad was a very good devotee of Baba. At the time he was a collector of Central Excise and Customs for West Bengal, Bihar, Orissa, and Assam. He had requested me beforehand to stay for two days in Calcutta for prachar. During these two days he organized several meetings in different places where I addressed tattvasabhas. On March 7 I returned to Jamalpur.

After reaching Jamalpur, I spent the next few days clearing up my backlog of office work. I also arranged the money to send the field workers their monthly allowance. It was a matter of great surprise to me that wherever I went for prachar work or to supervise the work in the field, a dynamic supernatural energy took hold of my body and mind. But while in Jamalpur, engaged with my office work, I felt physically dull, like an ill person. Swami Vivekanandajii said once that he could not personally do any work — an invisible power compelled him to work. Now I realized the significance of his pronouncement.

26
West Bengal Work

ON MARCH 21 I went to Calcutta. Ac. Dhiren, Jitendra Tyagijii, and Vishvanath Sarabjii met me at Howrah Station. We all went to the residence of Vishvanathjii and then Ac. Dhiren left for Behala. Jitendra Tyagi was from Merut but was residing in Delhi. Both Tyagijii and Prasadjii had taken initiation directly from Baba in the early days of Ananda Marga and both were ardent devotees. They were not only brother disciples; they were also classmates from childhood and best friends. I felt a great mental harmony with them and thus we felt very happy to be together.

As per the suggestion of Raghuvir Prasad, a meeting was organized among the workers. During the meeting Prasadjii said that since he was going to different areas for his official duties, wherever he was he would go to the local Ananda Marga unit after completing his official business and work for Ananda Marga in that area. Hearing his decision, the workers were much encouraged. Then Tyagijii said he would accompany Mr. Prasadjii. While Prasadjii was busy with his office work, he said, he would inform the local Margis and with their help organize a tattvasabha.

After completing the meeting, we three went to the residence of Mr. Prasadjii, where a small tattvasabha was held. Then Tyagi and myself returned to Vishvanathjii's residence.

The next morning Ac. Dhiren, Arun of Taherpur, and I started for Krishnagar. Ac. Sukhenjii had organized a meeting of volunteers for that evening. After the meeting Ac. Sukhenjii and I went for kapalik puja.

The next morning Balai-da and I started for Calcutta for the purpose of introducing him to the Margis and workers of West Bengal in regards to his new assignment, known as Amra Bengali. From there we caught a night train to Bankura where Ac. Master Dhiren and Amit came to receive us. We went to the residence of a Margi named Sri Rakhahari Chatterjee, who was once a reputed leader of the Hindu Mahasabha. That evening the local Margis and workers assembled and I introduced Balai-da to them and told them about his programme. From there we went to Durgapur and did the same at the residence of a Margi named Monoj Chakravarty, a high-school teacher. Then we went to Bardhaman.

At Bardhaman, I introduced Balai-da to Ac. Sachinandanjii and many other Margis and informed them that there would be a meeting for all of West Bengal in Indas, the village of Ac. Sachinandanjii. I requested them to see to it that the meeting was successful, and then we started for Siliguri.

When I arrived at Siliguri Station the next day, a crowd of Margis was waiting to receive me with garlands in their hands: Ranjit Rudra from Alipurduar, professor Ac. Dhruva Narainjii from Balurghat, Ac. Sripatijii from Galgalia (later Ac. Shraddhananda Avt), Ac. Anadinath from Jalpaiguri, and a local Margi, Jagadishjii, who had selected the place for the meeting. I addressed the meeting and introduced Balai-da. That evening Balai-da, Ac. Anadinath, Brajen, Ranjit, and I left for Indas. Indas is situated in the middle of West Bengal, which is why we chose it for the meeting. It had two local acharyas, a jagriti, and a good number of devotees. About fifty organizers from different parts of West Bengal attended the meeting. That evening Ac. Dhiren became an avadhuta and was thenceforth known as Ac. Nirmalananda Avadhuta. Balai-da and I returned to Jamalpur on April 1.

27
Malice

AFTER REACHING JAMALPUR I found that my office secretary, Rajesh, was not there. I learned from the ashram manager, Sri Madhav Jha, that the general secretary had sent him home, paying his train fare. It was clear to me then that P. K Chatterjee was still against the system of wholetime workers and avadhutas. It was a direct challenge. I was not in any way creating difficulties for him. So I appointed Sri Sudhir Kumar (later, Ac. Abhedananda Avt) as my office secretary and taught him the office work. Later I came to know that Rajesh did not go home. He went to Ac. Anadinath, a wholetime worker in North Bengal, to help him with his prachar work. He sent me a letter informing me that P. K. Chatterjee had compelled him to leave the ashram and so he had gone to Ac. Anadinathjii. I informed Baba about the matter and then brought him back to Jamalpur, where he took up his old job.

At that time the following wholetimers were working in West Bengal: in North Bengal, Ac. Anadinath; in Calcutta and 24 Parganas, Ac. Dhiren; in Bardhaman, Ac. Nimai; in Bankura, Ac. Master Dhiren; in Murshidabad, Ac. Amit. The local acharyas were Ac. Sukhenjii and Ac. Manas in Krishnagar; Ac. Sachinandan in Birbhum District; and Ac. Professor Druvadev Narain in West Dinajpur District. These local acharyas were working like wholetimers. In every area the Margis and acharyas were working in coordination and cooperation with each other, and with missionary zeal.

28
North India Tour

NEXT I ORGANIZED a tour of North India and sent a circular to the concerning workers of those areas: western U.P., Delhi, Punjab, Himachal Pradesh, Jammu, Kashmir, and Rajasthan. During the week leading up to my departure I met with Baba each morning and evening and he talked to me in detail about the areas I would be visiting and how best to do my work there.

I started from Jamalpur on April 7, with Ac. Ramashray accompanying me up to Arrah. At Patna, Ac. Vishokananda Avt. and a group of Margis came to meet me at the station. Ac. Ramashray got down at Arrah where another group of Margis came to meet me, and at Mughalsarai I changed trains for Kanpur. I reached Kanpur the next morning. Ac. Arun met me at the station along with a local Margi, Sri Krishna Singh, who was Deputy Superintendent of Central Excise. We went to the residence of Ac. Om Prakash Sethi in Swarup Nagar. He was also Deputy Superintendent of Central Excise. Ac. Shivananda Avt. was already there. That evening we went to the residence of Ac. Maheshwarjii for dinner and a tattvasabha arranged by our host for some high-ranking officials. I talked about samskara. Afterward I addressed another tattvasabha organized by Sri Peswarilaljii, who was the superintendent of Central Excise. All the Margis there were high-ranking officers. In the meantime Ac. Raghavjii telephoned me with a request to stop at Aligarh on my way to Delhi. I agreed and informed Delhi of the change in my programme.

That night Ac. Arun and I caught a train for Aligarh, reaching there in the morning. Ac. Raghavjii and some Margis met us at the station and took us to the residence of the unit secretary, the advocate Sri Brajakishorejii. He was a very good devotee and a gentleman. His father was leading a monk's life at Lakshmanjhula. During spiritual discussions Brajakishorejii would weep out of devotion.

In the afternoon I addressed a tattvasabha in Brajakishorejii's residence, explaining about Ananda Marga and its spiritual practices. Then Ac. Raghavjii saw us off at Aligarh Station. Ac. Raghavjii had graduated in engineering from the Bihar Institute of Technology in Ranchi. He had learned about Ananda Marga from me during his student days. When I asked him about his plans, he told me that he wanted to go to America. I asked him to first help me build up our mission. He agreed and after getting training he was working as a wholetimer. Later I allowed him to go to America, just as Ananda Marga was getting established there.

Delhi

Sri Tyagijii, Ac. Ramtanukjii, Ac. Ratneshjii, and Ac. Lalanjii came to receive us at Delhi Station. They took us to the residence Sri Shashi Rainjanjii at 93 North Avenue. He was a good devotee of Baba and a Member of Parliament. The next morning I discussed the organizational work with Ac. Ramtanukjii and Tyagijii. We made a plan to contact the DMK leader, Mr. Manoharan. We called and made an appointment and later that day I met with him at his MP quarters. From there I went to Tyagijii's residence. Ac. Om Prakash, a wholetimer working in Punjab, had reached there to accompany me during my tour of Punjab. Then we returned to Sri Shashi Rainjanjii's quarters.

Ac. Lalanjii had opened his RU office in Shashi Rainjan's residence and the next day he organized a meeting of local Margis. I addressed the meeting and talked about our system of work and the importance of sadhana. Professor Balaraj had came from Ambala and I met with him for some time. Sri Kulabhusanjii from the military camp also came to meet me. In the night Ac. Om Prakash and I started for Ambala.

Punjab

We reached Ambala early in the morning, about 4:00 a.m. Raja Sahab came to the station and took us to his residence. He had invited some intellectuals to attend a tattvasabha there at 10:30. In that tattvasabha I explained about the systematic and scientific sadhana of Ananda Marga, and afterward many learned sadhana from Ac. Om Prakash. Then we started for Patiala by bus.

The next morning I talked to the local Margis about the importance of sadhana. They were eager to work for the organization. In the evening a public meeting was organized. I talked about the philosophy of Ananda Marga and yoga sadhana.

On the thirteenth we started for Chandigarh by bus and reached there at 10:00 a.m. A Margi student from Chandigarh University named Nandalal met us at the bus stand and took us to his residence. We ate our meal at the residence of Dr. Devaraj Vora, a yoga teacher in the government yoga centre and a good Margi. He organized a tattvasabha in his yoga centre in the evening and I explained about Ashtanga yoga sadhana. Many of them took initiation.

Simla

In the morning Dr. Vora brought a group of students to meet me. Then I had a tour of Chandigarh, arguably the most beautiful town in Asia. It was a government bus tour and I had the feeling that I was touring a foreign country. In the meantime Nandalal brought our luggage to the bus stand and at 1:00 p.m. Om Prakash and I started for Simla. On the journey we passed through beautiful mountain scenery, including the two hill towns of Kalka and Solan, reaching Simla in the afternoon. It reminded me of Darjeeling. In Simla we stayed at the DMV school. It was bitterly cold. The principal of the school was an Ananda Margi but he was not doing sadhana properly. I made him understand the importance of sadhana.

The next morning we went to Gandhi Park in the middle of town from where we had a wonderful view of the Himalayas. Simla is in the foothills. The park was nicely decorated with benches and protection from the rain and sun. It is at the base of a thousand-foot hill, called Jakku Hill. We climbed the hill from where we had a stunning view of the Himalayas. At the top there was some level ground with a small gazebo and several benches. While we sat there, hundreds of monkeys were playing all around us. We remained there until late afternoon and then came back to the school.

The next day we went by train to Kalka, and from there to Amritsar, reaching at 6:00 a.m.

The Golden Temple

Ac. Jialaljii and some Margis met us at Amritsar Station and took us by car to Ac. Jialaljii's residence. Ac. Jialaljii was Assistant Collector of Central Excise posted in Amritsar and an ardent devotee of Baba. After lunch, Om Prakash, Jialaljii's eldest son, Ashok, and I went to visit the Golden Temple and Jallianwala Bagh.

When we arrived at the Golden Temple an attendant took our shoes and gave us entry tickets. He brought us to a washing area to wash our hands and feet. Another attendant gave us a towel to dry ourselves and handkerchiefs to cover our heads. Nobody is allowed inside the Golden Temple with their head uncovered. Another volunteer escorted us inside the temple, which resembled a fort.

The temple had a large central courtyard in which there was a large pond. In the middle of the pond there was a shrine where the Sikh's principal religious book, the Guru Granthasaheb, was kept. Bhajans and kirtans were being sung continuously around the Granthasaheb. The shrine was connected to the courtyard by a bridge and the entrance was guarded by a Sikh devotee in full uniform that included a big sword. The roof of the temple was covered with gold plating. This reflected on the pond and as a result the water was a golden colour. We crossed the bridge to the shrine where the gatekeeper told me to leave my staff. I told him that I was a monk and it was part of my uniform, so he allowed me to take the staff in with me.

After returning from the inner shrine to the temple proper, we toured the upstairs rooms where we found many monstrous oil paintings of the atrocities perpetrated on the Sikhs during Muslim rule. The weapons used at that time were also on display. Finally we left the temple, got our shoes, and returned the handkerchiefs. The attendants turned out to be volunteers from the Sikh community, including high-ranking officials who offered their services at least two hours a week. They did this with the feeling that they were fortunate to have the opportunity to serve the visitors to the temple, in the spirit that service to humanity is service to God.

Jalianwalabag
After visiting the Golden Temple we went to see Jallianwala Bagh. After entering the gate, we went to the reception office to get permission for the visit. Punjab is a long way from Bengal but the office secretary was Bengali. When we entered the park, we found many square wooden frames fixed to the wall. The frames enclosed the bullet marks from the Jallianwala Bagh massacre when thousands of Indian patriots lost their lives at the hands of the British. We proceeded to the huge well in which many scores of patriots jumped to save themselves from the hail of bullets, though they ultimately perished there. The well was protected by a wire net. After our visit the secretary invited us for light refreshments. At the table we talked about the massacre. Then we returned to the residence of Ac. Jialaljii. The local Margis met us there and I talked to them about the importance of sadhana and the need to form a spiritually based society.

Jammu and Kashmir
In the morning some people came to take initiation. At noon we started for Jammu by bus and reached at seven. The Margis of Jammu were waiting for us at the bus station with garlands. We accompanied them to the residence of Sri Amarnath Kapoor, where I gave a talk about the importance of spiritual practice in human life and then answered their individual questions and told Baba stories until 11:30.

On Saturday an enthusiastic Margi named Makhanlaljii organized a tattvasabha in the school where he was principal. About fifty people attended. Later Makhanlaljii and some other people requested me to tell something about the socio-economic theory of Ananda Marga. One German lady was present. She became inspired and took initiation from me. In the afternoon we went to see the town.

On April 22 Ac. Om Prakash and I started for Srinagar by bus. We spent the day enjoying the natural scenery of the Himalayan hills, the higher peaks covered by snow. We skirted a river basin where the water flowed in the natural canal between two mountains. From the road to the river basin there was a drop of two hundred feet. The road was full of twists and turns and we were acutely aware of the danger as the bus passed perilously close to the sheer drop to the river. Crossing one hill after another we reached Srinagar at 9.00 p.m., after a journey of thirteen hours. It was rainy season in Srinagar and time for paddy transplantation.

We spent the night in the government tourist lodge. It was so cold that we could not sleep properly, having brought insufficient warm clothing, and in the morning the incessant rain confined us to the lodge.

The rain stopped around noon and we went out to meet a Margi named Sri Radhakrishna in his office. He told us that a room has been booked for us in the Gaylord Hotel. That night was the new moon so we had to perform our kapalik puja at midnight in the cremation ground. Radhakrishnajii sent someone to show us where the cremation ground was and we made arrangements with the hotel manager to let us back in when we returned. We were able to complete our puja successfully that night but due to the rain and the excessive cold my left leg became numb. Om Prakash had to help me walk back to hotel. We made a fire in a fireplace and sat in front of it for at least an hour until I felt better. I considered that suffering to be a penance for past deeds. In Jammu, the Margis had told me repeatedly not to do my midnight puja in Srinagar. But my programme was fixed and I couldn't change it.

I felt poorly the next morning so I took rest until eleven. At noon we went to see Dal Lake, Salimar, and the Nisadbag gardens. We saw the floating gardens by boat on the waters of Dal Lake. After returning we went to Radhakrishnajii's office and talked about the importance of spiritual sadhana. The next day we returned to Jammu by bus.

The morning after reaching Jammu many Margis came to meet me. I talked with them for two hours on different aspects of Ananda Marga. In the afternoon we went to the school of Makhanlaljii where he organized a meeting.

On the 27 we started for Jalandhar by bus. In Jalandhar we stayed at the residence of Acharya Jialaljii's daughter Usha and his son-in-law, Sri R. K. Mahajan. Usha was well known to me from the many times she had visited to Jamalpur to attend Dharma Maha Chakra with her father. Her husband did not perform his sadhana regularly but he was a devoted person. At that time very few people in Jalandhar had taken initiation and there was no weekly dharmachakra. I gathered them together and talked about the importance of sadhana and the need for weekly dharmachakra. While I was there an ardent devotee of Baba, Doctor Rajkishan Mahendra from Ludhiana, came to talk to me about the programme in Ludhiana.

Vishwa Dharma Maha Sammelan

The next morning we started for Ludhiana and reached there about eleven. Two wholetime workers, acharyas Amaresh and Paras, had already reached. We went to the residence of Dr. Rajkishan Mahendra. He was very happy to have four acharyas at one time in his house. I was also happy to be staying with such an ardent devotee. His whole family was eager to serve us. Dr. Mahendrajii played devotional songs for us in both Bengali and Hindi.

In the afternoon I addressed a tattvasabha in town and after returning to the doctor's residence, a group of local people, some of whom had been present at the tattvasabha, requested Dr. Rajkishanjii to ask me if I could deliver a spiritual discourse at the Vishwa Dharma Maha Sammelan that was going on at that time in Ludhiana.

I told him it would not be possible. My programme had me leaving for Bekaner at 8 p.m. and the VDMS was to start at 7:00. While I was explaining this to Mahendrajii, members of the VDMS were waiting outside for my reply. After hearing that I could not attend, they came to me personally to renew their request. When I told them that my departure time was fixed for 8:00, the secretary of VDMS told me that I could give a talk from 7.00 to 7.30 and then they would take me by car to the railway station so I could catch my train. I was reluctant but when they supplicated me with folded hands I finally agreed.

That evening, as I was getting ready for my lecture, I knew that people from different parts of the world with different ideologies would be in the audience, many of them pundits and intellectuals. How would I be able to preserve the prestige of Ananda Marga? I left everything in Baba's hands and the moment I reached the dais Baba appeared within me.

The first two rows of seats were reserved for special delegates. Behind them about ten thousand people were in the audience. Exactly at 7.00 p.m. the bell rang. The secretary of VDMS introduced me and explained why I was the first person to talk. His introduction lasted five minutes and then I started my speech. The subject was the difference between dharma and religion. I had twenty-five minutes to complete my discourse and I completed it one minute before the final bell. I did namaskar to all and got up to leave.

The moment I tried to leave the dais, people started requesting the authorities in a loud voice that swamiji should remain one more day. The car was waiting for me but before I could leave, hundreds of people encircled it. A group of educated ladies stood by the car and asked me to please stay one more day to deliver a lecture on Ananda Marga philosophy and sadhana. Because of my lecture, they said, they had come to know about many new dimensions of spirituality and they were eager to know more. Faced with the situation, I acted like a child. I remained silent. Acharya Amaresh, Acharya Paras, Acharya Om Prakash, Dr. Mahendrajii, and the secretary of the VDMS tried to make them understand my difficulty. Still they were encircling the car, ladies on one side and gents on the other. Finally a few lady volunteers and a few male volunteers linked hands and opened a corridor for the car to pass. The moment the car started moving, the ladies started shoving each other to do pranam to me. It was a strange scene. Finally I reached the station and seconds after I boarded the train it started. Had I arrived even one minute later I would have missed it. Fortunately two Margi brothers had gone to the station to book my ticket and they were holding my bunk for me (I was traveling alone this time). When I lay down on the bunk I was overwhelmed by the spiritual wave. It took some time before my mind came back to its normal condition.

Rajasthan

When I awoke early in the morning I found that the passengers had left flowers by my feet. I was surprised to see the devotion that the people of that area felt for monks. After some time I reached Hisar, where I changed trains for Sodolpur and again at Sodolpur for Bikaner. From Hisar the desert began. Wherever I looked I found a vast expanse of sand baked by the scorching rays of the sun. The metre-gauge line jingled musically as the train rolled on in slow motion. Particles of sand filled the air in the compartment as we travelled, covering the bodies of the passengers. Here and there some thorny bushes appeared and we could see people going hither and thither on camels. From Sodolpur to Bikaner I did not see a single pond or even a single blade of grass. It was a new experience for me. At about 5 p.m. I reached Bikaner, which was also built on sand.

Two wholetimers, Acharya Vashistha and Acharya Mukunda, came to receive me at Bikaner Station along with few local Margis. They took me to the residence of a Margi professor, Tularamjii, where arrangements had been made for my stay. I was so dirty from the train trip that I couldn't enter the room, but the water crisis was critical so they could only spare one bucket for me to take bath. Vashisthajii collected my clothes and told me that he would get them washed in another place. That evening I addressed a tattvasabha and then returned to take my meal and talk with the Margis and wholetimers. I discovered that green vegetables were unavailable there. People were eating preparations made from gram flour and pickles. I could see the effect of the lack of green vegetables in the local people.

The next morning I addressed a tattvasabha and at noon I addressed a student meeting. In the afternoon I went to see the town. In the evening, Acharya Vashistha, Acharya Mukunda, and myself started for Jodhpur. We reached there the next morning. A group of Margis were waiting with flowers and garlands to receive us. They took us by car to the place that had been arranged for our stay. After meditation and breakfast they took us around the town and in the afternoon I addressed a tattvasabha at the Arya Samaj founded by Swami Dayananda. Most of the people who attended took initiation. It was said that Dayananda had died there after being poisoned by one of his disciples.

The high court of Rajasthan is in Jodhpur and many highly qualified persons live there. In India there are only two states where the capital and the high court are in different cities: Rajasthan and Uttar Pradesh. The capital of Rajasthan is Jaipur and Uttar Pradesh's capital is Lucknow, while its high court is in Allahabad.

In the evening we left for Udaipur and reached there at 11:00 a.m. Some local Margis were waiting at the station with garlands to receive us. They took us to the residence of Taj Singh and that afternoon a lawyer named Payarilal came to me with his questions. After I had replied to his questions, he said that I seemed very familiar to him. I told him that we Ananda Margis believed in reincarnation, so perhaps we had known each other in a previous life. I addressed a tattvasabha that afternoon and another in the evening.

The next morning a local advocate came to discuss Ananda Marga with me. While I was talking with him, the wife of Rajasthan's chief minister joined the discussion. After that I visited the town. The townspeople say that Udaipur is a second Kashmir. It is surrounded by beautiful hills and there is a lake in the middle of the town. There are a number of historical memorials for the Rajput kings. After that we visited a historical place named Chittor, which was once the kingdom of Maharaja Rana

Pratap Singh. We kept our belongings in a dharmasala and started on foot for Chittor Fort, one mile distant. The fort was set on a plateau and was protected by a high wall. Once it had been the capital of the Rajput kings and many historical events had taken place there. There was also a gorgeous Jain temple there and nearby we came upon another temple known as the Mirabai temple, which houses a statue of Lord Krishna. A little further on we discovered an old palace by the side of a pond. The pond had a bathing ghat. It is said that once, when Queen Padmini was bathing at that ghat, the emperor of Delhi saw her wet clothed body from the window and was stupefied by her beauty. He attacked Chittor in order to have her for himself but she committed self-immolation to protect her chastity.

That night we left for Ajmer and reached there the next morning. We stayed in a dharmasala. I was ill so my programme was postponed but many Margis came to meet me while I was taking bed rest. Some of them requested me to go to their house to recuperate but I did not think it proper to go to a family residence in that condition. In the evening I felt a little better and we took a bus to Jaipur, reaching about 10:00 p.m. Two Margis came to the bus stand to receive us with flowers and garlands: Sri Mangal Biharijii, the IAS Commissioner of Jaipur, and Sri Manoharlal Agarwal, the principal of Agarwal College. They took me to the residence of Manoharlaljii.

Though I was still not well, I addressed the Margis the next afternoon after the weekly dharmachakra about the importance of sadhana and then left for Agra by the night train.

Taj Mahal

I reached Agra at 8:00 p.m. Acharya Raghavjii and some local Margis came to the station to receive me. The next afternoon they took me to see the Agra fort and the Taj Mahal. I saw the tower where Aurangzeb had confined his father Shah Jahan and his sister. We went to the top of the fort from where a Rajput king on horseback had jumped the palace moat, breaking the horse's waist bone in the jump. There was a stone statue of the horse at that spot. The king had then escaped on another horse. In the tower where Shah Jahan had been confined, hundreds of small glass globes had been fitted in the wall at Shah Jahan's request. Each globe reflected the Taj Mahal, which was one mile from the fort. It was his desire to be able to see the Taj Mahal at every moment and from whatever direction he faced. One of those glass globes was still there and I was able to see the reflection. The rest had been removed, leaving hundreds of vacant pits in the wall.

After visiting the Agra fort, we went on foot to see the Taj Mahal. Entering the main gate we found a beautiful garden with many fountains. We proceeded towards the tomb through a garden path, climbing a set of steps into the courtyard. On one side of the entrance was a beautiful garden and on the other side the blue waters of the Yamuna River. Between the two was the huge, intricately carved mausoleum of white marble. On the outer wall was written spiritual passages from the Koran. It was a most attractive atmosphere and very calm. Inside we saw the tomb of Mumtaz Mahal. The Taj Mahal was built by Shah Jahan in memory of his wife, Mumtaz. It is a vivid example of the great love of a husband for his wife.

After exiting the tomb, we stood for a while in the courtyard, enjoying the natural beauty of the Yamuna River. From there we went to the other side of the Taj Mahal to visit the botanical garden. We were about to leave when a party from Calcutta told us that only on a moonlit night can one enjoy the full majesty of the Taj Mahal. Without seeing the Taj in the moonlight our visit would be incomplete. The sky was perfectly clear so we took some food and waited there until evening for the moon to rise. When the moon appeared we entered the courtyard. When the moonlight shone, the stones of the Taj Mahal glittered like diamonds, reflected in the night like a dazzling blanket of stars, overcoming us with its beauty. The gentleman who advised us to stay had been right.

On the way back, my companions asked me what I thought of the Taj Mahal. I told them that our country was a country of poor and distressed people while the Taj was a vivid example of the luxurious lives of kings and of physical desire.

That night I left for Jamalpur along with Acharya Om Prakash, Acharya Amaresh, and Acharya Paresh. Altogether we were eight persons. The next morning at Allahabad Station many Margis came and brought us food, and Acharya Arun Kumar joined us. At Patna and Bar stations many Margis came to see us with flowers and garlands, shouting slogans like *Ananda Marga Amar Hai*. The same scene repeated itself when we reached Jamalpur Junction.

Ananda Purnima

The eighth of May was Ananda Purnima. Hundreds of devotees came to Jamalpur from different parts of the country to attend the birthday celebration of Baba Anandamurtijii. The singing of devotional songs began early in the morning. All the wholetime workers attended and many of their relatives came to meet their affectionate sons. The courtyard of the jagriti was nicely decorated and there were many activities: puja, bhajan and kirtan, collective meals. At noon I went to bring Baba to the jagriti by car. The moment the car reached the jagriti everyone started shouting Baba Anandamurtijii ki Jai. Then Baba sat in his room on the cot and the devotees gathered round. He remained there for one hour with the devotees and then returned home by car. After dropping Baba off I engaged myself with different programmes.

Dharma Maha Chakra was held on the twelfth in Monghyr's Goenka Dharmasala. Thousands of devotees attended. During the programme Baba came twice a day. We held classes for the wholetime workers thrice a day. On the fifteenth I gave the necessary advice, train fare, and monthly allowance to the wholetimers and sent them to their fields. At that time there were about fifty wholetime workers. I also left the same day to visit Birbhum, Krishnagar, Calcutta, and Ranchi. While I was gone Baba did not come to the jagriti since there was no one to drive his car.

29
Disaster

*A*FTER THE DEPARTURE of the wholetime workers for their respective fields I entrained for Indas, where I conducted training classes. On the eighteenth Acharya Sachinandanjii and myself started for Krishnagar. We reached Navadip Station at midnight and went to the waiting hall to take rest for the night. At that time a state of emergency had been imposed throughout the country due to Chinese aggression. Taking advantage of this, many innocent people were being harassed. Five minutes after our arrival three policemen came and interrogated us. We told the truth and they left.

Again early in the morning four or five policemen came with their in-charge and asked Dr. Sachinandanjii many questions. After half an hour I got up and asked them why they were harassing us. What was our fault? They replied that it was the government's order that if they had any doubt about anyone then they could bring them to the police station in order to verify their story. I told them that we were happy to help them and asked if they had brought a police van to take us. The in-charge said that the police van was out of order so they would have to take us in a rickshaw. I told them to please ask the concerning officer to interrogate us and if he was satisfied then he should allow us to proceed to our destination; or if he had doubts then he should inform our people at Krishnagar that we had been detained and thus were unable to reach at the appointed time. The officer told us that his in-charge would come at 10 a.m., so I asked him to make arrangements for our morning duties and puja, since I was a monk. He then directed a constable to show me where I could perform my morning duties. At 10:00 a.m. the officer-in-charge arrived and called us for interrogation. I explained the situation and he scolded the officer for not recognizing that we were innocents and not antisocial elements. Then he told us we were free to go.

30
Calcutta

W̲E REACHED KRISHNAGAR at noon and stayed in the Bashasri Hotel because the work in Krishnagar had not been done properly. Dr. Sachinandanjii went to invite the Margis to attend a meeting in the hotel. When the news reached Ac Sukhenjii and Balai-da they were shocked and came to take me to their residence. I told them that I had taken the huge responsibility of Baba's mission and depended on them. If they would not cooperate with me then there was no place for me to stay except a hotel. The devotees admitted their fault and assured me that in the future they would not commit any such mistakes. Many started weeping. At last Balai-da and Ac. Sukhenjii took me to the residence of Balai-da. In the evening there was the weekly dharmachakra where I gave them their respective responsibilities.

The next morning I started for Calcutta. Prasadjii sent his car to receive me. It took me to the central excise office on Strand Road. I passed the day in his office lounge. At noon, Brigadier Dubeyjii came to meet me and I talked with him about the philosophy and yoga sadhana of Ananda Marga. In the evening Prasadjii arranged a tattvasabha in his office. Then Prasadjii and I went to his residence where we found the Commissioner of Jaipur, Sri Mangal Biharijii waiting for us. He had recently had Baba's darshan in Jamalpur. We passed our time in a joyful spiritual atmosphere.

The next day I did my office work, which I had brought with me. In the evening I discussed Ananda Marga and Baba with Prasadjii and his family.

On the twenty-second, Brigadier Dubeyjii and three friends came to meet me. I talked with them for some time and we took breakfast together. At noon Sri Vishvanath Sarab and the Assistant Collector of Central Excise, Ac. Virendra Asthana, and Ac. Sachinandanjii, an important businessman of Gorakhpur, dropped by. In the evening they went to Howrah Station to see off Mr. Dubeyjii. In the meantime Vishvanathjii and I went to the residence of the Assistant Collector Central Excise, Mr. Agarwal. He was a new Margi. In the meantime Prasadjii, Ac. V. K. Asthana, and Ac. Sachinandanjii returned from Howrah Station and then accompanied me back to the station to see off me for Ranchi.

I reached Ranchi at 8:00 a.m. Ac. Kedarjii, Ac. Kshitishjii, and Balendujii, the District Mining Officer and district secretary of Ananda Marga in Ranchi came to receive me. They took me to the residence of Balendujii. Thereafter I visited the local units of Ananda Marga and in the evening I taught a class for the workers.

The next day there was a meeting of the unit secretaries of Ranchi District. Afterward I went to Mander Missionary Hospital to take an x-ray of my hand. In the afternoon I taught a class in the training camp and then started for Gaya by bus. Ac. Satyanarainjii came with a car to receive me and take me to his residence.

The next day Ac. Satyanarainjii and I went to Patna. We stayed for a few hours at the residence of Sri Biharilaljii, the district secretary of Ananda Marga in Patna. Many Margis came there to meet me. In the evening I boarded a train for Jamalpur.

While I was in Jamalpur my work was as follows: 1) Answer the letters of the wholetime workers; 2) Send them their monthly allowance; 3) Send my tour programme to the different units with the necessary directions; 4) Maintain the office records; 5) Arrange personal contact with Baba for newly initiated Margis; 6) Organize tattvika classes in the morning and evening; 7) Train the wholetime workers and local workers; 8) Drive the Jeep; 9) Teach acharya training classes.

I was busy the entire day from morning to night.

31
ERAWS

AT THIS TIME Baba started a new department named the Education, Relief and Welfare Section. The general secretary was appointed as ERAWS secretary and Ac. Sambuddhananda as the assistant ERAWS secretary. Before starting this department there were two schools, one at Pathargama in Dumka District and the other at Lahariasarai in Darbhanga District, and one children's home at Patna under the supervision of Ac. Sambuddhananda. The work of this department was to start schools and children's homes in different places and to help the people at the time of natural calamities.

PROUT (Progressive Utilization Theory)
To preach the socio-economic theory given by Baba, an independent organization was created. It was named Progressive Federation of India (PFI) with its headquarters at Patna under the supervision of Ac. Vishokananda. Its main work was to publish newspapers and magazines propagating Prout.

After a few months the concerned authorities saw that the work of ERAWS was not satisfactory. I was made the secretary of the ERAWS steering committee, so all the responsibility for that section now came on my head. The papers and magazines were not published properly, so that responsibility was also given to me. Gradually the pressure of work increased so much that I was only able to rest three or four hours a night.

32
Interview

I WENT TO CALCUTTA on the sixth of June because Ac. Lalan, the in-charge of RU at Delhi, requested me to help him meet some of the top intellectuals and invite them to the Renaissance Universal Club. He also reached Calcutta at the same time. On June 7, Sri R. Prasadjii, Lalan, and I met Sri Satyen Bose, Sri Suniti Chatterjee, Dr Radhavinod Pal (secretary of the International Jurist Commission), and Sri Niharainjan Dutta Mazumdar. They were men of ethical knowledge and highly placed in West Bengal. We met them in their residences and told them about our mission and Ananda Marga philosophy and yoga sadhana.

After meeting with them Lalanjii went back to Delhi. The next day I organized a meeting among the Margis. In the meeting local Margis requested me to arrange tattvika classes for them. I agreed because I knew that without proper knowledge the prachar work would not be successful. They were happy and the next day I returned to Jamalpur.

33
Malaria

*A*FTER REACHING JAMALPUR I became ill with malaria. My illness lasted two weeks but the pressure of work was so great that even in my weakened condition I continued my work. On July 2, I went to Asansol and stayed at the residence of my initiate Sri Durga Mukherjee. The next day Ac. Ramakanta came to meet me and also Sri Vikram from Chirkunda with some Margis. I organized a large tattvasabha in Subhash Samiti. Afterward many wanted to take initiation. I introduced them to Ac. Ramakanta and directed him to give them initiation.

The next day I went to Baglata where I toured the area with Sambuddhananda and Tarapada, a local Margi from Chitmu village. A surveyor named Kunju came with a map of the area but we found it difficult to conduct a proper survey. For that reason Sambuddhananda and I went to the district headquarters, Purulia, where we met the JLR, the DFO and the Tribal Welfare Officer. They told us that the matter could only be solved at the ministerial level. After two days we returned to Baglata and called a meeting of the surrounding villagers but we were unable to come up with a solution. Then I went to Dhanbad while Sambuddhananda returned to Jamalpur.

In Dhanbad I met the local Margis and we passed the evening in bhajan and kirtan. Kshitishjii had come from Ranchi and he was a very good singer. The next morning Kshitishjii and I left for Calcutta. We stayed at 7 Hare Street, which had been arranged by Prasadjii. Then I accompanied Ac. Dhiren and a Margi, Mr. Khanna, to attend dharmachakra in Behala.

On July 14 there was a dharmachakra at Dalhousie followed by a tattvasabha attended by many members of the public. I explained for one hour the philosophy and yoga sadhana of Ananda Marga. Then we came back to Hare Street where I found that Ac. Sukhenjii and Balai-da had come from Krishnagar. The district secretary of Ananda Marga, Sri Pratap Banerjee, also brought one person for initiation.

34
Tattvika Class at Calcutta

*T*HE NEXT MORNING Ac. Sukhenjii, Balai-da, and I went to the Forward Block office where we talked about Ananda Marga for one hour. After returning, Pratap Banerjee, Sanjiv, Ahuja, and I went to meet the barrister Sri Nihar Rainjan Dutta Mazumdar, who had taken initiation a few days earlier. I advised him to attend the proposed tattvika class. I saw Balai-da and Sukhenjii off at Sealdah Station and when I returned Prasadjii was waiting for me. He came thrice a day — morning, noon and evening, to inquire about the progress of my missionary work in Calcutta. He was always alert to remove any inconvenience that I might be facing.

Though he was a customs and excise collector for four states he had no vanity and lived a simple life, one reason why I loved him so much. He was the final authority for a smuggling case involving a huge amount of money for which big businessmen had offered him a bribe. He told them that he would prefer to eat dry bread as a virtuous man rather than accept any illegal gratification. By ignoring them he had to face a lot of difficulty from the central ministers. This happened to him on a number of different occasions. His birthplace was Bareilly in Uttar Pradesh and he took initiation directly from Baba in the year 1955. He was an ardent devotee of Baba.

At the time there were a good number of Margis in Calcutta, but they did not know the philosophy of Ananda Marga, nor much about our yoga sadhana. I organized a tattvika class for them at Dalhousie Square in the Hindi Siksha Kendra hall. About fifty Margis attended. After the class I returned to Hare Street where I met with the chairman of the PSP, Sri Sunil Dasjii.

The next day I gave initiations and taught a tattvika class. Prasadjii dropped by at least six times to see if I needed anything. Sri Pratap Banerjee came to meet me at noon and stayed until evening to attend tattvika class. Ac. Mani Mitra from Barrackpore and Ac. Hara Prasad from Krishnagar also came to meet me along with Sri Jitendra Tyagijii. After evening tattvika class I went to Krishnagar to perform my kapalik puja.

The next morning at 8:00 a.m. a meeting was organized at Calcutta. Balai-da and I came back to Calcutta by the early train. We were half an hour late. About one hundred people were waiting for us to arrive. I addressed the meeting for one hour and there was one hour for questions and answers. Everyone was fully satisfied.

On the twenty-second, after teaching evening tattvika class, Balai-da, Pratap, and I went to meet Major Satya Gupta, who was Netajii Subhash Chandra Bose's right-hand man. He told us many things about his work with Netajii.

On the twenty-third at 8:00 a.m. Prasadjii and I went to meet with the forest minister, Fajlur Rahaman, to discuss the disputed land at Baglata. A few of the plots that had been donated to us by the zamindar had been appropriated by the forest department. The forest minister did not give us a favourable reply.

At 2:00 p.m. Pratap, Ac. Master Dhiren, Sanjiv Babu, and I went to meet a famous lawyer, Dr. Radhavinod Pal, who had recently taken initiation from Ac. Lalanjii. We had a very cordial talk. At the end he said that he was ready to work for the welfare of his countrymen. I told him that we had plans to meet the top intellectuals of Calcutta in the near future.

35
Penance

WHEN WE RETURNED, Prasadjii and Tyagijii were waiting for me with a car. Mr. Hadda, the general manager of Birla Company, had organized a large tattvasabha at New Alipur for 5:00 p.m. When we reached the meeting hall we found the thousand-seat hall full to overflowing. Many people had to stand. I walked to the dais and started my lecture. Glancing around, I could see that the audience was highly educated. Accordingly I selected the subject and talked for an hour and a half. Then Prasadjii talked for a few minutes.

Afterward Mr. Hadda took us to the back rooms to take some tiffin. I told them that I could not eat anything until I had done my evening puja. We passed through several rooms, one after another, all air conditioned and sumptuously decorated. When we reached the dining room we found a great variety of fruits and sweets. They repeatedly requested me to at least take some fruit juice but I refused. Then Tyagijii said, "Dada! Surely you can take liquid before puja." Hearing this, they immediately prepared some fruit juice from grapes and pomegranates and pressed me to take it. To save Tyagijii's prestige I was compelled to drink it. Then they insisted that we take some fruits back with us in the car but I told Tyagijii no. Once we were in the car I scolded him. After reaching Hare Street, Tyagijii held his ears and did tic-tics as punishment. Even then I told Tyagijii that I would have to face the consequences for drinking that juice because Baba told us never take any food from non-Margi capitalists. Just a few days earlier the divisional superintendent of the Howrah division of the railway, Sri Shyamnarainjii, had attended a party thrown by a capitalist and Baba had gotten annoyed.

The next morning while passing stool a quantity of fresh blood came out exactly equal to the quantity of juice I had taken. I told Tyagijii about it and he became anxious and wanted to arrange some medicines but I told him not to worry. I was quite okay and in fact was free from all anxiety after having done my penance. Similar incidents have occurred many times in my life when I knowingly committed some transgression in the interest of the organization and later had to face the consequences.

On July 24 the tattvika classes ended. I then held oral exams. The next day Sanjiv, Pratap, Amulya, Ac. Dhiren, and I went to meet Mr. K. K. Hazara in his residence. We discussed Ananda Marga and its social outlook, and afterward he said he was ready to do social work. He was India's first ICS officer during British rule. He was a pious, honest, and ethical person. After that we had an appointment with the barrister Sri Niharainjan Dutta Muzumdar. Dr. Radhavinod Pal, also came. We discussed how to spread out our ideology among the intellectuals of West Bengal.

Since tattvika classes were over, I had asked the participants to bring me candidates for initiation. These initiations took up the whole day. Prasadjii had arranged a tattvasabha at the Central Services Club that evening. Ac. Dhiren, Prasadjii, and I addressed the meeting. When we returned to Hare Street a group of Margis were waiting for me. I sat with them and told them that we needed an office of our own in Calcutta. I directed them to search for a suitable house. Then I formed a district committee for Ananda Marga in Calcutta. The next day Prasadjii found a house at New Alipur for the Ananda Marga offices.

36
Asansol

On the twenty-ninth Prasadjii saw off me at Howrah Station, from where I caught a train for Asansol. After reaching Asansol Station I found many local Margis waiting to receive me. I went with them to the residence of Durga Babu where I met Acharya Ramakanta, Ac. Sahadev, Sri Manoj Kumar, and Sri Arindam. They had organized a tattvasabha for me that evening in old Asansol. I gave a lecture about the philosophy and yoga sadhana of Ananda Marga and then introduced Ac. Sahadev to the persons who wanted to take initiation. The next day at noon I addressed a meeting of young men at the bar library. Many were inspired to take initiation. I made a list of them and handed it to the local acharya for initiation, though Ac. Ramakanta initiated some persons then and there.

The next day I went to Dhanbad where an accounts officer, Ac. Maheshwarijii, had organized a tattvasabha at an old dharmasala. Many people wanted to take initiation and I gave them the address of Ac. Maheshwarijii. On Ac. Maheshwarijii's request, I initiated his senior accounts officer, Sri Ananda Biharijii. A Margi student of Sindri Engineering College invited me to address a meeting the next morning at his college. I went there and explained about physico-psycho-spiritual parallelism and how to achieve the goal of life through yoga sadhana. Afterward I left for Garh Jaipur via Purulia.

At Garh Jaipur I met Ac. Amulyajii and Ac. Sambuddhananda. We went over the Baglata land papers with the son of the raja and made plans to meet again the next Monday. In the evening I addressed a tattvasabha in the Garh Jaipur higher secondary school and initiated some students. Then I went to Ranchi where I met with our general secretary, Ac. Pranay Kumar Chatterjee, about the Baglata land. I stayed at the residence of Ac. Kshitishjii and on Monday the three of us went to Garh Jaipur. After completing our work I went to Baglata to look for local persons who wanted to exchange their land with us. I measured the area with the help of the surveyor Kunju, an ashramite, Ram Kishore, and a local Margi, Gana. In the meantime a Margi named Suresh arrived with a letter from the general secretary.

Then I returned to Jamalpur for three days. I had many letters to answer and circulars to send out to the wholetime workers. On August

14 I left for Indas to teach organizational classes to the workers of West Bengal. On the way many Margis met me in the Bhagalpur and Sahebganj stations. I reached Indas on the fifteenth and in the evening I gave avadhuta initiation to Acharya Master Dhiren, Ac. Rajesh, and Ac. Anadinath. Henceforth they were known as Ac. Vijayananda Avadhuta, Ac. Ajayananda Avadhuta, and Ac. Lokeshvarananda Avadhuta. The next day classes began and continued up to the twenty-first. Then I gave them their organizational duties.

37
Shantiniketan

ON AUGUST 22 everyone left for their respective areas. I went to Bolpur where I saw both Shantiniketan and Sriniketan. I saw the earthen house of Kabiguru Rabindranath and the place where he started classes under the trees. This made a great impression on me. It inspired me to build up the project in Baglata. From Bolpur I went to Calcutta where I had two principal works planned. I wanted to divide Calcutta Region into four districts and form four district committees. I also wanted to meet the postmaster general to made arrangements for our ashram residents to open a post office at Baglata.

38
Baglata Post Office

I CALLED A MEETING of the Margis of greater Calcutta and told them that I was going to divide Calcutta into four parts that would be known as districts. Accordingly I formed four district committees and gave them their respective duties. Then Prasadjii and I went to meet the postmaster general. I requested him to open a post office at Baglata that our Ananda Marga ashram members would run. After listening to my request, he directed his personal assistant to take care of it. The postmaster general was a friend of Prasadjii, which greatly helped our cause. At that time Purulia was under the control of the postal superintendent of Bankura. I accompanied the PA to his chambers where he telephoned the Bankura postal superintendent and told him that as per order of the postmaster general a new post office was to be opened by tomorrow in the village of Baglata in Purulia District, near the Pundag railway station, and that a special messenger was on his way with the necessary papers.

After completing my work I returned to Jamalpur on August 31. At this time Baba changed the name of the area from Baglata to Anandanagar. He said that both the name of the post office and the railway station should be Anandanagar. I tried but it was too late to get the name of the post office changed. To change the name of the railway station I approached the general manager of South Eastern Railway. He told me he would try to change the name but as I expected my request went into cold storage. Nevertheless we started to use the name Anandanagar on our office stamp, office pad, and other correspondence.

I went to Anandanagar on September 3 and shifted the wholetimer training centre there. Ac. Prithivi Saran was helping me to teach the classes. The next day he reached Anandanagar with the trainees. I stayed there for three days, teaching classes for the trainees and helping Kunju to survey the lands. On September 7, I went to meet with the local MLA, Sri Deven Mahato, about the land matters and then with the deputy commissioner of Purulia District for the same purpose. Then I left for Calcutta by the night train.

While in Calcutta I met with a minister from Purulia, Sri Tarapada Ray, and then went to the Midland Hotel to meet with Sri Deven Mahato. I gave copies of our land papers to each of them. Then Pratap, Ac. Vijayananda, and I met with the minister, Fazlur Rahaman. We talked about our difficulties with the land and about our plans to open a charitable dispensary and educational institutions in that neglected, backward area to uplift the standard of the local people. From there we went to the board of education to learn the rules and regulations required to run our educational institutions. Then again we met with Sri Tarapada Ray. After spending the whole day meeting different officials, I addressed a meeting of the RU Club in the evening.

On September 12, Pratap, Ac. Vijayananda Avt., Sushil Ganguli, and I went to meet with the chief minister, Sri Prafulla Sen, about the land at Anandanagar. After meeting with these different ministers I came to the conclusion that while they were eloquent I doubted they would do much for public welfare. After that I attended the evening dharmachakra and gave a spiritual talk. I did not take my meal that night for the purposes of self-purification.

39
Gorakhpur Dharma Maha Chakra

THE NEXT DAY I went to Ranchi and informed the general secretary about the progress with the land and my talks with the different ministers. I left the same day for Patna where there was a workers meeting. I addressed the meeting and gave them the necessary instructions. In the night I left for Gorakhpur to attend the DMC. After reaching there, I met with Baba and then went to the dharmasala where the General Margis were staying. Then I sat with those who wanted to become wholetime workers, after which I sent them to the training centre at Anandanagar. After that I met with the Margis from Lucknow and gave them instructions for prachar work.

The next day was occupied with organizational meetings and Baba's DMC. That night Baba and I left for Jamalpur by train. At every station along the way groups of Margis came to meet Baba with garlands and food, shouting slogans like *Ananda Marga Amar Hai* and *Baba Anandamurtijii ki Jai*.

At Jamalpur I remained engaged with my organizational work until September 23. Then I left for Anandanagar and dealt with the problems of the training centre. From there I went to Kotshila where the GS and Ac. Kedarjii were waiting to accompany me to Purulia to meet with the minister, Sri Tarapada Ray. After that we returned to Ranchi in Kedarjii's car.

40
Anandanagar High School Building

ON SEPTEMBER 28 I returned to Anandanagar from Ranchi. After my arrival Ac. Prithivi Saran, the trainer of the wholetime workers, asked for a few days leave to go to his home at Muzaffarpur. The post office had opened but in order for it to become permanent we needed to show a sufficient volume of correspondence, so we began posting all our central office correspondence from Baglata. In the meantime I was teaching the wholetimer trainee classes, working to exchange land with the local people, replying to the letters of the workers, sending their monthly allowance, and sending circulars to the workers about organizational programmes. Now we began a new work: the construction of the high school building. It was a difficult work because there were no roads to and from Anandanagar, making it impossible to get bricks. An earthen structure would not be completed within the deadline for the school opening. I consulted with the local people and they suggested that since there were a lot of stones and stone masons in the area we should build stone walls. We would also be able to find people to prepare tiles from local materials and to collect bamboo and wood. That way we could construct the school building without depending on outside materials.

I selected a site near an old neem tree and made a drawing of the construction, which would have nine rooms measuring twenty feet by fourteen feet with a seven-foot-wide veranda. I engaged about fifty villagers and some bullock carts to carry the stones, as well as some masons who knew the art of constructing stone walls. The local tribals, *adivasis*, collected bamboo and wood for me according to my need. A tile-making team also came. I calculated that they would need two months to raise the walls and another two months for the rest of the work — in total four months, just enough time to get the building ready for the start of classes in February.

Ac. P. Saran returned on October 11. I filled him in on the work and then left for Jamalpur. When I returned after three days all the work had stopped. Ac. P Saran was from Bihar and he had no experience dealing with Bengali labourers. I called the labourers together and got them to go back to work. Once everything was back in full swing, I spent a full day with Kunju measuring the land and then in the night I left for Calcutta.

41
Jabbalpur Dharma Maha Chakra

THERE WAS A DMC at Jabbalpur planned for October 26. Baba was scheduled to go there via Calcutta. In the meantime Shashi Rainjanjii reached Calcutta on the twenty-second. I took him to meet with the minister Sailya Mukherjee about the Baglata land matters. Baba reached Calcutta on the twenty-fourth. Thenceforth I was busy with Baba's programme and looking after the Margis. Baba remained the whole day in Calcutta and left in the evening by train. I saw him off at Howrah Station and then met with those Margis who wanted to become wholetime workers. The other workers left for Indas to attend their provincial conference. On October 25 I left Calcutta to attend the Jabbalpur DMC. Prasadjii dropped me at Howrah station. I respected him as much as an avadhuta because he loved Ananda Marga wholeheartedly and was mad for the ideology. He laboured much for the progress of the organization; therefore I called him a householder avadhuta.

The next morning, on the way to Jabbalpur, a group of Margis came to meet me at Dehri-on-Sone Station. Srimati Kalavati, the wife of the deputy superintendent of police, Rajeshrijii, brought food that she had prepared for my journey. The entire family were Margis. They had been ardent devotees of Baba since 1955 and thus were well known to me. Sri Rajeshrijii had been unable to give up wine, thus he was ashamed to come before me, but he had intense love for Baba. His wife was like a sister to me. When she saw me she was beside herself with joy.

I talked with the Margis until the train started. A group of Margis met me at noon in Allahabad Station. I took my bath and meal there, since the stoppage was more than half an hour. I reached Jabbalpur at 8:00 p.m. Ac. Narendrajii, Dhyanananda Avt., and Shyambiharijii came to the station to receive me. When I reached the DMC site, Baba had nearly finished his discourse. Afterward I met with Baba and we talked about organizational matters. Then I held different organizational meetings with the Margis. In this DMC sixteen young men took the decision to become wholetime workers. I gave them their train fare and money for food and accompanied them up to Allahabad before they continued on to the Anandanagar training centre. At Allahabad I went to the residence of the Ananda Marga district secretary, the advocate Sri Gulson Jaina. Baba reached Allahabad the next day at 11:00 a.m. He was on his way to the Ara DMC. I accompanied him.

42
Ara Dharma Maha Chakra

*T*HE MOMENT THE train reached Ara Station, hundreds of devotees with flowers and garlands came to receive Baba, shouting slogans like *Ananda Marga Amar Hai* and *Baba Anandamurtijii ki Jai*. They started garlanding Baba but the shoving got out of control so I closed the compartment door. The volunteers were not able to control the crowd. Then Baba appeared in the doorway, his smiling face fascinating one and all. Then and there the devotees started to dance and sing spiritual songs. All became intoxicated with spiritual emotion. They took Baba in a procession to the place fixed for his stay. I and the other Margis went to the dharmasala. That evening we celebrated the DMC. The next morning, before his departure, Baba gave another discourse. Then we went by car to Danapur and from there by train to Jamalpur. During the short journey, groups of Margis came to see Baba in nearly every station, carrying flowers and garlands and shouting slogans.

From October 30 to November 3 I remained engaged with these programmes. For the yearly volunteers social service camp I wrote a leaflet, which Baba approved and which remained forever unforgettable. On November 3 I left for Gaya by the night train and stayed at the residence of Ac. Satyanarainjii. Then I went to Ranchi for two days. After completing my work in Ranchi I went to Anandanagar for a few days to take care of the new wholetimer trainees. I made sure they were meditating properly, taught some of their classes, and explained the importance of sadhana. I also looked after the construction of the school building. The yearly volunteer social service camp was to be held at Anandanagar beginning December 15. More than two hundred volunteers were expected to attend. I had to make arrangements for their food and lodging, which was a difficult job in this jungle area. Baba had given instructions for the high school to open in January, so I was extremely busy in this regard.

43
Hostel Construction

*A*FTER REACHING ANANDANAGAR I found that there was insufficient space for trainees. The cold season had begun and I had purchased some tents in Calcutta for the central camp, so the trainees and I started living in those tents.

After my arrival, Sri P. Saran went home for a few days to solve some urgent family problems. In the meantime I was faced with the problem of collecting sufficient vegetables to feed everyone. We were also running out of stones for construction and needed a supply of bricks to build the hostel. In the meantime there was some good news: Ananda Marga has been officially registered under the social act of the West Bengal government, with its headquarters at Anandanagar. Now it was the duty of the general secretary to establish the central office there, and for that purpose he sent a young wholetime worker named Ratandhar Jha to be the ashram manager. Now there were three permanent residents: Sri Ram Kishore, P. Saran, and Ratandhar.

At that time there was an outdoor vegetable market twice a week in Ropo village, three kilometres from Anandanagar. We depended on that market but it would not be sufficient once the VSS camp began in the second half of December. I decided to start a local vegetable market in Anandanagar and announced it to the surrounding villages by beating the drum and by spreading the word in the Ropo market. We started the market at the present site of the polytechnic. We also announced that at the close of the market we would buy all the unsold produce at market rate. The vegetable market got off to a good start. After some time, by request of the local people and the stationmaster, the market shifted to the railway station.

I organized a meeting of local Margis to discuss the brick situation. I told them that I wanted to prepare bricks for the hostel construction and asked them if there were any locals who knew how to prepare bricks and what would be the rate per thousand. Within two days everything was arranged and the brick-making work began. We decided that the hostel would have a brick kitchen and storeroom and a veranda on both sides. The hostel construction began forthwith, so work was going on on both buildings simultaneously.

On his return P. Saran was posted as construction in-charge as well as the wholetimer trainer but I continued to supervise the construction of the high school building.

44
Mitigation of Sorrow

I BROUGHT P. SARAN up to speed on the construction works and then on November 22 I went to Ranchi where I taught classes at the jagriti for the trainees. On the twenty-fifth Kshitishjii and I went to Chaibasa where we stayed at the residence of Ac. Rajmohanjii Mishra. Rajmohanjii was the SDO of the irrigation department. He lived with his wife in their government quarters. He was an old Margi who loved me very much. I had stayed with him many times. When I arrived at his residence his wife became afraid. In jest somebody had told her that Satyananda would come to her residence and make Rajmohanjii an avadhuta. After taking our noon meal, she came to me with tears in her eyes and said that the Margis had frightened her. They told her that since she was already twenty-five and had no child, Dadajii was going to make her husband an avadhuta. She fell to my feet and begged me not to make her shelterless and to kindly bless her so that she would be the mother of a child. I restrained my impulse to laugh. Instead I asked her if she had so much faith in me that she believed that whatever I said would be a boon. "Dada!" she said, "Baba said that you are our mini-Baba." I told her that if she had cent per cent faith in me then by the grace of Baba she would become the mother of a child very soon. I also told her that I would not make Rajmohanjii an avadhuta, that those Margis were only joking with her. Her anxiety disappeared and keeping a portion of her sari on her shoulder she did pranam with joyful tears. After that she remained in a blissful state, serving us with a radiant smiling face. Ac. Rajmohan was like Sadashiva and his wife had the same nature. Both were ardent devotees of Baba — Baba Margis. They were leading an ideal family life. Within one year she gave birth to a boy. It just so happened that she gave birth the day I reached Chaibasa on tour. She had a caesarian birth and later on she became the mother of a second child.

That same day Rajmohanjii, a new Margi named Anjan Babu, and I went to see a Tantra piitha, which was located a little ways from Chaibasa. After completing evening puja there I went to the residence of Balendujii, a district mining officer who had come from Ranchi where he was the district secretary of Ananda Marga. When I reached his house he left all his work to spend time with me. It was his desire that whenever I came to his town I should stay in his residence. But since both were great devotees and Baba Margis, I made a compromise. I told them that one time I would stay at the residence of Rajmohanjii and the next time I would stay with Sri Balendujii. A few years later Balendujii died in a Jeep accident.

The next afternoon I went to Tata where Ac. Chandradeojii was waiting for me. We held a meeting for the Margis in his residence. After halting there for the night I started for Calcutta. From Howrah Station I went to Hare Street where Ac. Vijayananda Avadhuta and Tyagijii were waiting for me.

45
Gopenjii

*A*T THAT TIME the Behala unit, run by Ac. Gopenjii, was behaving in a whimsical way. Two other householder acharyas had joined it and they were not paying heed to the directions of the district secretary or the wholetime workers. Long before, Baba had given some spiritual power to Gopenjii. Taking advantage of the power of Gopenjii, the local Margis had violated the system of Ananda Marga by starting what they called "madhuchakra" in place of the weekly dharmachakra. I tried in vain to make them understand. At last Baba came to know of their unruly activities. Then he withdrew Gopen's spiritual power along with his acharyaship and the acharyaship of the other two acharyas. Gopenjii became an ordinary man. After that he did not come among the Margis anymore.

After some months Baba went to Calcutta for DMC but Gopenjii did not attend. Still Baba could not remain separate from him. During his walk Baba asked me if I knew where Gopen lived. I told him that I did not. Baba asked me to find someone who knew where he lived because he wanted to meet him, but that I should not tell anyone about the meeting. Sri Manohar Guptajii (a Baba Margi) knew where he lived so I took him with us and advised both him and the driver to keep Baba's visit secret. When we arrived at Gopenjii's residence at Behala, Baba remained in the car while I went to inform Gopenjii about his arrival. He was wearing a towel when he opened the door, having just come from the bathroom. He was surprised to see me. When I told him that Baba had come to meet him and was waiting in the car, he started weeping loudly. Like a child he ran to the car and fell down before Baba. Baba consoled him. All the time Gopenjii was saying, "Baba, please forgive me, please forgive me." Seeing that exchange between bhakta and Bhagavan on the road, we also could not control our tears. Baba again and again told him that he forgave him. Gopenjii was so emotional I had to carry him in my arms back to his residence. After that we returned to Camac Street and celebrated the DMC. The next day Baba returned to Jamalpur.

On November 29 I again went to meet the postmaster general to change the name of the Baglata post office to the Anandanagar post office but it was not possible to do so. In the evening Sri Sailen Ghosh invited me to attend the Salkia dharmachakra. All his family members were ardent devotees of Baba. Later his second son became an avadhuta. After my arrival he organized a programme of spiritual songs. I spent the night there and the next day I started for Jamalpur, where I remained for one week to complete my work. Then I went to Anandanagar.

46
Anandanagar VSS Central Camp

IN ANANDANAGAR THE All-India Volunteer Social Service Camp was scheduled to last for fifteen days and I was to serve as commander-in-chief. Two hundred and fifty volunteers were expected to attend the camp from different parts of India. Arranging their food and lodging was a difficult job so I decided to take the help of the nearest strong Ananda Marga unit, Ranchi, and went there to make the arrangements. The tents, utensils, and vegetables would be collected from there. So far as the vegetables were concerned, I made arrangements for one Margi under the guidance of Ac. Kshitishjii to send vegetables everyday by the morning train, which reached Anandanagar at 1:00 p.m. This solved our biggest problem for the camp.

On December 16 most of the wholetime workers reached. By then everything else we needed from Ranchi had arrived. The wholetime workers then became engaged raising the tents, making ovens, erecting the pandal, etc. They completed everything within a day. The expected 250 volunteers arrived and the camp went off smoothly, even as the construction work continued in full swing. During the second half of December, Anandanagar looked like a country fair.

47
Behind the curtain

AFTER THE FIRST week of the central camp, I came to know that the father of Ac. Amitananda Avt., Sri Shiv Dhyan Singh, had lodged a kidnapping case against Baba, myself, and Sri P. K. Chatterjee at Monghyr Court, alleging that his son was a minor. I informed Amitananda and asked him what he wanted to do? He told me that he would do whatever

I thought best, and that he could prove that he was an adult by his college certificate. Under no circumstances would he return to his parents. Without disclosing it to anybody, I sent him back to Kerala that same night. In the morning, when others saw that Amitananda was not at Anandanagar, they thought he had left the organization without notice. Ac. Lalan started to propagate that Amitananda had left the organization due to the misbehaviour of Ac. Satyananda Avt, He organized a meeting at Calcutta that included Prasadjii, Tyagijii, Ac. Asthanajii, and Shashi Rainjanjii and tried to turn their minds against me. He, P. K. Chatterjee and Lalan were against my activities but they had mostly remained silent because I had Baba's support. At the time I did not know about the meeting in Calcutta.

48
Anandanagar High School

*A*FTER THE VSS camp many workers became avadhutas. In order to open the high school, I directed some wholetime workers to remain at Anandanagar as teachers. Then I sent Ram Kishore to the surrounding villages to invite the villagers to a meeting about the high school on January 2. I also directed the wholetime workers in the field to send students to the school, assuring them that the hostel would be finished in time to house them.

On January 1, 1964 the first New Year's Day celebration was held at Anandanagar. As per *Ananda Marga Caryacarya*, it was celebrated with collective meditation and meals and children's games. After the strict discipline of the fifteen-day camp, everyone was happy to join in the festivities.

The next afternoon people came from the surrounding villages to attend the meeting about the high school. We told them about the different activities in Anandanagar, distributed the prizes from the children's games from the day before, and then informed them that we had decided to open a high school at Anandanagar where their children would have the opportunity to study through class ten. This was the gist of my talk:

"The first time when I visited Baglata I looked at these barren hills and wondered how I would possibly be able to build up Anandanagar. I did know how we could materialize our plans to open different welfare projects on this land. But now I find that with the cooperation of all of you, along with the blessings of Parama Purusha, within a few months we have been able to open a charitable dispensary in an area where the closest dispensary was ten kilometres away. In the future we will open a hospital as well so we can be able to serve you in a better way. When I came here there was no post office, so it was nearly impossible to communicate with your distant relatives. I personally met with the postmaster general in Calcutta and was able to establish a post office at Baglata. For buying and selling your agricultural products we opened a local market here. We also successfully petitioned the railway to get the Ranchi Express to stop at Pundag station. Now I am thinking about the education of your children. In the next few days we are going to open the high school. I had hoped that we would be able to start the classes in the newly constructed building but the construction is not complete due to the lack of roads and other communication problems. But I hope that within two months the school building will be completed. In the meantime we shall start classes in the tents that were set up during the volunteers camp. Therefore I shall request you to send your children for admission starting tomorrow so that the children will not waste their valuable time. In March the classes will shift to the new building. The hostel building is also going up and will be completed by the end of February so that students from outside the area will also be able to study in the Anandanagar High School. I feel proud starting classes underneath a tent because that is how Kabiguru Rabindranath Tagore started his classes at Shantiniketan. Now that institution is one of the most renowned education centres in the world — Vishwabharati University. So again I shall request you to send your children for admission from tomorrow. I have given the necessary instruction to our teachers. We will do everything we can for local welfare but your cooperation is urgently needed. Our effort and your cooperation will enable us to build up Anandanagar in a systematic way. You have come here today with great zeal. For this I give you many, many thanks."

Once the meeting concluded we served everyone bread fried in ghee and sweets. I remained at Anandanagar up to January 7, conducting workers meetings, surveying the land, and supervising the construction. I sent the workers to their respective fields on January 8 and then returned to Jamalpur.

49
Control

*E*VERY MONTH I sent the wholetime workers their monthly allowance for working in the field. They did not know how much difficulty I faced to collect that money. It was a rule that every worker had to submit a monthly account of their expenditure. I discovered that there was no uniformity in their expenditures. Many workers spent money beyond their actual needs. Sometimes even a great deal more. By then many Ananda Marga units had been formed in different parts of the country. In those units the workers were getting their food and lodging from the Margis. Accordingly I fixed certain amount for their monthly allowance and told them that nobody would get more than the fixed amount. Some non-avadhuta workers commented that since I was an avadhuta and leading a life of hardship, I was compelling them to do the same. But this was not the case. I alone had to collect the total amount for the wholetime workers' monthly expenditure and my means were limited. After some time I set the system right. Many workers began to maintain themselves with less than the fixed amount and returned the rest of the money to me. Gradually they understood the difficulties I faced in discharging my responsibility and all misunderstandings were removed.

50
Forest Department Case

*A*FTER BECOMING AN avadhuta I looked after the avadhuta work as the sole member of a one-man avadhuta board. Now that the number of avadhutas and wholetime workers had increased significantly, I added two more avadhutas to the board to make it strong. From January 8 to 10, the workers came to Jamalpur for Baba's darshan and then I sent them to their respective areas. On January 11, Yogananda Avt. and myself left for Gorakhpur, where we were met at the station by Ac. Raghunathjii and Ac. Sachinandanjii. After proceeding to Ac. Sachinandanjii's residence, I addressed a meeting of the local Margis. Then I went to see Gorakhapur University and the Gita press with Ac.

Raghunathjii. On the walls of the Gita Press, I found many artistic pictures of Ramliila and Krishnaliila. That night I returned to Jamalpur.

After reaching Jamalpur I consulted with Baba on different issues, then went over the accounts with Ramtanukjii and Raghujii. I also talked with Ac. Abhedananda about the construction in Anandanagar. On the fifteenth morning I reached Anandanagar and on the sixteenth P. Saran, some local Margis, and I went to Purulia by Jeep to attend court. The forest department had lodged a case against P. Saran and myself for damaging forest land at Anandanagar, specifically the small plot of land where we had made a charitable dispensary, land they had claimed despite the fact that we had the registered deed to the land.

I returned to Jamalpur on the twenty-second. The next day I went to Monghyr Court with Ramtanukjii to obtain bail on the kidnapping case that the father of Amitananda Avt. had lodged against Baba, the GS and me. A warrant had been issued for me. Baba and P. K. Chatterjee had already taken bail. The magistrate of the court was an acharya of Ananda Marga, Ac. Bal Mukunda Rastogir, so I had only to sit in the court compound while Ac. Ramtanukjii made the arrangements.

51
Ghazipur Dharma Maha Chakra

*T*HE NEXT DAY I accompanied Baba to Ghazipur for DMC. Baba and I stayed at the residence of the advocate Ac. Keshav Prasad. The following morning I supervised the personal contacts until 12:00 p.m. Then Baba went for his bath and meal while I completed organizational meetings with the wholetime workers and acharyas. Afterward Ac. V. K. Asthana made a remark that I could not answer. I told Baba about it and he said, "You do not know that Lalan in Calcutta has been spreading the rumour that Ac. Amitananda left the organization due to your misbehaviour. There is no need to respond to Asthana's remarks. After the DMC you contact them and tell them what actually happened. They love you very much. When they hear the facts, you see that their doubts and confusion and reaction will be removed."

The next day Baba and I went to Begusarai. At Chapra Station many Margis came with flowers and garlands to see Baba. After reaching Begusarai we went to the residence of Ac. Himachal Prasad Akhouri. At that time he was Additional Police Superintendent of Monghyr District. Ac. Amitananda Avt. was then at the residence of our law secretary, Ac. Ramtanukjii, in Begusarai, because he was going to give a statement before the magistrate of Monghyr court about the kidnapping case lodged by his father. Before giving the statement he came to Akhourijii's residence to talk with Baba and on the twenty-ninth we returned to Jamalpur via Monghyr.

52
Removal of Doubts

On February 1, I started for Calcutta, where I met with Prasadjii, Tyagijii, Asthana, and the others. I told them what had happened with Ac. Amitananda as per Baba's advice. After hearing everything, they were extremely pleased. The next day Tyagijii left for Delhi to put an end to the propaganda against me. I stayed in Calcutta for two days for organizational work. On the fourth I went to Tata and addressed a workers meeting. The next day I went to Chaibasa for another workers meeting at the residence of Balendujii. Then I left for Ranchi where Ac. P. K. Chatterjee was being interviewed by a radio station about Ananda Marga.

53
Seva Dharma Mission

The next day P. Saran and I went to Anandanagar. I stayed there up to February 13 to complete my pending works. I issued a circular to the workers and did the various accounts. On the thirteenth I left for South India for a long tour programme. I had less pressure of work in Anandanagar since several persons had been posted there in different sections. But it was not safe to keep the workers training centre there, since we were facing various troubles. A few days earlier an engineering student named Jayanta, the son of Dr. Anjani Prasad of Patna, had reached the Anandanagar training centre from America, where he had gone for further studies. His arrival created a problem. The Bihar government filed an action against us over his joining, so we decided to shift the training centre to Varanasi and to register an independent organization in Lucknow under the society act named Seva Dharma Mission with its headquarters at Varanasi. This mission would take over the training of workers and prachar work. For the time being I took the responsibility for the new organization. Accordingly I decided to shift my activities to Varanasi. I advised the concerning workers to find a rented building to serve as my office. Then after taking a circular tour ticket I went to Calcutta and left for South India on an all-India tour, intending to visit all the states on the way. It was the first time that I was going to South India.

54
Orissa

I PASSED THE FOURTEENTH in Calcutta with Prasadjii, Tyagijii, Peshwarilaljii, Ac. Vijayananda Avadhuta, and others, and that evening Mantu and I boarded the Puri Express. Mantu was a very devoted young man. He had expressed a desire to go with me as my attendant and I also needed an attendant for such a long organizational tour. When I was engaged with my work I neglected my personal needs and I was liable to fall sick. He was a fit young man, physically strong, active, disciplined, and devoted — the perfect person.

The next day we reached Bhubaneshwar, where a wholetime worker, Ac. Devashish, came to receive us along with a group of local Margis. They took us to the residence of Ac. Prayagjii, where I addressed the local Margis on the philosophy of Ananda Marga and the importance of sadhana. In the afternoon we visited an ancient spiritual centre in Udaigiri and then some Buddhist, Jain, and Nath temples in Khandagiri. In these temples we enjoyed the art and architecture of those bygone days. After returning I addressed a tattvasabha for one and a half hours. Then we started for Puri, where Mantu, Devashish, and I visited the Jagannath temple.

In the temple we saw the famous Jagannath idol. The room it was kept in was very dark. A single electric bulb hung in front of the seemingly half-finished idol. The place was very lonely. If somebody killed a person there, nobody would know it was happening. Why am I mentioning this? Because there are many stories of Sri Chaitanya Mahaprabhu in connection with this temple. About five hundred years ago Mahaprabhu went there and abolished the caste system of the temple, which made him an enemy of the priests. When Mahaprabhu went there a second time he disappeared. Some said that he drowned in the sea, others that he had merged with Jagannath, and still others that he was killed by the priests and his body disposed of.

On the outside walls of the Jagannath temple there are many engravings of sexual scenes that are not accepted by the culture of the twentieth century. Many people give it a philosophical explanation but having such types of engravings and statues in a religious temple will encourage transgressions in society and have an adverse effect on spiritualists. As a monk I did not want to stay in such an environment. We left there for the seashore where we sat on the sand and gazed out at the waves. It was the first time I had seen the sea and the waves greatly attracted me. Some people came over to talk to us and I discussed with them about the philosophy of Ananda Marga. Then we walked along the beach and played in the waves. That night we caught the Puri–Hyderabad Express. Acharya Devashish got down at Khurda Road and Mantu and I continued on to Waltair.

We reached Waltair at noon the next day. Waltair is also called Vishakapatnam. After taking our meal we went to the residence of Dr. Payaraju. Ac. Ramlal Dani had come from Raipur to meet me. I gave him the necessary instructions for his area. As of yet there had been no prachar done in Waltair. Dr. Payaraju was not an Ananda Margi but he was a spiritually minded man.

55
Madras

ON FEBRUARY 19 we left Waltair for Madras. We did not get a reservation so we went standing until we could get a seat. We reached Madras the next morning. Ac. Shivananda and a Margi advocate named Bhasyan came to receive us. They took us to the Lalit lodge, where some students came to discuss with me about Ananda Marga. In the evening a tattvasabha was organized at the residence of Bhasyan.

The next morning we toured Madras by bus. We made a round of the town and got down on the coast near Presidency College. We sat on the beach and after a few minutes a Margi student brought some students for a talk. Later we started for Dindigul.

On December 22 there was a volunteers camp near Dindigul at Angunagar. Angunagar was once Tipu Sultan's capital. We went to visit the Tipu Sultan fort, which was situated on the top of a small hill, before returning to Dindigul. In the meantime Sri S. V. Sundaram came from Madurai by car to take me there. On the way the road bifurcated, one way going to Madurai and the other to Kodaikanal Hill. Sundaramjii had a strong desire to show me Kodaikanal Hill. We had time so we went there. It was about seven-thousand-feet high, one of the most attractive places in South India. At the top there was a training centre for Christian missionaries. We reached there at sunset and made a round of the area by car. We found many residences of foreigners, including the in-charges of different sections of the mission and some priests. They were from a cold Western country and could not tolerate hot weather very well, so they made a village of their own at the top of the hill. Trainees were walking around in different groups. Then we left for Madurai, reaching there about 9:00 p.m.

The next day we went with Sundaram to visit the famous Minakshi Temple. Its great attraction is the towering Shiva temple where images of different mythological gods and goddesses are carved on the outside walls. It attracts religious people from all over the world. The circumference of the temple compound was nearly one mile and it was encircled by a thick brick wall about ten feet high. The same images were carved into the walls as well. The Tamil Nadu government had sanctioned 2.6 million rupees for repainting and other decorations. The compound had a small market and a small pond. It is said that Lord Shiva used to take a boat out on the pond. The walls by the pond depicted many stories related to Lord Shiva.

We went inside where Minakshi Devi used to sit. People were leaving offerings there. Then we went to where Lord Shiva used to sit, some twenty yards away. The spot was encircled by white stone elephants. The moment I went to that side of the temple I felt a spiritual wave vibrating my whole body. After some time Mantu told me that he was also feeling a strong vibration. I explained to him that about seven thousand years ago Lord Sadashiva used to sit there; therefore his spiritual wave could still be felt. Next we saw the place where Lord Shiva had sat with his devotees. South Indian temples were like forts with strong iron gates and high walls. Perhaps they were made to protect the people from enemies or to take shelter in during invasions. In Kerala, Karnataka, and Andhra Pradesh the temples were made in the same style. It was said about this particular temple that the princess of Madurai, Kumari Minakshi, set out to conquer the whole country. She won the war and at last went to fight Lord Shiva, but when she saw his great personality she surrendered to him. Later Sadashiva married her and came to South India and ruled the country from here. Since that time people have been visiting this temple.

Next we went to see the Rameshwaram temple and after spending the night in a retiring room we started for Dhanuskodi by train, reaching there about 9:30 a.m. The railway station was on the coast. It was a temporary station with a small vegetarian restaurant. We walked along the beach for about one furlong and then sat on the sand. The waves were crashing on both sides of us. It was a beautiful scene. At one end there was a small inlet where hundreds of pilgrims were taking bath. I hesitated to do so, thinking that after taking bath in the salty water I would need another bath to wash off the salt, but later I took bath there under the pressure of circumstances.

Afterward we went to the nearby hill where it was said that Sri Ramchandra had devised a plan to rescue his wife Sita from Sri Lanka. It is also said that when Ravana threw his shakti weapon at Laxman, Hanuman carried the Gandha Madan hill to that place. On that hill there was a small temple where supposedly the footprints of Ramchandra can still be seen. The view of the sea from the top of the hill was beautiful; our minds expanded and our thoughts grew spiritual. We sat for meditation and then returned to see the Rameshwaram temple. There also the activities of Lord Shiva were depicted on the walls of the temple. There was also a Shiva lingam.

After that we returned to Madurai. Ac. Pranavananda Avadhuta, Ac. Shivananda Avadhuta, and Ac. Shiva Prasad came by car and took us to the residence of Sundaramjii. From there we went to see Napur Ganga. We came back at 7:00 p.m., by which time some Margis had come for guidance and to talk about Ananda Marga.

56
Kerala

On February 26, Mantu, Acharya Pranavananda Avadhuta, who was posted in Kerala, and I started for Thiruvananthapuram. We reached there at 7:00 p.m. and went to the jagriti where a group of Margis had gathered to talk to me.

In the morning we went to visit the town zoo. I would not enter any of the temples in Kerala because there was a rule that men had to remove their upper garments in order to enter the temples and I did not want to encourage such superstitions fomented by the orthodox Hindu priests.

At noon we were invited to take lunch at the residence of a local acharya named Manikyam. Afterward we started for Kanyakumari by bus and reached there in the evening. We took our lodging in a dharmasala and then went down to the sea. A triangular delta ended in a bathing ghat. On the left was the Bay of Bengal and on the right the Indian Ocean. Innumerable waves from both sides were striking the coast. Just in front of the bathing ghat there was a small stone mound to protect the ghat from the high waves. It appeared that the sea and ocean were dancing in rhythm. Due to the protection afforded by the stone mound, pilgrims were able to take bath without any danger. We sat on the cement bathing platform until 9:00 p.m., enjoying the harmonious atmosphere and listening to the murmur of the sea. We decided to return there in the morning to catch the sunrise, so we went to bed earlier than usual.

The next morning the sky was clear. Many tourists were standing near the Kanyakumari temple with their cameras, ready to catch the rising sun. All were at attention, looking at the horizon, waiting for the sun to come up over the sea so they could catch in their cameras its crimson glow shining on the water. We also stood with them. After the glorious sunrise we went to the second story of the Mahatma Gandhi Memorial and did our meditation there overlooking the sea.

We returned to Thiruvananthapuram in the afternoon and I sat with the Margis to explain about the philosophy of Ananda Marga and the importance of spiritual practices. After that we went to see an exhibition of agricultural products near the jagriti.

The next morning we started for Cochin by train, reaching at 8:00 p.m. We went to the place that had been arranged for our stay and had a discussion with the Margis about sadhana.

On the morning of March 15 the port chairman of Cochin harbour, Sri P. R. Subramanium, took us by car to see Cochin Port. He had been recently initiated into Ananda Marga. We made a round of the harbour by motorboat and then went out into the deep ocean from where we saw the ships approaching the port. Then he showed us a place where the fishermen were fishing with a special technique practiced in that region. After that we returned to Sri Subramaniumjii's residence for breakfast and then he took us by car to Kalady.

Kalady was the birthplace of Jagatguru Adi Shankaracharya. The house he had been born in, which was well preserved, was on a river, facing a cement ghat. It was said that at the age of five Sri Shankaracharya wanted to take permission from his mother, who worshipped Lord Krishna, to become a monk, but she would not give him permission. One day he was taking a bath at the ghat with his mother when a crocodile caught his leg and started pulling him into the water. His mother caught his hand, trying to save him, but she was also being dragged in. Shankaracharya cried out to his mother that if she would allow him to become a monk then the crocodile would let him go. In her desperation she gave him permission and the crocodile let him go. By the side of the ghat there were a few small temples related to his childhood.

After visiting Kalady, we returned to Cochin. Cochin and Ernakulam are sister cities divided by a canal. In the afternoon I addressed a public meeting and in the evening we attended dharmachakra where I talked about the importance of spiritual sadhana. After dharmachakra we started for Calicut by train.

Pranavananda, Mantu, and I reached Calicut early in the morning and went to a dharmasala in which one room was reserved for the Ananda Marga office and for weekly dharmachakra. I discussed different aspects of Ananda Marga with the Margis in the morning and after lunch we went to visit the town. We saw the famous timber factory, the biggest factory in Asia, and then went to the coast to see the sunset. In the evening some Margis came from Kalady to meet me. We sang bhajans and kirtan for more than an hour. Then we meditated and I told them about the importance of spiritual sadhana in human life.

57
Madras

ON THE MORNING of March 3 we started for Coimbatore by train. Natarajan and some other Margis saw off us at the railway station. He was a good devotee. He remained with us throughout the time we were in Calicut, helping us with whatever we needed.. We reached Coimbatore Station at 5:00 p.m. Acharya Shivananda Avadhuta, Sundaramjii from Madurai, and a few local Margis came to receive us. We went with them to Shivanandajii's place where I discussed sadhana with the Margis. Later I met with the wholetime workers and gave them the necessary instructions.

The next morning Acharya Hariram from Bangalore arrived and took us by car to Bangalore. He proposed that we visit Otakamand and we agreed. Along the way we saw the hydroelectric project at Paikar. We performed our evening puja in a park in Otakamand and then drove around this hill town before returning to Coimbatore. Otakamand is the district headquarters of Nilgiri District. It is eight thousand feet above sea level so the weather is quite cold. Otherwise there is no winter season in the south, which is why many people from the South like to visit there.

The next morning we went with Acharya Hariramjii to visit a Shiva temple and then caught a train for Salem. Acharya Pranavananda went back to Kerala but Acharya Shivanandajii remained with us. Acharya Narain Swami and some local Margis were waiting when we arrived. They took us to the Theosophical Society where we had a room for our pracharakas. Then we attended the weekly dharmachakra at the residence of Balsubramaniumjii. Afterward I talked about the science of sadhana. Then we visited the school where Narain Swamijii was the headmaster.

58
Mysore

THE NEXT MORNING I discussed different aspects of the philosophy with the Margis. Then we started for Bangalore by train. Acharya

Narain Swamijii and Acharya Shivanandajii saw off us at the station. We reached Bangalore in the evening. Acharya Cidghanananda Avadhuta, who was posted in that area, received us along with Acharya Nagaraj and a few local Margis.

The next day we all went to visit the town. At 3:00 p.m. we started for Mysore by train. We reached there in the evening and the next morning we went to see the Mysore palace and a few other places. In the evening Mantu and I caught a train for Landa.

59
Goa

WE REACHED LANDA Station at 5:00 p.m. Our pracharaka in Maharastra, Ac. Shantananda Avadhuta, was waiting for us. We performed puja in the waiting room and then caught our connecting train. In the morning we got down at Vasco da Gama Station. From there we went by taxi to Kurnal and then by motorboat to the capital of Goa, Panjim. The town is encircled by the sea and is full of natural beauty. It is quite different from the rest of the country because it was ruled for a long period by the Portuguese.

At 11:00 a.m. we went to the bus stand to catch a bus for Sountabari. While we were waiting for our bus many people crowded round us, eager to show us their palms and know their future. But I did not encourage them. As far as I know, the science of palmistry has no scientific basis. The lines of the hand are always changing.

60
Maharastra

WE REACHED SOUNTABARI about 7:00 p.m. A group of Margis were waiting to receive us. We went with them to the jagriti and then to a public meeting in which I talked about the philosophy of Ananda Marga. Afterward I talked to the Margis about the importance of sadhana and we had a collective feast. I could see that they were great devotees of Lord Anandamurtijii. During my talks many of them were weeping. I was surprised to see that they were from different sections of society. They had forsworn their superstitions and caste beliefs.

The next morning we started for Belgram. Acharya Cidghanananda Avadhuta had gone there earlier to prepare our programme. We reached Belgram at noon and had a programme with the local Margis. At 3:00 p.m. we left for Pune by train.

When Mantu, Acharya Shantananda, and I got down at Pune Station early the next morning we saw a group with garlands and flowers waiting to receive somebody. I asked Acharya Shantananda who they were. As per the reports I had received, Pune only had one or two Margis. Shantananda did not know who they were but we soon discovered that they had come to receive me. One of them, Mr. Chowla, took us to his car. All were reputed men and they had all come in their cars. Still we did not know who they were or where we were going. On the way I asked Mr. Chowla and he said that all arrangements had been made for us at the residence of Brigadier Saheb. I told him that as per my programme we were to stay in the Gargey Dharmasala, and that he should kindly drop me there, but he requested me to please first go to the residence of Brigadier Saheb. After bath and meal they would bring us to the dharmasala. I replied that I would give a programme for them that evening at the residence of Brigadier Saheb, but for the time being he should drop me at the dharmasala.

When I got down at the dharmasala all were surprised. They rushed to my car and peppered me with questions. I explained to them why I had gotten down there. Then all left and only Mr. Chowla remained with me. I asked him how they had come to know about my Pune programme and why they were so interested. He told me that my programme had been published in the newspaper. The people who had come to the station were all high-ranking government officers and co-disciples of the same guru. Their guru, at the time of his physical departure, had told them that a spiritual mission named Ananda Marga had been started in Bihar and that they should cooperate to the best of their capacity with their missionary work. The founder of Ananda Marga, Shrii Shrii Anandamurtijii, is the Jagatguru, the maker of the age, he told them. Mr. Chowla was an executive engineer in Pune. He took two days leave to remain with me.

After reaching the dharmasala we learned that Acharya Chandranathjii had come from Mahabaleshwar to meet me. I had not seen him for a long time and we passed the morning sharing stories of Baba. A doctor invited us for lunch at his residence but he was not an Ananda Margi so I remained behind with Chandranathjii. Shantananda and Cidghanananda went instead. Later that day the doctor took initiation from me.

In the afternoon I addressed a tattvasabha at the residence of Brigadier Saheb. From there I went to the residence of a Margi, Mr. Ghosh, who was Assistant Collector Central Excise, for another tattvasabha. Many were ready to take initiation and I directed Acharya Shantananda to give them initiation later on.

On the thirteenth, Ac Shantananda, Ac. Cidghanananda, Ac. Chandranathjii, Mantu, and I started for Bombay by the 7:00 a.m. train. At Bombay the director of Akashvani, Acharya Chandradeo Varma, came to receive us and take us to his residence. Lalan had also come from Delhi. We old Margis were seeing each other after a long interval and we soon created a spiritual atmosphere. We chalked out a programme to see the town and on the way back I addressed a meeting of the Margis in a Central Excise building. That night we kapaliks went to Bital Bari for midnight puja.

61
Gujrat

THE NEXT MORNING Shantananda and I left for Baroda. Mantu's official leave was over, so he left for Calcutta. Ac. Cidghanananda left for Patna, and Acharya Chandranathjii left for Mahabaleshwar. We reached Baroda at 4:00 p.m. Ac. Dipak came to receive us. He accompanied us to a central lodge where I talked for some time with a Margi inspector of Central Excise. Then Ac. Dipak and I started for Ahmedabad, along with Ac. Shantananda.

62
Rajasthan

THE NEXT MORNING, after arriving in Ahmedabad, we went to the bus stand to buy tickets for Mount Abu but unfortunately no tickets were available so we cancelled our programme and informed Mangal

Biharijii by telegram that I was coming to Udaipur. Ac. Shantananda stayed behind.

I reached Udaipur the next day and was met there by Ac. Shankarananda Avt. and Ac. Krishna Murari, along with a group of Margis. Sri Mangal Biharijii, an IAS officer, and Sri Kotoyanijii also came with a car and I accompanied Sri Mangal Biharijii to his residence. I completed my meetings there with the Margis and workers and in the evening there was a public meeting. After returning from the public meeting we sang bhajans and kirtan. This created a divine atmosphere and as a result the old Margis became spiritually intoxicated.

On March 18 I attended the local dharmachakra at the residence of Arjunjii. After that Mangal Biharijii, Srimati Vimala Vashisthajii (later she became Avadhutika Ananda Bharati), and I went to the Udaipur lake where we boarded a boat. In the middle of the lake there was a brick building. In ancient times rajas and maharajas used to go there for pleasure trips. While in the boat we talked about the different spiritual expressions of Baba and the philosophy and sadhana of Ananda Marga. Srimati Vashisthajii not yet seen Baba, therefore she expressed her desire to go to Jamalpur for the coming Dharma Maha Chakra on the occasion of Vaishakhi Purnima, the birthday of Baba Anandamurtijii. Then we visited the palace of Udaipur. Here Sri Arjunjii, Ac. Shankarananda, and Ac. Krishna Murari joined us. From there we went to the residence of Srimati Vashistha's daughter Sabita. Her husband was the police superintendent of Udaipur District. Sabita sang such wonderful bhajans it seemed as if she were the great devotee Mirabai. While singing bhajans she would weep, merged in the feeling of the Lord. That evening a tattvasabha was organized at her place in which I explained the philosophy of Ananda Marga for one hour. From there we went to the residence of a Margi named Teja Singh and then returned to the residence of Mangal Biharijii.

The next morning Shankarananda, Krishna Murari, Ram Prasad, and I left for Jaipur in Mangal Biharijii's car. On the way we got a flat tire and then later another tire went flat. With the help of a truck at Vijaynagar we repaired both tires. That evening I addressed a meeting in Jaipur.

63
Punjab

*T*HE NEXT MORNING some students came to meet me and at 11:00 a.m. we started for Hisar, a day earlier than planned. Ac. Shankarananda accompanied me. We reached Hisar at 9:00 p.m. and went to a nearby dharmasala without informing the Margis. Due to the constant traveling my health had broken down so I took rest there for the next twenty-four hours.

The next evening I went to the railway station at the time that I had originally been scheduled to arrive. Ac. Om Prakash, the local pracharaka, and a group of Margis were waiting for my train. We came up behind them and did namaskar. They were all surprised. After we explained the mystery of our arrival, we took our bags from the dharmasala and went to the residence of a Margi advocate named Krishnachandrajii. That night Ac. Shankarananda had to return to Rajasthan.

The next day was Sunday. A public meeting was organized at 10:00 a.m. in which I talked about the philosophy of Ananda Marga. At 2:00 p.m. Ac. Om Prakash and I started for Ludhiana, reaching there at 9:00 p.m. A group of Margis with garlands and flowers was waiting at the station to receive us. They took us to the residence of an ardent devotee, Dr. Rajkishan Mahendra. We talked for some time with the Margis and then went to bed.

The next day I was engaged with different programmes. I addressed three tattvasabhas and one meeting with the Margis. This went up to 11:00 p.m. without any pause.

On March 24, Ac. Amaresh, Vishwabandhu, and I started for Pathankot. Due to an illness Om Prakash could not go with us. Many Margis met with me along the way, at Jalandhar and Amritsar stations, but the Margis of Batala compelled me to get down there and stay for a day. Accordingly I sent Ac. Amaresh to Pathankot to inform them about the change in my programme. The next day I started for Pathankot with Ac. Vishwabandhu. We met Ac. Amaresh there and the pracharaka of Jammu, Ac. Parosh, and accompanied them to the residence of the brother of Ac. Jialaljii. Afterward Ac. Parosh and I left for Jammu.

64
Jammu

WE REACHED JAMMU at 6:00 p.m. A group of Margis had come with flowers and garlands to receive us at the bus stand. We went with them to the residence of a devotee, Makhanlaljii, where we attended dharmachakra.

The next morning I talked to the people who were arriving one by one. In the afternoon we went to a hospital to see a Margi patient named Vishnudasjii and in the evening I addressed a public meeting. After that I went to the house of Maharajkishanjii. Later on, Maharajkishan and Makhanlal became acharyas of Ananda Marga.

On March 2 we left for Kathua. We got down at the village of Janglot in Kathua District where Major Payer Singh was waiting with a car to receive us. He took us to his residence for a tattvasabha. I explained to the invitees about the philosophy of Ananda Marga and then answered the personal questions of Major Singh. He was a new Margi but very interested in sadhana. He was a moralist as well as a religious person. Once he had been a cabinet minister of the Jammu and Kashmir government. He told me a story about his days in the ministry. During his time many projects were undertaken, including some bridges. Once, when the concerning papers for the construction of a bridge reached his table for signing, he went to inspect the place. He found that there was no bridge at all. After returning he raised the matter in a cabinet session but to no avail. Since no action was taken against the party responsible for this fraud, he resigned from the cabinet in protest.

65
Ambala

EARLY THE NEXT morning I started for the Pathankot railway station. Major Singh and Acharya Parosh brought me to the station by car and at Ludhiana Acharya Satyanarayan and a local Margi, Dr. Rajkishanjii, brought me a meal. When I reached Ambala station, Acharya Om Prakash and a local Margi, Raja Saheb, and his son were there to receive me and bring me to the residence of Raja Saheb.

The next morning I met with Ac. Gurudas Khanna and a group of Margis from Patiala. Afterward there was a tattvasabha in which I explained the ideology of Ananda Marga and its social outlook. Then I went to see a piece of land that was being donated to Ananda Marga by Raja Saheb. Afterward I started for Delhi. After arriving there I went to the quarters of Sri Shashi Rainjanjii at 93 North Avenue. All sorts of Ananda Marga activities were going on there. Lalanjii had opened his RU office there. In the night Ac. Om Prakash, Lalan, Ac. Shuddhananda, Shashi Rainjanjii and myself passed our time in spiritual discussions and talks about Baba. It was a glorious time.

66
Vrindavan

ON MARCH 30, Ac. Om Prakash, Ac. Shuddhananda, and I went to visit Vrindavan, the birthplace of Lord Krishna near Mathura, but due to the rude behaviour of the Brahmin priests we were about to leave without seeing it. In the meantime an old priest named Jaharlal saw what was happening. He hurried over to us and requested us with folded hands not to leave Mathura. "I will show you these places," he said, "and nobody will bother you." We went with him and saw the places related to Lord Krishna. When we reached Vrindavan, a priest offered to accompany us. I told him it would be better not to remain with us because of how the priests had misbehaved with us in Mathura. He told us that Vrindavan was the divine land of Lord Krishna. Nobody would misbehave with us there. I told him that he was earning money from the tourists but we would not pay anything. Even so, he wanted to stay with us and said that he would not ask for money.

He took us to a place where five hundred widows from Bengal were sitting and chanting the name of Lord Krishna. Those who were taking part in the bhajans were getting free food from a spiritual trust. From there we went to a stage named Rasaliila. A teenage boy and girl wearing the dress of Lord Krishna and Radha were performing the Rasaliila. From there we went to see the so-called tamal tree where people tied pieces of cloth of different colours. It is said that Lord Krishna hid the clothes of the gopis by the tamal tree while they were taking bath in the river Yamuna. The different-coloured pieces of cloth tied to the branches of the trees were symbols of the gopis throwing off their clothes. This was how the priest explained it but I scolded him and said that the Krishna whom I loved was the composer of the Gita and the statesman of the Mahabharata. I did not like to hear the name of Krishna associated with a lascivious role with the gopis. The priest said, "Swamijii! Lord Krishna wanted to make them understand that everything comes from him and goes back to him; why should they be ashamed to be with him." I was happy with this philosophical explanation. After that we went to the temple of Lala Babu. It was made in the South Indian style. In the courtyard there was a gold palm tree. Finally we went to a garden with a small brick room. Inside the room was a beautifully decorated bed known as *kunjavan*. There are many mythological stories about this bed. When we returned to the bus stand, I tried to give the priest ten rupees but he refused to take it. I told him I was giving him this money so that he could buy sweets for his children. Then he accepted. From there we returned to Delhi.

67
Delhi

*W*E REACHED DELHI at noon. Ac. Manoharjii had come from Jaipur to meet me. I talked with him for some time and in the meantime Shashi Rainjanjii arrived. He and I went to the bus stand to see off Manoharjii. In the evening I addressed a tattvasabha for one hour.

The next morning I went to the residence of Jitendra Tyagijii where a meeting had been organized for the unit secretaries and pracharakas of that area. I collected their progress reports and gave them the necessary directions. When Ac. Om Prakash and I arrived back at 93 North Avenue, the Margis of Delhi were complaining about Lalanjii's acts of sabotage in the organization. I had told them about what had happened in the case of Ac. Amitananda, both in Bombay and in Delhi. Shashi Rainjanjii wanted me to sit with Lalanjii and discuss the matter, but Lalanjii did not want to sit. Finally he agreed but he said he would remain hostile to me. I told him that I had not come there as an individual but as a representative of the organization and that such a hostile attitude would bring harm to the organization. Still he said he would not stop. In the meantime Shashi Rainjanjii brought a photo of Baba and asked us both to touch it and take an oath that in the future we would not act against each other. I took the oath but Lalan did not. He said that he would not compromise under any circumstances. Seeing this, the Margis understood the situation and afterward no one gave any importance to his actions.

68
Dehradun

ON THE MORNING of April 2, I started for Dehradun by train. The pracharaka of Uttar Pradesh, Acharya Yogananda, accompanied me. We reached Dehradun at 7:00 p.m. Ac. Srinandan, Ac. Maheshwarjii, and a group of Margis were waiting at the station to receive us. I went with them to the Jain dharmasala. We completed our evening puja there and then went to the residence of Ac. Maheshwarjii for our meal and a talk with the local Margis.

The next morning Yogananda and I took a bus to Mussoorie. It was a popular hill town close to Dehradun. Many men with horses were waiting at the bus station to take the tourists to the top. We went up to Laldibba. From there the Himalayan ranges were clearly visible. We could see the clouds moving among the mountains. It was an attractive scene for the tourists. After some time we went to the opposite side of the hill, to the town market. The town looked like a picture. On our way back we stopped at a sulphur spring where many people were taking bath to cure their skin diseases.

69
Laxmanjhula

ON THE FOURTH I addressed a tattvasabha at the residence of Ac. Maheshwarjii. Then we went by bus to Rishikesh. From there we hired a tonga for Laxmanjhula. There was a hanging bridge over the Ganges and on the other side there was a vacant dharmasala where we kept our bags. Then we went to see the area. Only monks and retired males who wished to lead a spiritual life could live there. By the side of the Ganges were many huts for sadhana and a few ashrams, such as Gita Bhavan and Svargashram. In most places there were only monks.

As we were walking along the bank of the Ganges we came across a signboard in the jungle on which was written Shankaracharya Nagar. Intrigued, we entered the jungle and found a hut in which a monk dressed in white was sitting on a cot giving spiritual instruction to a foreigner. After taking his permission to enter, we introduced ourselves and came to know that he was Maharishi Mahesh Yogi. I asked him about his activities and how the society would be economically benefited from them. But he was not able to give a proper answer. Earlier I had told Yogananda that we would listen to everybody but not argue with them, because we had gone there to study the environment of monks. Accordingly, we maintained a cordial conversation with him and left the place without any arguments. In Rishikesh non-vegetarian diet was prohibited.

The suspension bridge at Laxmanjhula was 450 feet long and 60 feet above the Ganges. It was similar to Howrah Bridge in Calcutta, supported by two pillars at each end. It was only six feet wide so no vehicle could cross it. By the side of the bridge a cement ghat led down to the water. In the water near the ghat we saw large fish fearlessly eating gram from the hands of the tourists. If a person entered the water the fish would encircle him and allow him to pass his hand lightly over their backs, just like a pet. One furlong from there, in the Kali Kamli Baba ghat, even larger fish weighing upward of fifty pounds would behave the same way with the tourists. Boats would pass by there so the tourists could give them gram to eat. It was said to be somewhat risky to go into the water because if the fish struck a person they could injure them. Legally nobody is allowed to kill any animal in this area. I had seen fish coming out to eat gram in Ballygunge Lake at Calcutta but here in the free atmosphere of the Ganges they were playing with the tourists like pet fish.

In the afternoon we found different groups of monks moving hither and thither. Some were sitting on the rocks. I asked them if there was any realized monk in the area. They said that they were begging for their food and were not concerned with such persons. But one of them said that there was a sadhu who sat on a tiger's skin under a tree and knew many things. He would come at 8:00 a.m. and remain up to 3:00 p.m. A shopkeeper also told us that there was a yogi living in the jungle about twelve kilometres away on the way to the Nilkanth who was a realized mahatma. He was popularly known as Chintabala Baba.

The next morning we set out to meet Chintabala Baba. We followed a zigzag road through the jungle and after two hours we came upon a stone on a hill with an arrow marking the way to Chintabala Baba. A little further on we found a black person sitting on top of a rock. When I asked him where Chintabala Baba's ashram was he said that he was Chintabala Baba. He said he had no ashram but lived in a cave. We asked him if he could give us some drinking water and he directed us to a nearby spring. Then we went with him to see his cave. By the side of his cave there was another small cave in which his disciple lived. His disciple had gone to Laxmanjhula to bring puris, fried bread, from the Kali Kamli Baba ashram. The ashram would give five puris daily for each person free of cost. Then I asked him about his spiritual realization. He said, "I am Lakkar Baba. Every day I require three mounds of wood to heat my body." I asked what was the purpose of heating his body. He said that constantly heating his body was an ascetic discipline. When I suggested that he could do this near Laxmanjhula and thus wouldn't need to bring food from such a long distance, he said that the government would not allow him to cut the branches of the trees near Laxmanjhula. In the meantime a fifteen-year-old boy returned with puris from Laxmanjhula. I asked the boy where he was from. He said he was from the nearby hills. By then I had realized that our journey had been fruitless. I asked him if he knew if there were any other spiritually elevated persons in that area. He said in the Bhutnath hills near Laxmanjhula there were many caves occupied by sadhus.

When we returned to Laxmanjhula we came across a group of naga sadhus sitting on the rocks under the sun. Their bodies were covered with ash, they had matted locks, and they were wearing nothing but a lungota. We asked them about their spiritual activities but they were not interested in discussing it. Many of them were wearing the saffron dress out of poverty so that they could beg successfully. Some were criminal absconders. They hid themselves behind the saffron dress to avoid legal punishment and weren't concerned with spiritual practice. Most of them were illiterate. But one young naga monk was sitting at a little distance on a rock. I approached him and asked him why he was sitting alone? I told him that we wanted to know something about spiritual sadhana. "Sadhana is nothing but to meditate on the chakras and control the respiration," he said. "Then you can walk on water and air. If you meditate on the guru, he will do everything for you. Once, at the time of my meditation, I wanted sixty rupees from my guru and I got it. Later I repented asking for that because I did not get peace but rather unrest. Ultimately I sent back the money to my guru and then I got relief."

We left him and went looking for the sadhu who sat under a tree on a tiger's skin from 8:00 a.m. to 3:00 p.m. We sat by his side with folded hands. After some time he opened his eyes and starting speaking on different scriptures in Hindi, English, Sanskrit, and Bengali. When he finished I asked him about sadhana and his achievement. He said that all the Vedas existed within him. But after five minutes of discussion his stock was depleted. In the meantime some tourists were coming down the path. Seeing them, he asked us to please wait for some time to let the tourists pass. He closed his eyes but as soon as they approached he started the discussion again. After they had passed by, he revealed that he was sitting under that tree to earn money. "I am from East Bengal," he said. "I came to India as a refugee during the partition and came here to earn my livelihood. This puja is only for outward show; actually I am a householder."

We left there to take our dinner and afterward we went to Bhutnath Hill to meet the sadhus who lived in the different caves. It was close to Laxmanjhula. First we went to a cave near the bottom of the hill where we met a sadhu with matted locks. When he saw us he became reacted. Seeing his behaviour we became stupefied. He looked like a criminal. Perhaps he was hiding himself in the garb of a sadhu and did not like public contact for fear of his identity being exposed. In the next cave we met a well-behaved sadhu who told us that he didn't practice sadhana but simply repeated mantra. In the next cave a young sadhu was cutting a gourd. When I asked about it, he said that he ate only fruits and raw vegetables. He did not practice sadhana but also only repeated mantra. I asked him where he got his food from. He said that people who were there for spiritual purposes could register their names to get free food from the Kali Kamli Baba ashram or the Punjabi Kshetra ashram, enough to meet their minimum requirements. He said that if we wanted to know about spiritual sadhana we should visit a Bengali sadhu who lived at the top of the hill. "He is a very old," he said, "and has been living here for a long time. He does not like to meet anybody but you can try."

We went to meet the Bengali sadhu. At the mouth of his cave we did namaskar and he asked us about the purpose of our visit. When I told him, he cordially invited us inside and offered us a blanket to sit on. Then he brought some sweets and water for us. He told Yogananda that since he was a young man he would request him to bring a bucket of water from the spring so that he could cook rice for us. I told him that we had already ordered food at the Marwari restaurant, therefore there was no need to take any trouble for us. Thinking perhaps that we were hesitating because he had asked us to fetch water, he said, "Please don't mind that I have asked you to bring water. I am an old man and I am unable to go up and down this hill for it. But I shall be fortunate to have a chance to serve you."

I said that the sadhus who lived in the caves at the foot of the hill caves had told us that he did not allow anybody to come to his ashram but we had found the truth to be otherwise. "We are charmed by your cordial behaviour and your eagerness to serve," I said. "Now my age is seventy-eight," he replied. "I have been living in this cave for thirty-two years. Thirty-two years ago Laxmanjhula was a heaven. Now the atmosphere has been polluted by deceivers living here in saffron garb. During the day they pretend to be sadhus but at night they kill the jungle hens and fish from the Ganges and eat them. Many antisocial elements are here who have committed crimes and absconded disguised as sadhus. Nevertheless they have registered their names for free food either in the Kali Kamli Baba ashram or Punjabi Kshetra ashram. I do not belong to any ashram. I have many disciples in Calcutta and Bangladesh. They look after my maintenance. I live alone, so I don't need much."

After that we started discussing spirituality. He said he practiced yoga as per the prescribed rules but had no great achievement. "Now I feel that without the grace of the Lord nothing can be achieved," he said. I told him that we were under the guidance of a sadguru and were serving the society. But if the day came when we returned to sit for deep meditation would he help us? He was delighted and said that he would be fortunate to have a chance to give whatever help he could. Then he took us to another cave just nearby. He said it was under his control and we were welcome to stay there if we returned. When I asked him how we would get food and clothing, he said that he would arrange everything. He would make arrangements with his disciples for after his physical departure.

After taking permission, I entered into the cave to do meditation. During meditation I felt a deep silence and was overwhelmed with emotion. Inside the cave my mind became concentrated within moments and became unified with the Lord, while outside some time was required. We thanked him and returned to the dharmasala for rest.

In the afternoon we walked along the Ganges up to the Garur inn. Once this road was used to go to Kedarnath on foot. On the way we met the young naga monk. I asked him to teach us something. Then and there on the stone-chipped ground he started to show us different asanas. I advised him to stop because the stone chips would hurt his body. Furthermore, I said, we were not interested in learning asanas. We wanted to learn yoga sadhana. After some time he said that he could see that we were both practicing yoga sadhana. We left him and went ahead to a hillside village where there was a dharmasala by the road. We took some rest there and before sunset we headed back to Laxmanjhula. While we were returning it grew dark. I saw the surrounding area full of spiritual effulgence and my mind was flooded with spiritual vibrations. I realized the glory of that place. The feet of innumerable sadhus and the spiritual waves they generated had made this place heaven. I became completely indifferent to the world. It felt as if I had returned to my homeland. We sat down by the banks of the Ganges and sang some bhajans. We performed our puja there and then returned to our dharmasala.

The next morning we left Laxmanjhula for Haridwar via Rishikesh. Keeping our bags in a locked room we went to purchase a kamandulu water pot. Then we walked along the Ganges for some time, seeing the sights, before catching the evening train for Lucknow.

70
Lucknow

THE NEXT MORNING Ac. Goutamjii and his wife, Ac. Rataneshjii, and a group of Margis were waiting for us at Lucknow station. Ac. Goutamjii was the district secretary of Ananda Marga and a high-ranking government officer. The whole day Margis came to meet me at Goutamjii's residence. Another devotee, Doctor Badalajii of Lucknow Medical College, lived right across the street. At noon I went with him to the medical college for my checkup. In the afternoon I met with a very old Margi, Chamanlal Sethi, and then went with Ac. Rataneshjii to the market. In Lucknow there are two main markets — one is at Hazaratganj and another at Aminabad. Lucknow was a town of nabobs and everything was in the nabobi style. Lucknow's imumbaras, a Mogul religious hall, were very famous. The locals call them bhulbhulia because they have hundreds of rooms and if you go inside without a guide it is almost impossible to find your way out. Another special attraction is the zoo. Here also you can see the formal nabobi style and the strong influence of Urdu.

The next afternoon I caught the Punjab Mail for Varanasi. Ac. Indrajitjii from Ghazipur and a group of Margis came with garlands and flowers to receive us at the station. Before going to South India I had instructed Ac. lndrajitjii to establish an office for Seva Dharma Mission in Varanasi. The next morning we went to search for a suitable house for the SDM office. We saw a few houses with a Margi advocate named Golap Singh but could not finalize anything. After that we started for Jamalpur.

71
Raipur Dharma Maha Chakra

*A*FTER REACHING JAMALPUR I heard that Baba and P. K. Chatterjee would be out of town for fifteen days. I remained there for two days to reply to the letters of the workers. On the twelfth I left for Calcutta. There I met with Ac. Vijayananda and Ac. Lokeshvarananda and went with them to Hare Street to meet with Tyagijii and Prasadjii about organizational matters. Then I caught a train for Chaibasa where I met with Balendujii and Ac. Rajmohanjii for organizational talks. I also met Ac. Dhanananda and Ac. Gagandeojii for the same purpose. Then I left for the Raipur Dharma Maha Chakra. Ac. Narendrajii, Ac. Kailashjii, and Ac. Shambhusaran came to receive me and I went with them to Shantinagar to meet Baba. After meeting with Baba I went to the dharmasala where the General Margis were staying. I held a student meeting and then went to look after the arrangements for Dharma Maha Chakra. In the evening I brought Baba to the DMC. After the DMC I collected the workers and gave them the necessary instructions.

The next morning I officiated two intercaste marriages as per the Ananda Marga system. In the meantime Baba and the general secretary went to visit the surrounding area. During the noon General Darshan Baba blessed the newly married couples. After this I left for Ranchi where I spent the day with Ac. Kshitishjii.

On April 18 I reached Anandanagar and visited the construction. I found that money was being wasted. This especially bothered me because I had faced a lot of difficulty to collect that money. During my long absence no one had properly overseen the work.

The next day I told everyone about my all-India tour and the progress of Ananda Marga throughout India. The next day I left for Jamalpur. Baba was back by then and I talked with him about the tour and the various works. The following day Ac. Ramtanukjii and I went to Monghyr court for the Amitananda case.

72
Jammu Dharma Maha Chakra

ON APRIL 25, Baba, P. K. Chatterjee, and I started for Varanasi. Acharya Ramtanukjii accompanied us up to Patna. We reached Varanasi in the evening and stayed at the Ananda Bazar Lodge for the night. Devotees from Ghazipur, Azamgarh, Gorakhpur, and other places came for Baba's darshan. In the morning Baba gave personal contact to the new Margis and at noon he went to the dharmasala for General Darshan. Baba gave a lecture and then enjoyed the bhajans and kirtan sung by the devotees. After that he returned to the lodge and gave personal contact to the rest of the new Margis. Then he met with the senior Margis and local acharyas in a homely atmosphere before taking rest for the night.

The next morning Baba left by plane for Jammu with the general secretary. We saw Baba off at the airport and then with the help of Ac. Keshavjii, Ac. Raghunathjii, and Golap Singh we started looking for a rented building to serve as the SDM office. We saw a few buildings but none were suitable. I remained at Varanasi for two more days to complete my office work and on the twenty-seventh I left for Jamalpur via Patna. Baba was scheduled to reach Patna from Jammu at noon on the twenty-eighth. Accordingly I and one Patna Margi went by car to the airport to receive Baba. On the way one of the rear wheels fell off and we narrowly escaped harm. Another car was also coming to receive Baba. We flagged it down and went in that car to the airport. I oversaw Baba's programmes in Patna and then accompanied him to Jamalpur by train.

73
Transfer

*T*HE NEXT DAY Acharya Ramtanukjii arrived. We had an organizational meeting with the general secretary and then Ramtanukjii left for Anandanagar. I packed up the office records and sent them to Varanasi with Rajendrajii. From now on, the dharma prachar and workers training would be conducted at Varanasi under the auspices of Seva Dharma Mission. They were to have no organizational relation to Ananda Marga. But they requested me to continue supervising the work at Anandanagar until a competent man became available.

On May 2, I left Jamalpur for Varanasi. It was decided that Acharya Prakashananda would remain there as the chief secretary of Seva Dharma Mission so I instructed him in the office work related to that section. I stayed there for two days to complete his training as well as to look for a building for the office. Then I left for Calcutta via Jamalpur.

74
Printing Press

*A*T THIS TIME our priority in Calcutta was to purchase a printing press. I talked with Prasadjii, Tyagijii, and Peshwarilaljii about it and finalized the programme. We purchased the press and the letter moulds and sent them by truck to Anandanagar. In the meantime I held organizational meetings with Vijayananda, Lokeshvarananda, and Nirmalananda. On May 11 I went to Krishnagar with Nirmalananda for kapalik puja. Then we returned to Jamalpur.

75
Ananda Purnima Dharma Maha Chakra

*A*FTER REACHING JAMALPUR Baba called me. After completing my talks with Baba I went to meet the general secretary in his residence. The next day I went to Patna to see to the arrangements for DMC. There

I consulted with a doctor and took some medicine and rest. The next day I went to Varanasi to help the Seva Dharma Mission work. I remained there for two days, doing my office work and searching for a suitable building for the SDM office. Then I returned to Jamalpur.

At Jamalpur we were preparing to celebrate Ananda Purnima, the birthday celebration of Baba Anandamurtijii. The DMC would be held at Patna. I was extremely busy organizing those programmes. Devotees and their families came from different parts of the country to attend Baba's birthday programme. They all wanted to be physically close to Baba. It was my duty to arrange for their stay and teach the tattvika classes. I was also busy organizing the Patna DMC, giving the new organizational programmes to the workers, and overseeing personal contact for the new Margis. In the meantime Baba came to the ashram each morning and evening so I was alert to utilize Baba's valuable time in a proper way. One week passed in this way. On the twenty-sixth we celebrated Ananda Purnima. All the wholetime workers came to attend this holy function.

Each year my worldly family attended Ananda Purnima. On this occasion my younger brother, Satchidananda, got married in the Jamalpur ashram as per the Ananda Marga system. Baba blessed them in the evening when he came to attend the function.

The next day I left for Patna. With the help of the local Margis and workers I completed all the necessary arrangements, and on the twenty-ninth Baba arrived by train. Innumerable Margis came to Patna Junction with flags and festoons to receive Baba. Due to the heavy crowd I was afraid that Baba's security might be hampered. Therefore when Baba reached the station we brought him directly to the DMC site and informed the General Margis at Patna Junction that Baba had already reached the site. The DMC programme lasted for two days and was highly successful.

A remarkable event took place during this DMC. A few senior Margis asked that a second cot be kept on the dais for Baba's wife so that she could sit by him during the DMC. A doubt arose in my mind. If I allowed this to take place without taking permission from Baba I could get in trouble, so I told Baba what the Margis had proposed. When he heard this he said: "In Dharma Maha Chakra Anandamurti is a singular Entity; there is no second existence apart from Him."

We removed the cot that had been placed for his wife. A few years later we realized the significance of his pronouncement when his wife left him.

76
Varanasi Office

*A*FTER COMPLETING THE DMC programme, I returned to Jamalpur with Baba. On June 4 I started for Varanasi. When I reached the station I found Sri Sailen Ghosh of Howrah and his family waiting to catch the train home. All were Ananda Margis. Whenever I went to Howrah I would stay with him. I talked with them for some time in the station and once they boarded the train I went to the SDM office. We had finally found a suitable building for the office at D 57/60 C Sigra. It was a second-story flat in a building situated on the main road near the railway station. The owner of the house lived on the ground floor with his family. We put a signboard on the wall of the main road so that visitors could find it without any problem.

I remained with workers up to June 12 and gradually sent them to their respective areas. In the meantime an American student named Richard took initiation from me. On new moon night twenty of us kapaliks went to the other side of the Ganges to perform our midnight puja. We crossed the Ganges by boat and started singing bhajans. The helmsman became intoxicated with our singing. The atmosphere was delightful and rhythmic. After completing our midnight puja we remained the whole night lying on the sand. In the morning some of us crossed the Ganges by boat and the rest of us swam across. So many workers gathering together at one place for a few days created a heavenly atmosphere. We all experienced divine happiness.

77
Central Office at Anandanagar

I RETURNED TO JAMALPUR with Richard and he met Baba. I left the next day for Anandanagar and went to Purulia to attend the court case lodged by the forest department. Acharya Svarupananda accompanied me. After reaching Purulia we learned that the date was not the seventeenth but the eighteenth so we returned the next day. Several sections of the central office had shifted to Anandanagar from Jamalpur and from time to time the general secretary came there to supervise the work. I talked with him about organizational matters and then left for Ranchi, Chaibasa, and Calcutta, where I held different organizational meetings. I returned to Jamalpur on the twenty-fourth to attend the court in Monghyr for Amitananda's case. On the twenty-ninth I left for Patna and then Varanasi.

I remained at Varanasi till July 3, seeing to the office work and giving training to the workers. I posted Acharya Shuddhananda Avadhuta there. He was a wise man and a philosopher. I asked him to take over those administrative responsibilities that Prakashananda was unable to handle. While I was in Varanasi I went every evening to the other side of the Ganges by boat to sit in a solitary place on the sand for meditation.

78
Maha Mahopadhya Sri Gopinath Kabiraj

ON JULY 1, Sri Gopinath Kabiraj's attendant, Sri Sadananda, came to convey a request from Gopinath that I meet with him in his residence. He told me that Gopinath had a deep desire to meet me. Sadananda had come twice before for the same purpose but both times I had avoided going on some pretext. This time I asked him why Gopinath did not come here himself if he was so eager to meet me? Sadananda said that Kabirajjii was now seventy-seven years old and living in a second-story flat. He was not able to come down to the ground floor. After hearing this I accompanied him to Kabirajjii's residence.

The house was on the main road, about one furlong from our Sigra office. His name was written in marble at the main gate, beside a swirl of madhabilata flowers. Sadananda and I climbed to the second story where we found him teaching a class to a group of professors. The moment I entered the room he ended the class and asked his students to leave. He asked Sadananda to bring a chair and place it by the side of his cot.

Gopinath lived very simply. He was short in stature and wore a dhoti up to the knee. His upper body was bare. He was lying on the bed, supporting his head on his hand. While we were talking he mostly kept his eyes closed. It appeared that he had strong spiritual feelings. He began to discuss Ananda Marga with me, but after some time he wanted to know about the life of Baba Anandamurtijii. Since it was my first meeting with him, I remained reserved. We talked for one hour and then I returned to the office. At the time of my departure he requested me repeatedly to visit to him whenever I came to Varanasi and I agreed.

The next time I met him he was also teaching a class on different subjects to professors who came from different parts of the country for his guidance in their pursuit of a doctorate degree. Again he stopped the class and started our discussion. In the meantime two monks came to meet him but he directed them to wait outside for some time.

While Baba and I were returning by car from the Bhurkunda Dharma Maha Chakra, I told him about my discussions with Gopinath. Acharya Amulya Ratan Sarangi was also in the car. Baba started to narrate the life history of Kabirajjii, though Baba had never met him. Baba said that he was the world's preeminent pundit. Universities from Calcutta, Patna, and Benares had authorized him to give doctorate degrees to successful candidates in Hindi, Bengali, English, and Sanskrit. I told Baba that he seemed to be a good devotee. Tears rolled down his cheeks when he took the name of God. Baba said that when a person reached the culminating point of theoretical knowledge of God but was not realized, his condition was like that. When I told Baba that he had requested me to meet him whenever I came to Varanasi, Baba said that if he felt happy when he met me then I should meet him whenever I went to Varanasi.

When I returned to Varanasi after completing my tour programme, Acharya Shuddhananda told me that during my absence Sadananda had come twice to our Varanasi office to inquire as to when I would return. So I went to meet Gopinath. Again he was teaching a class to professors and students. As soon as he was informed of my arrival, he stopped the class, asked me to sit by the side of his cot, and started to ask about Baba. I explained as much as possible. He also said many things about sadguru. He said again and again that without the grace of sadguru the vision of Parama Purusha is not possible.

While he was talking about the importance of sadguru in spiritual life, tears continued to flow from his eyes. On this occasion he told me some wonderful events from his spiritual life. He was a disciple of Vishuddhananda Sarasvati, whose ashram was near the Varanasi railway station. Vishuddhananda had established a panchamundi seat there for spiritual practice. He had acquired some occult powers and would give demonstrations about spiritual processes. Gopinath told a miraculous story during our discussion. After Vishuddhanandajii's death, Gopinath's wife fell seriously ill. The doctors despaired of her life and Kabirajjii was very affected by this. He thought that since all his worldly efforts had failed, there was nothing left to do but to surrender unto the feet of the sadguru. Thinking this, he sat for puja as per the system his guru had taught him. After some time the whole room was filled with a sweet spiritual fragrance, the same fragrance that would emanate from the physical body of his guru when he was alive. He felt as if his guru were in the room. At that moment his wife, who had been lying unconscious in her bed for the last two days, regained consciousness and looking around for Kabirajjii. He was performing puja by the side of her bed. He approached her and she said that gurudeva had come to her and was sitting beside her, caressing her forehead with his hand.

Then he said, "Anandamurtijii is a sadguru. Kindly tell some stories about him, because without the grace of a sadguru a human being cannot attain spiritual realization."

I went out again on tour and after a few days I returned to Varanasi and went to visit Kabirajjii in his residence. He was teaching a class on Vaisnava Tantra to a group of professors from Bengal. He stopped the class when he saw me but this time I requested him to continue because I also wanted to participate. "You are a world-renowned scholar," I said. "I am eager to acquire philosophical knowledge from you." So he continued, explaining the Asta Sakhis of Lord Krishna. He explained twice but one of the professors could not understand properly. He scolded him little and said that the dry theoretical knowledge will not appeal to the heart. It requires spiritual practice under the guidance of a sadguru. When one follows the spiritual path, the inner rhythmic flow of spiritual feeling helps one to understand the fundamental truth.

After he ended his class he sat with me. He asked me about different aspects of yoga in Ananda Marga and what sorts of formulas should be adopted in one's life. When I was leaving I told him that I was going to South India and would only return to Varanasi after a long interval. But I assured him that when I returned I would come to meet him.

In the first week of November I returned from South India and went to meet Kabirajjii. He was teaching class and I requested him to continue so that I could learn from him. In reply, he said that I was eating butter while he was describing buttermilk. But he continued his class. His discourse was on the creation of the universe and the activities of maya. He explained that the creation was like a circle. From the nucleus of the universe, known as Purushottama, the centrifugal and centripetal forces acted in tandem to create a circle. Due to the desire of the cognitive principle, the veil of illusion (Mahamaya) influenced and covered reality. To get liberation from the veil of illusion one must follow the path of yoga under the guidance of a sadguru. Through his grace the aspirant will be liberated from the veil of illusion and will merge with Parama Purusha. After completing the class we talked. He expressed his desire to learn yoga from me. I told him that to learn the yoga of Ananda Marga one would have to follow certain rules. He said that it would be difficult for him to leave certain social customs. Accordingly I taught him a certain process as per the system. He said that due to his social obligations he could not come to Ananda Marga openly. Gopinath attended the programmes of Anandamayi Ma. He had helped her to become popular among the intellectuals of India.

The next time I saw Baba I requested him to tell us something about maya. Seeing my eagerness, Baba said that he would explain about maya in an upcoming Dharma Maha Chakra and that I should note it down. Baba gave this explanation in the Dhurua DMC, along with a demonstration.

79
Touring Bihar, UP, and Bengal

On July 3, I left Varanasi to go on tour. I went first to Lucknow, where I stayed with Acharya Om Prakash. Other Margis, such as Acharya Goutamjii, Acharya Ratnesh, an editor, and Dr. Badalajii of Lucknow Medical College, requested me to visit their residences. I also met a good devotee of Baba named Sanwar Prasad at Telibag. The wholetime workers from the surrounding areas came to meet me, including Acharya Yogananda Avadhuta, Acharya Sumangal, and Acharya Dipanananda Avadhuta. I gave them the necessary organizational instructions and then left for Gonda on July 6.

I spent one day in Gonda and then went to Gorakhpur. Acharya Raghunathjii and Acharya Sachinandanjii came to the station to receive me. I went with them to the residence of Acharya Sachinandanjii after which we went to meet with an advocate about organizational matters. That night Acharya Raghunathjii and I went for kapalik puja.

The next morning I met with the acharyas and unit secretaries. In the evening I addressed a tattvasabha at the residence of Acharya Pratapaditya. The next day I went to Motihari via Muzaffarpur. Acharya

Ramashray and Ranajit accompanied me from Muzaffarpur. After reaching Motihari in the evening I addressed a workers meeting and then went to the residence of Paramanandajii for the night. The next morning Paramanandajii and I went to the Bethia ashram. The local devotees had made a beautiful ashram and led by Paramanandajii we passed our time chanting bhajans and other devotional songs. In the evening I held an organizational meeting. The next morning a devotee named Ramakantajii invited us to go to Muzaffarpur with him by Jeep. On the way there we passed by a village named Chakia, which was the birthplace of Acharya Abhedananda Avadhuta. Hearing that we would be passing through, his father, Sri Raj Mangaljii, blocked the road and requested me to go to his residence for few minutes. We went with him to his house for some time and then continued on to Muzaffarpur.

We reached Muzaffarpur in the evening. I went to the residence of Acharya Gangasaran to attend dharmachakra and then to the residence of Acharya Sakaldipjii, who requested me to visit an ill Margi who was suffering from a complicated stomach condition. The doctor had advised him that without an operation he would not survive, and his family was afraid. Acharya Sakaldipjii, who was our district secretary, had told them that the spiritual son of Baba Anandamurtijii, the first avadhuta of Ananda Marga, was coming to Muzaffarpur and that they should get his blessings for a successful operation. The whole family came to take me to their residence. I wanted to avoid it by giving some pretext, but other Margis also insisted, so ultimately I was compelled to go. When I met the ill man I took Baba's name and asked Baba to bless him. I wished him a successful operation. Later on I came to know that his operation was successful and he gradually resumed his normal life.

On July 13 Acharya Ramashray, a rich Margi businessman from Bethia named Sitaram Rajgoria, and I went to Mokama from Muzaffarpur in Sitaram's car. We stayed at the government guesthouse. When a Margi student named Madhu got the news of our arrival, he rushed to the guesthouse and stayed the whole day with us. At night we caught the train to Jamalpur.

I stayed in Jamalpur for three days. Most of that time I spent with Baba, taking his guidance in all respects, physically, mentally, and spiritually. He gave me some instructions that were very helpful for my future work. On the sixteenth night I left Jamalpur for West Bengal. The next morning Ac. Ajayananda Avt. and a group of Margis received me at Howrah Station. The following day I went to Shrirampur, where I addressed a meeting of the Margis. The next day I addressed a tattvasabha in Calcutta organized by a devotee named Yadram. From there I went to see a rented house at Khidirpur but it was not suitable for our office. In the night I attended the weekly dharmachakra at Camac Street. The next day I was not feeling well so I passed my time with Sri Jitendra Tyagi.

On the twenty-first, Ac. Ajayananda Avt., Ac. Purnananda Avt., and I went to Tamluk in Midnapore District where we contacted some students and Margis. One student named Subal was very determined and courageous. He organized a public meeting at the Bargabhuma Temple. About two hundred people attended and there was pin-drop silence during my talk.

The next day I went to Midnapore by bus. Some Margi students arranged for our food and lodging in their student hostel. Here the prachar work was done mostly among the students. They organized a public meeting at the Basic School. The next day I went to Bankura. Here the Margis were very enthusiastic and made different arrangements for us. In the evening I explained to them about the importance of spiritual sadhana. A senior Margi named Sri Rakhahari Chatterjee was also present.

The next day we left for Purulia. I met Acharya P. Saran there and went with him to attend the court in the case lodged against us by the forest department. Then we attended Dharma Maha Chakra at Bhurkunda in Hazaribagh District. Bhurkunda is a colliery area and those materialistic elements started to create disturbances. Therefore we completed the DMC early and left the place. Many families attended the DMC so we did not want to run the risk of some undesirable incident. After the DMC, Baba left for Jamalpur by car. Acharya Svarupananda Avadhuta was Baba's attending secretary. The car was driven by Acharya Amulya Ratan Sarangi and I sat beside Baba. I talked with Baba about Maha Mahopadhya Gopinath Kabiraj during that trip.

I remained up to July 31 in Jamalpur, getting spiritual and organizational guidance from Baba. Then I left for Patna to give some necessary instructions to Vishokananda for PFI (Progressive Federation of India), which was running under my supervision. The next day the in-charge of Seva Dharma Mission for Bihar, Acharya Ramashray, arrived. He was searching for a rented house to serve as the SDM office in Patna. After meeting with him I returned to Jamalpur and remained there up to August 7, doing various organizational works. During my stay in Jamalpur, Baba came to the jagriti every morning and evening. As a result of my close association with Baba I did not feel any pressure despite my heavy workload. Then I left for Patna and Delhi after making the necessary preparations for the Lucknow Dharma Maha Chakra.

80
Vox Populi

*A*FTER AMITANANDA GAVE his statement in the court that he was not a minor and had joined Ananda Marga of his own free will, his father became frustrated and set out to tarnish the image of Ananda Marga. He published a booklet entitled *Vox Populi* and circulated it throughout India, especially among government officials, bar associations, and universities. My main work at Delhi was to combat that *Vox Populi*.

I prepared and published a booklet in Amitananda's name that was circulated in the same venues his father's was. At this time Amitananda was staying in Bharat Sadhu Samaj in Delhi under the supervision of the Central Home Minister, Sri Guljarilal Nanda, out of fear of reprisals by his father. In the meantime I addressed a meeting at the International Hotel and then left on August 13 to attend the Lucknow Dharma Maha Chakra.

81
Lucknow Dharma Maha Chakra

*T*HE NEXT MORNING Acharya Yogananda and Swarup Narayan Mathur (Assistant Collector Central Excise) came to Lucknow Station to receive me. I remain engaged throughout the day with the DMC arrangements and in the evening I explained the importance of spiritual sadhana to the members of Mathurjii's family.

The next morning Dr. Badalajii came to take me to his residence. Earlier he had requested me to stay with his him and his family. From there I went to see to the food and lodging for the devotees who would attend the DMC. In the evening I went to receive Baba at the railway station. His train was several hours late, reaching at 2:30 a.m. We took

Baba to the residence of the district secretary of Ananda Marga, Acharya Goutamjii. This was just across the road from Dr. Badalajii's residence, where I was staying.

The next day was the DMC and it was my duty to make sure everything went off without a hitch. I remained with Baba during the programmes and the rest of the time I remained with the devotees, answering their questions and helping them with whatever problems arose. The morning after Baba's DMC discourse I arranged personal contact with Baba for the new Margis.

Baba and I left Lucknow for Varanasi by the Punjab Mail at two p.m. Baba stayed at the K. V. Hotel. I stayed in SDM office but spent most of my time at the hotel organizing Baba's programme. Margis came from the surrounding areas to meet Baba. At 11:00 p.m. Baba took rest for the night and the next morning I made arrangements for General Darshan. Then I saw Baba off at the station for Jamalpur.

I remained busy at the SDM office until August 18, teaching classes to the new trainees and doing my office work. On the twenty-sixth I left for Anandanagar and remained there for three days, completing pending works with the general secretary and with Dr Sachinandanjii. Then I went to Ranchi and from there to Chaibasa, Tata, and Calcutta for different organizational works, reaching Calcutta on September 4. On the sixth, after completing organizational talks with the workers and senior Margis of Calcutta, I returned to Jamalpur.

Shortly after reaching the jagriti, Baba called me for some organizational talks. Then he sat with the devotees. It was Sunday morning and on that day devotees came from different places for Baba's darshan. They encircled Baba singing bhajans and kirtan, creating a heavenly atmosphere. Baba came again in the afternoon and after completing some organizational talks with me, he sat on his cot encircled by the devotees until evening. That night I went out for kapalik puja.

82
Siliguri Dharma Maha Chakra

On September 8 I left for Varanasi. I stayed there for two days for important office work and then returned to Jamalpur. On the twelfth I attended Monghyr court and then crossed the Ganges and caught the train for Siliguri, where Acharya Ajayananda Avadhuta and Acharya Lokeshvarananda Avadhuta received me. Baba had already reached Siliguri for DMC. As soon as I reached I went to the DMC site to look after the arrangements. There were very few Margis there; therefore we workers had to make all the necessary arrangements.

The next day Baba visited Kalimpong. In the meantime I met with the workers, unit secretaries, and students. The following day I accompanied Baba to Katihar. Arrangements for Baba's stay were made at the residence of Acharya Indradeo Gupta, a professor at Katihar College.

On September 16 I accompanied Baba by train to Jamalpur. We travelled in the same compartment and throughout the journey Baba told many interesting stories. Kash flowers were blooming on the banks of the Ganges, beautifying the atmosphere. Seeing this, Baba told us a story about how most of the time we neglect the smallest things, but occasionally the smallest things are the root cause of the biggest thing. Then he explained it through a rhyme:

> *Kshudra kush kassmuley, atal anal jvaley,*
> *Kshudra niharika garey shato shato dhara,*
> *Hriday ta bhengey churay kshudra ashru vindu jharey,*
> *Kshudra navishasey hoy sara pran vora.*

> Sparks from a tiny piece of the root of kush grass can burn a vast area; similarly a small nebula can create many hundreds of worlds, tremendous heart-rending pain can be expressed by a small teardrop, and a small navel respiration maintains the whole of life. No matter how small, nothing should be neglected because big things are hidden within small things.

Hearing this rhyme I came to know that a never-ending process is going on in the universe, from small to great and great to small, and that no one can truly understand it in all its inherent complexity.

When we reached Sahebpur Kamal Station, we changed trains for Monghyr Ghat Station. There we crossed the Ganges by steamer. On the way Baba told many different stories to the devotees. From Monghyr we took a taxi to Jamalpur, reaching at 8·00 p.m. The next evening I accompanied Baba on field walk. In the field we sat on the tiger's grave and Baba explained about different aspects of spiritual sadhana. It was a heavenly atmosphere.

The next day Acharya Ramtanukjii and I left Jamalpur by train. Ramtanukjii went to Varanasi and I got down at Patna to see the new SDM office opened by Acharya Ramashrayjii. I completed some organizational work and then took the night train for Varanasi along with Nirmeghananada Avt.

I remained at Varanasi from September 19 to 26, keeping busy with the office work and teaching classes to the trainees. On the twenty-sixth I went Patna to supervise the work of the Seva Dharma Mission office and on the twenty-seventh afternoon I reached Jamalpur. Baba was still sitting with the devotees in the jagriti when I arrived. In the evening I went with him to the field. We stayed up to 10:00 p.m. on the tiger's grave and then I accompanied Baba to his house.

The next morning I met with Baba in the jagriti for some urgent organizational work and in the evening I went on field walk with him. After returning from field walk I left for Calcutta where I accompanied Ac. Ajayananda Avt. and Ac. Lokeshvarananda Avt. to our new office at Bhuban Banerjee Lane.

On October 18 I went to Tatanagar where I stayed with Ac. Chandradeojii. It was ekadashi and I was forced to take rest due to illness. But despite running a temperature, I went to Chaibasa that evening by bus as per my programme. From the bus stand I went to the residence of Balendujii where I found Acharya Kshitishjii waiting for me. He had come for some organizational advice. In the evening we performed collective sadhana and then passed our time telling Baba stories. The next day we went to the hospital to see the wife of Ac. Rajmohanjii, who was having problems with her delivery. The doctor advised her to have a caesarean. Ac. Rajmohanjii asked me to give her my blessings. I remembered Baba and blessed her for a successful delivery. She delivered a male child and both mother and child were healthy. In the evening I went to Tata by Jeep and caught the Ranchi Express for Anandanagar.

83
Inquiry

I REACHED ANANDANAGAR AT 1:00 p.m. and was talking with Dr. Sachinandanjii when four persons came up to us and asked if Acharya Satyananda Avadhuta had arrived in Anandanagar. They had come from

Calcutta to see him. When I asked them their identity, they said they were from the intelligence department and had come to know about the activities of Anandanagar and Acharya Satyananda. I directed them to inquire at the central office of Ananda Marga and pointed out where it was. "Please ask the general secretary," I said. "I'm sure he will be able to answer all your questions." There they met with the general secretary and were satisfied with his answers.

It turned out that a young man from Srirampur, who was living at Anandanagar as a worker, was actually an informer for the Intelligence Bureau. When I had been in Calcutta he had also been present there and he had informed the IB of my schedule. However, I was engaged in no such illegal activities that would concern the IB. My work was to create the proper atmosphere for holding Dharma Maha Chakra in every state of India and abroad, and at the same time to open education, relief, and welfare centres to serve the society, especially the downtrodden and the suffering people of the country. By creating moralists through dharma prachar the government would also be benefited. I was sure that their interest was due to the influence of the *Vox Populi* circulated by the father of Amitananda Avt.

84
Jaipur and Bombay Dharma Maha Chakra

ON OCTOBER 7 I left Anandanagar for Jamalpur. Two days later I left for Varanasi. I completed my urgent office work there and the next day I received Baba at Mughalsarai Station and accompanied him and a few Margis to Sarnath. This was the place where Lord Buddha gave his first sermon to his first disciples, Sariputta and Moggallana. Many stone inscriptions from the time of Lord Buddha were still there. We found these ancient ruins throughout the area. Baba explained the history in detail. Then we went to see the modern Chinese-made Buddha temple. Inside the temple, the icon of Lord Buddha and the arts and crafts were in the Chinese style.

After visiting Sarnath we returned to Varanasi. Baba was due to leave the next day by train for the Jaipur DMC. In the meantime many Margis came to get personal contact and attend General Darshan. I was extremely busy organizing these two programmes.

In the evening Baba boarded a large boat with some close disciples and floated down the Ganges for one hour. During this time he talked about many things, including why Indian society had given such high status to Varanasi, why the rajas and maharajas had built so many buildings there, and why it was considered the cultural centre of India. When our boat reached Manikarnika Ghat, Baba explained how the ghat had gotten its name: "Once the wife of Lord Shiva was taking bath at this ghat and she lost a valuable gold earring. Since that time the ghat became known as Manikarnika Ghat (*mani* means "jewel" and *kan* means "ear"). This ghat was the family ghat of Lord Shiva. At present some twenty to twenty-five bodies are cremated there daily, so it has become a dismal cremation ground."

On the eleventh morning Baba and I boarded the train at Mughalsarai Station. Baba was suffering from piles, so it was difficult for him to move. He lay down during the trip and we took care of him. At Agra Station, the pracharaka of Uttar Pradesh, Ac. Yogananda Avadhuta, and Ac. Dipananda Avt. came to receive Baba. They took him to a hotel for the night and the next morning we resumed our journey, reaching Jaipur in the afternoon. Hundreds of Margis came to the station with flowers and garlands to receive Baba. They took him to the residence of Mangal Biharijii. We also stayed there.

The next day I remained engaged with Baba's programme. While Baba was giving personal contact to the new Margis, Lalanjii started an altercation. He was by nature a quarrelsome person. I completed the personal contacts as per system and then went to see to the arrangements for DMC. Then I came back to escort Baba to the DMC. That night, due to misbehaviour of Lalanjii, I did not take food.

On the fourteenth I was again engaged with the personal contacts until 1 p.m. In the afternoon at four Baba and I left for Bombay by plane. In the plane Baba said that he was feeling unwell so he would not be able to do any work that evening. Many devotees of Bombay came to the airport to receive Baba.

From the airport we went to the residence of the district secretary, Anandajii. Since Baba was not feeling well, he did not sit for General Darshan. Instead he sent me as his representative. I sat for one hour and explained about the importance of spiritual sadhana in everyday life. Then I returned to where Baba was staying.

The next morning Baba was feeling better and his programme proceeded as normal. Acharya Chandranathjii was also there. He had been posted at Mahabaleshwar as CID DSP. Baba loved him very much and so did I. In the evening Baba delivered a lecture for the Margis at National College and the next day I accompanied Baba to see the Elephantine Caves. On the way back I stopped to see the Seva Dharma Mission office near Juhu Beach. It was surrounded by a garden, creating a nice ashram atmosphere. Later I held a workers meeting and then went to see to the arrangements for Dharma Maha Chakra. In the evening the DMC went off very nicely.

On October 17 Baba and I flew to Calcutta on a C-175 Caravell. We reached Dum-Dum Airport (now known as Netajii Subhash Chandra Bose Airport) at 9:00 a.m. Hundreds of devotees were there to receive Baba. From there we went to the residence of an ardent devotee, Sri Manoharjii, at Gorcha Road. After completing our bath and puja we went to the Camac Street school where arrangements had been made for personal contact and General Darshan. At 9:00 p.m. Baba left by train for Jamalpur. I remained a few days more in Calcutta for organizational work, teaching tattvika classes and meeting with the workers.

On the twenty-fourth evening I took the same 13-up train to Jamalpur and reached there in the morning. The twenty-fifth was a Sunday so Baba came to the jagriti to sit with the devotees. He gave personal contact and General Darshan in the morning and then came again in the afternoon.

The next morning Baba came to the jagriti for some urgent work with me and I spent the rest of the day in office work. In the evening I went with Baba on field walk and the next day I left for Patna. There I gave some instructions about SDM to Acharya Ramashrayjii and then continued on to Varanasi. I had a great deal of work pending there for the Varanasi SDM office. I remained there up to November 12 to complete it. In the meantime I taught classes to the new wholetime workers twice a day. I also answered the letters of the workers working in the field and sent out circulars. Sri Baman Das Mukherjee came to Varanasi from Shyamnagar for one month and we often went for a walk in the evening at Dashasvamedh Ghat. Sometimes we crossed the Ganges by boat and sat on the sand on the other side. Mostly we told different stories of Baba. I also met Gopinathjii each week while I was there. Occasionally Baman Dasjii and Acharya Suddhananda accompanied me.

Then Baba sent word that he wanted me to come to Jamalpur. I arrived on the thirteenth, stayed for one day, and then went to Calcutta, Tatanagar, Chaibasa and finally Dhurua for the Dharma Maha Chakra.

85
Dhurua Dharma Maha Chakra

*D*HURUA IS NEAR Ranchi. The Dharma Maha Chakra was celebrated on November 20 at Dhurua High School. The classrooms encircled a field and from the outside no one could look in. Two thousand devotees assembled to hear Baba deliver his lecture, which was on Maya — Mahamaya, Vishnumaya, Vidyamaya, Avidyamaya, Yogamaya, and Anumaya — and how to liberate oneself from the veil of Maya. After attending the class of Maha Mahopadhya Gopinath Kabiraj on Maya I had requested Baba to tell me something about Maya and he had said that he would explain it in a DMC. This was that DMC. He said that Maya is the creation of Parama Purusha and as such is under his control. If any ardent devotee, by dint of sadhana, surrenders unto the feet of Parama Purusha, then Parama Purusha will rescue him from the veil of Maya. No one can part the veil of Maya by his own efforts. Baba also said if he withdrew Maya for some time then we would lose our balance and become emotionally mad. We would not be able to maintain our separate existence but would be converted into one.

On request of the devotees Baba allowed us to do guru puja. He blessed us and said that now, as per desire of Parama Purusha, he would be withdrawing Maya for two minutes. Then and there all the devotees lost their self-existence and entered into trance. All were weeping loudly and embracing each other without any distinction, floating in an unending flow of bliss. I have no capacity to express the feelings we felt that night.

At the time I was standing next to Baba, acting as his bodyguard. Baba looked like a child in an abnormal condition. The moment the great emotional wave touched me I began to lose my balance. But then I thought that if I became abnormal there would be no one to look after Baba. Immediately I left the compound to save myself. There was a car near the gate. I approached and saw that a devotee of Baba, Dhanbad Police Superintendent Sri Sachidananda Srivastav, was waiting there. He had arrived late and thus could not get entry. I told him to remain ready, that I would now bring Baba to his car so that he could take him to his residence. Without any delay I returned, caught Baba's hand, and took him from the dais to the car, handing him over to Sachidanandajii. Then I went inside the compound. The situation was still abnormal. High-ranking officers, government servants, professors, doctors, and farmers were embracing each other and weeping. It was like the water of canals, streams, and rivers running into the ocean. They were not able to maintain their separate existence. Lord Krishna has said about Maya:

Daevii hyeśá guńamayii mama máyá duratyayá;
Mámeva ye prapadyante máyámetám taranti te.

According to my desire, Maya has covered the reality of the universe. Therefore nobody can cross the realm of Maya by his own effort. The devotee who surrenders to me with intense love, I shall rescue him from the illusory world.

The next day after General Darshan, Baba left for Jamalpur by car. Ac. Dhyanananda Avt., Ac. Svarupananda Avt., and I went to Anandanagar via Ranchi. After completing my work there I left for Jamalpur on the twenty-fifth. As soon as I arrived I went to meet Baba. When he saw me he said, "You wanted to know about Maya. That is why I talked about it at Dhurua. I think you might have understood. What you saw there is what happens when a man is liberated from the influence of Maya." "Yes, Baba," I replied. "I not only understood it but I felt it practically in my heart." Then I told him that the sadguru was always doing his duty by giving both theoretical and practical demonstrations while the pundits only explained things theoretically. I compared his lecture to the lectures of Gopinathjii. Baba was in a very jolly mood. Laughing, he said that once a pundit described a horse by giving many examples to make his disciples understand and the disciples noted down the exact explanation and got full marks. On the other hand, when a disciple asked a spiritual guru to describe a horse the guru took his disciple to the stable without speaking and showed him a horse. The next day the disciple of the pundit met the disciple of the spiritual guru. At that moment an ass was passing by on the road. Seeing the ass, the disciple of the pundit said, "Look, there is a horse passing by." The disciple of the guru said, "That is not a horse. It must be some other animal." Then the disciple of the pundit opened his notebook and read out the description of a horse but he could not influence the disciple of the spiritual guru. Seeing this, he became angry, but the disciple of the spiritual guru said politely, "There is no need to argue. There is a stable nearby. Let us go there and see what a horse looks like." When they reached the stable and saw a horse the disciple of the pundit became ashamed and bowed his head. He burnt his notebook and took the shelter of the sadguru, becoming his disciple.

Mathitvácatváro vedán sarvasháastrańi caeva hi
Sáram tu yogibhih piitam takram pivanti pańditáh.

Churning the four Vedas and other scriptures produces butter and buttermilk. The yogis eat the butter while the pundits are left to fight over the buttermilk. Knowledge acquired through spiritual practice is actual knowledge and all other knowledge is relative knowledge.

86
Salem Dharma Maha Chakra

AFTER MEETING WITH Baba, I returned to the jagriti. The PFI in-charge, Ac. Vishokananda, Avt. had come from Patna. I gave him some organizational instructions and then did my office work. The next day I went to Monghyr to attend court for the Amitananda case. Acharya Ramtanukjii came from his home in Begusarai to accompany me. The next day Baba came to the jagriti at 9:00 a.m. and afterward I went to Varanasi and remained there for two days to reply to the letters of the workers in the field. On December 2, I returned to Jamalpur. Then taking Baba's programme for the Calcutta, Madras, and Salem DMCs, I left for Calcutta to organize the programme there.

The next morning I met Ac. Ajayananda Avt. and Ac. Lokeshvarananda Avt. at Howrah Station and went to our office at Bhuban Banerjee Lane. Just after my arrival the local Margis came in a group to find out about Baba's programme in Calcutta. The DMC was to be held at the Vishuddhananda school. The Margis helped with the arrangements. The next morning, December 6, hundreds of Margis went to Howrah Station to receive Baba, bringing flowers and garlands and shouting slogans. Baba stayed at the Vishuddhananda school, as did the devotees. Baba gave General Darshan, DMC, and personal contact, and in the evening Baba, Ac. Ramtanukjii, and I left for Madras. When the plane touched down at Minambakkam Airport, hundreds of devotees were there to offer rose garlands. Baba's entire body was completely covered with garlands.

We stayed in a dharmasala and Baba gave personal contact before taking rest for the night. It was the first time that Baba had visited South India.

The next morning we left for Salem in the car of a local Margi named Vasyam. We went up to Jalarpet with him. From there Baba and Ramtanukjii continued in the car of Ac. Hariramjii while I went by train. In the evening I checked the arrangements for DMC. It was a very nice place, a large dharmasala with all facilities. Margis had come from all over South India. I made a list of the new Margis for personal contact, which was conducted in a room on the second floor. The DMC was also celebrated on the second floor in a big hall.

The next day I was busy with Baba's programme. Baba completed one work after another without any wastage of time. In the evening he gave a talk and then went for field walk. In the meantime I held a workers meeting. When Baba came back he again gave personal contact.

The following day, December 9, was the DMC. Since it was Baba's first time in South India, most of the Margis were new, and it was the policy for Baba to give personal contact to all new Margis. Thus the personal contacts continued throughout the day. In the evening Baba gave his DMC talk on the way of liberation. It was Baba's first lecture in English. I was very curious to hear the Baba give a lecture in English. He explained the complicated philosophical ontology in a simple way. The devotees were spellbound. They had come from five states: Tamil Nadu, Kerala, Karnataka, Andhra Pradesh, and Maharastra.

The morning after the DMC, Baba went for a walk with the acharyas to Yercaud Hill. On the way up we found many coffee trees. It was a new tree for us and they were full of fruits. When we left there I took some branches with fruits to show the Margis in Jamalpur. In North India there was no cultivation of coffee, only tea. Tea is made from the leaves while coffee is made from the fruits. In the evening I accompanied Baba to the railway station, where he took a train for Madras.

Due to the excessive labour of the past few days I was feeling unwell and took rest. The next day the local acharyas who had accompanied Baba to Madras Airport returned. That night Ac. Pranavananda Avt., Ac. Shivananda Avt., and I left for Coimbatore. From there we boarded a train for Ooty.

Ooty is eight thousand feet above sea level and was terribly cold. We remained there for two days and then went to Calicut, where we visited the Alka Hill lake.

87
South India and Kerala

On the sixteenth morning Ac. Pranavananda Avt. and I left for Calicut by bus. We reached there at 1:30 p.m. and went to a dharmasala that was being used as the Ananda Marga office. The road from Ooty to Calicut was a serpentine path that passed through hilly jungles. It was a new experience for me and going from a cold area to a hot area my skin became cracked. In the afternoon a tattvasabha was organized at the Theosophical Society. I addressed the tattvasabha and then went to the seashore and sat on the sand for some time.

In Malayalam *ker* means "coconut" and *la* means "land." Thus Kerala means "the land of coconuts." In fact the whole state looks like one huge coconut garden. I also saw coloured bananas that I have not seen anywhere else in India. The skin of one banana was deep red. Another was a full foot long but when it ripened it remained hard. It had to be boiled before eating. In Kerala they prepare chips from this banana and export them. There is also a large cashew-nut factory that exports the nuts. Fish are also exported from this state. The state is famous for all these things but especially for coconut products.

The next morning I talked with the Margis about sadhana and then Ac. Pranavananda Avt. and I left for Kolandi. Dr. Kunjilal met us at the station and took us to his residence. That evening both Margis and non-margiis came to discuss the ideology of Ananda Marga. Afterward we gave initiation to several people.

The following morning I, Ac. Pranavananda Avt., and a Margi named Bhim Rao left for Ernakulam. The local Margis took us to the Woodland Lodge. On the twentieth I addressed a tattvasabha on the topic of yoga sadhana. In the meantime Dr. Basudevan sent his car so that we could visit the surrounding area. We visited the Tirka Temple, Tirupunitura Temple, and the palaces of Cochin Maharaja. After that I addressed a tattvasabha in the residence of Dr. Ray.

On the twenty-first we started for Kurnal. Bhim Rao and Ac. Piram saw us off at the station. We reached there at 1:30 p.m. and the local Margis put us up at the Kyashino Hotel. In the evening there was a tattvasabha at a yoga centre. I delivered a lecture about the yoga system of Ananda Marga.

The next morning we went to Thiruvananthapuram. The upstairs office of S. V. Sundaram was reserved for the work of Ananda Marga. We kept our luggage there and went to meet the local acharya, Ac. Manikyam. He took us to visit Kavalam, situated in the lap of the Indian Ocean. There are wide stretches of sand, stony hills, and long rows of coconut palms decorating the royal palace. Both Indians and foreigners are always visiting this attractive place.

88
Vivekananda Rock

THE NEXT MORNING we went to Nagarcoil, where we met with the local Margis, and the following day we went to Kanyakumari. Two friends of Sundaramjii came to show me the famous rock out in the ocean where a temple of Swami Vivekananda would be built. I asked them to tell me the story behind it. They said that Swamijii had wanted to go to America. He became ensconced in a spiritual trance and dove into the ocean to swim to America. After two furlongs he became tired and took shelter on that rock and meditated there for two days. In his memory they wanted to build a temple there with a statue of the swami. They also said that a Christian named Stephen had been the first to go there and for that reason it was a disputed matter. I joked with them that so far as I knew, Swamijii was a learned and conscientious spiritualist who would not for a moment consider swimming across the roaring waves of that infinite ocean to America. Nor could I believe that he sat on that rock soaking wet and meditated for two days. "As a monk," I said, "I know that the mind can sometimes become confused. If, as you say, Swamijii really jumped into the ocean to swim to America then I will say that this rock saved his life. On the other hand, whether or not he actually went there it is now a matter of sentiment. No matter what really happened, you have come to take me to this rock and I must go with you. But today it is not possible. Tomorrow morning at 9:30 I will be ready to go with you." They were happy and agreed to take me there the next morning.

After their departure, Ac. Manikyam from Thiruvananthapuram arrived. The Kanyakumari Temple is surrounded by a high wall with a big iron gate. In order to enter, it was required to remove one's upper dress. I did not support this sort of superstition and thus would not enter any temple in this state. Once Swami Vivekananda was not allowed to enter the temples in Kerala because he was considered a shudra, a low caste person. We passed by the Gandhi Memorial on our way to the sea and walked along the sand telling many stories of Baba in that beautiful place. Fishermen were catching fish and there were many boulders scattered around. There was a statue on one of the boulders. Sunset was near at hand. We waited to see the sun set on the horizon over the sea.

On Christmas morning the men who wished to build the Vivekananda temple came to take me to the rock. We went with them by boat. The waves were very high that morning and it was difficult to climb into the boat. We tried three times but eight-foot waves were making the boat dance on the water. Each time we tried we had to run back to the shore. With the help of the boatman and others we were finally able to climb into the boat on the fourth attempt and cross over to the rock. Two steps had been carved out on the rock but everywhere else was slippery with algae. We make a round of the rock and then sat on a flat stone to perform meditation and enjoy the beautiful scenery. On one side was the Bay of Bengal and on the other the Indian Ocean. The engineers spread lime to demarcate the dimensions of the proposed temple. After one hour we again fought the waves to return to shore. Then they took us to see the quarry where stones for the project were being collected. There were also engravings of different designs for the temple. At 3:00 p.m. Ac. Pranavananda and I left for Trinelvali by bus.

We arrived at 7:00 p.m. Ac. Shivananda Avt. and a group of Margis were waiting to receive us. We attended dharmachakra and afterward I talked about sadhana. The next morning I answered the Margis' questions about sadhana. After lunch I went with them to see the Manimukta Dam. The local people call the dam "Rescue from Sins." The next day we passed with the Margis.

Then Ac. Shivananda Avt. and I left for Madurai by bus, while Ac. Pranavananda Avt. returned to Ernakulam. On the twenty-ninth two Margi brothers, Sri Sundaram and Rangarajanjii, organized a tattvasabha. I delivered a lecture and afterward we went to a beautiful hill where Mahatma Gandhi had lived. I saw his furniture and other possessions. By the side of the hill I saw many engraved statues from Buddhist Tantra. There was also a large stone statue of an ox. I guessed that there had once been a Tantra piitha there. After returning we started for Coimbatore by train. We reached there the next morning. Acharya Hariramjii met us at the station. He had organized a tattvasabha at the Ramakrishna Vidyalaya. We went directly to the school and I gave a talk for the students and professors on education for liberation. After the lecture the principal took us to see the polytechnic workshop. This gave me the inspiration to build up our workshop at Anandanagar. After a ten-minute talk with the swamijii of their mission I returned to the residence of Ac. Hariramjii. He was originally from Sindh Pradesh, which was now part of Pakistan. After partition his family had migrated to India. Some of his relatives had settled in Bombay and some in Coimbatore. In the evening I addressed a tattvasabha at the Theosophical lodge.

89
Mysore

ON NEW YEARS Eve I started for Bangalore accompanied by Ac. Shiva Prasad. Ac. Cidananda Avt. and Ac. Nagaraj (later he became Vimalananda Avt.) were waiting for us at the station with a group of Margis. We went with them for dharmachakra.

The next day the preparations for the New Year's celebration were in full swing. In the morning the Margis came to take me to the ashram. We celebrated the New Year as per *Caryacarya* and I gave a talk on Ananda Marga and the importance of sadhana. From there I went to the residence of Ramchandrajii where some young men were waiting to talk with me. After this I visited Nandi Hill with Ac. Cidananda Avt., Ac. Nagaraj, Ac. Shiva Prasad, and a local excise superintendent, Rammurtijii. It is said that Agastha Muni and Chanak Muni lived on Nandi Hill. We saw the caves in which they had lived. Then we went to see the nearby fort of Tipu Sultan.

In the evening there was a public meeting that was very well attended. I talked about Ananda Marga for one hour and afterward many people were eager to learn the spiritual science. From the dais I went to inaugurate the Mysore Seva Dharma Mission office and then returned to the residence of Ramchandrajii. Some intellectuals were waiting there to meet me. When I was getting ready for bed, Ac. Cidananda Avt. came to my room and said, "Dada, in the morning Ramchandrajii came to massage you but you did not allow him. Since then he has been observing fast and weeping, saying that he is a sinner and for that reason Dada would not accept his service." I told Cidananda, "Please make him understand that he is not a sinner but rather a pious man who is much older than me. As per avadhuta rules I cannot personally accept physical service from anybody unless I am ill. If I feel ill then I will call him." "Dada, the whole day we tried to make him understand this but we failed." When I heard this I thought that he really must be a very pious man. Remembering Baba, I decided to accept his service in order to remove his despondent state of mind.

I asked Cidananda to send Ramchandrajii to my room. When he came, I said, "Ramchandrajii, the whole day I am so busy that I forget my physical troubles. It is only in the night, when I take rest, that I remember my aches and pains. Now I have a headache. Would you be able to massage my head for some time?" When he heard this he became extremely happy. He took my head on his lap and started massaging me with a smiling face. I told him that if I fell asleep during the massage then he should go and take some rest himself. Like this I passed half an hour with Ramchandrajii, talking of spiritual matters. Later on I slept. The next morning I inquired about his mental condition. Cidananda that he was now in a very jolly mood.

This was the second time I had toured South India and it was clear to me that the people of these states were more devotional than those in other parts of India. Ninety percent of the people in the South would go to the temple and put devotional ashes on their heads. That is why the Britishers, after seeing all of India, said that the Madrasis were devotional, Bombay people emotional, and Bengalees sentimental. After touring all of India I realized that what the Britishers had said about Indians was true.

90
Brindavan Gardens

THE NEXT MORNING Ac. Cidananda Avt., Ac. Nagaraj, Ac. Shiva Prasad, and I left for Mysore. Ramchandrajii, his wife, and Rammurtijii saw us off at the station. During the journey a group of Margis came to meet us at Mandaya Station. Among them was a remarkable young man named Shiva Nangia Goura. Recently he had obtained a Masters of Science degree from Benares Hindu University. His ever-cheerful face was so clean and simple, so fresh and pure. There was no dirt in his heart. In the Salem DMC he became a favourite of Baba's. It was like a magnet and iron.

After reaching Mysore we went to a dharmasala whose owner was an Ananda Margi. He had sent a man to the station to guide us. Afterward we went to see the cremation ground, since that night was the new moon, and on the way back we visited the Mysore Emporium, famed for its sandalwood crafts. Then we took a bus to the Brindavan Gardens. It is one of the most beautiful places in India, a two-hour journey from Mysore. The gardens are next to the Krishna Raja Sagara Dam, from which the water passes gently like a spring. There was a reservoir in the middle of the flower gardens and a beautiful fountain. The water of the reservoir was lit by different coloured electric lights. It only opened twice a week, Wednesday and Saturday, and on these days shopkeepers came and made it seem like a fair. Nearly a hundred buses brought passengers from different parts to enjoy the beautiful scenery. We reached there one hour before sunset and remained for two hours to see the beauty, then returned to Mysore by government bus. There were buses every fifteen minutes going and coming. After reaching Mysore we left for the cremation ground to do our kapalik puja.

91
Srirangapattanam

ON JANUARY 3 we started for Mandaya by train. Shiva Nangia Goura and a group of Margis met us at the station and took us to a government guesthouse where arrangements had been made for our stay. I talked to the devotees for some time about the importance of yoga sadhana and then on request of Gourajii we took our meal at his residence. After that we visited the historic Srirangapattanam, which had once been the capital of Tipu Sultan. We saw the Daliabag, Diwaniam, Dewanikhas, the historical paintings in the war palace, the stables, the armoury and so on. Then we went to see where the two parts of the Kaveri River joined. The confluence of the two branches of the Kaveri River encircled the capital of Tipu Sultan. We sat there for some time to enjoy the beautiful scene. On the way back we visited the Ranganath Temple and stopped at Gangur, the village of Gourajii. Then we went to see the Ganjam Temple.

That night I addressed a tattvasabha and then had dinner at the house of professor Rajappa, who related to us much of the history of that area.

The next morning we left for Bangalore. Ac. Pranavananda Avt. and Ac. Ajay Kumar met us at the station and took us to the residence of Ramanandajii. In the evening I met with the Margis and talked with them about the importance of spiritual practice in daily life.

92
Telegram

On January 5 I received a telegram from Jamalpur requesting me to return. I tried to contact the Varanasi office by telephone but could not get a connection. I decided to briefly see some local sights before leaving. Accordingly I visited Bangalore, the capital of Mysore state — the assembly house, the high court, Shankaracharya Math, the Ramakrishna Mission gardens, and the airplane workshop. Then I started for Jamalpur by train. Ac. Ajay Kumar accompanied me up to Vijayawara. At Waltair I came to know that the train was running late. As a result I spent the sixth and seventh on the train and only reached Howrah Station on the eighth morning. Ac. Ajayananda Avt., Ac. Lokeshvarananda Avt., and Ac. Amritananda Avt. were there to receive me. I went with them to the office at Bhuban Banerjee Lane and in the evening Sri Baman Das Mukherjee from Shyamnagar and Sri Sailen Ghosh from Salkia came to meet me. I started for Jamalpur by the 9:00 train.

On the ninth morning I reached Jamalpur and went to the jagriti. After completing my puja I went to the residence of the general secretary. His mother had died two days earlier and I consoled him as best I could. After returning to the ashram, Baba arrived. He called me along with his PA, Ac. Abhedananda Avt., and Vishokananda and discussed with us different organizational matters. Then he sat with the devotees. In the evening I accompanied Baba on his evening walk.

On the tenth I started for Purulia. Prithivi Saranjii came from Anandanagar with the papers of the case lodged against us by the forest department. We attended court and stayed in a dharmashala for the night. The next morning we went to Anandanagar. I stayed there two days to oversee the various works. I also shared my experiences from my tour of South India. On the sixteenth I went to Ranchi where I visited a new school opened in the jagriti. Then I returned to Jamalpur.

It was Sunday morning when I reached Jamalpur and went to the jagriti. Just after I completed my puja, Baba arrived. He told me that my presence at Varanasi was urgently needed and that I should leave that night.

I passed the morning and evening with Baba and then left for Varanasi by the night train. In the morning Acharya Svarupananda was waiting for me at the station. After completing his work with me he left Varanasi. On the twentieth training classes began. I prepared a timetable for the different activities. Every day there were three classes: morning, noon, and evening. I taught the classes and spent the rest of my time engaged with office work. Due to my long absence, a lot of work was pending. Classes continued up to the twenty-eighth. On the twenty-third, Baba stopped at Varanasi for the night on his way to the Rewa Dharma Maha Chakra. In the morning we saw him off at Mughalsarai Station. On the 29th I started for Jamalpur.

The next morning Baba came to the jagriti at 9:00 a.m. I remained with him throughout the day. In the evening I went to meet his wife at the Rampur Colony railway quarters where Baba was living with his family. One quarter was allotted in the name of Baba and another in the name of his brother. During the day one quarter would be vacant and the devotees sometimes came there to meet his wife. Abhedananda and I met her and then returned to the ashram.

The next day was Sunday. and Baba came to the ashram in the morning and evening. The following day, February 1, after discussing organizational matters with Baba, I left for Varanasi. I stayed there till the twelfth to complete the training of the trainees as well as my office work. In the meantime I sent Ac. Ajayananda to Assam to look after the arrangements for the Assam Dharma Maha Chakra. Then I left for Calcutta, en route to Assam.

I reached Calcutta on the thirteenth and Baba reached the next day. We received him at Howrah Station and Baba and I went to the residence of Sri Manoharjii, where arrangements had been made for Baba's stay. I spent the rest of the day looking after Baba's programme.

The next morning I was ill so I was unable to go to Assam to attend the DMC. I could not even go to the airport to see Baba off. Acharya Rajmohanjii, Sri Balendujii, and Ac. Chandradeojii from Tata had come to Calcutta to attend Baba's programme there. The next evening I was feeling better and on their request I went with them to Chaibasa and then to Tata and finally to Anandanagar. From there I went to Purulia to attend the court and then returned to Anandanagar. By this time the general secretary was living in Anandanagar with his family to look after the central office. On the twentieth I went to Ranchi and remained there for a day before continuing on to Jamalpur. I remained there one day with Baba and then went to Varanasi.

I reached Varanasi on twenty-third. Ac. Ajayananda had just come back from the Assam DMC and he gave me a detailed report. The next day I went to Azamgarh with Amaresh and stayed at the residence of Sri Ram Kishore Tiwarijii, a sales tax officer and a good devotee. Two meetings were arranged, one for the Margis and one for the public. I addressed both meetings. At this time the construction of a three-story jagriti building in Azamgarh was going on under the supervision of Sri R. K. Tiwarijii. The next day a tattvasabha was organized for professors. I addressed it and then left for Varanasi.

Ac. Ajayananda was my office secretary in the Varanasi office and Ac. Sambuddhananda was my personal secretary. He accompanied me like a shadow. I taught the training classes and did my office work with the help of Ac. Ajayananda. Ac. Yogananda came from Lucknow to discuss my tour programme. I gave him my programme for his area and another for Punjab, adjusting with the Ludhiana DMC that was scheduled for March 18.

93
Uttar Pradesh and Punjab

*A*S PER MY programme I went to Lucknow with Acharya Sambuddhananda accompanying me as my personal assistant. Acharya Svarupananda also came to Lucknow with me. In the evening I addressed a tattvasabha and then met with the workers.

The next morning I met with the Margis of that area. In the afternoon Ac. Yogananda, Ac. Sambuddhananda, and I left for Dehradun by train. We reached there at 10:00 a.m. In the evening Ac. Maheshwarjii arranged a tattvasabha in his residence and the next day we attended dharmachakra there. Afterward I talked to the Margis about the importance of spiritual sadhana. In the afternoon we all went to see the Sahasra Dhara.

The next morning some students came to meet me at the dharmasala where I was staying. I talked with them about the philosophy. In the afternoon we started for Mansurpur by train. We got down at Saharanpur Station and completed the journey by taxi. At Mansurpur there was a sugar factory. The general manager of the factory was an Ananda Margi. We stayed at the factory guesthouse. The general manager organized a tattvasabha among the factory officers. Later on, he organized a second meeting where 250 persons attended. I talked about the spiritual science for one hour.

The next morning I addressed the local Margis and at noon we started for Delhi by train. Upon arrival we went to the quarters of Sri Shashi Rainjanjii at 93 North Avenue. I remained in Delhi from the ninth to the fifteenth. Then I went to Ludhiana to attend Dharma Maha Chakra. On the tenth I went to see the prime minister's house, the president's house, etc. The next day Ac. Nirmohananda from Punjab, Ac. Shankarananda from Rajasthan, Ac. Paras from Jammu-Kashmir, and Ac. Pradip from Himachal Pradesh came to meet me on organizational matters. I passed the day giving them new programmes to implement in their areas.

On the twelfth they left Delhi for their areas. On the thirteenth a charity show was organized by the Margis. I talked to them about the programme and then went to see the Mogul garden. On the fifteenth I went to the parliament house to hear the no-confidence motion against the Nehru government. MP Sri Shashi Rainjanjii made the necessary arrangements for me to attend.

94
Ludhiana Dharma Maha Chakra

ON THE SIXTEENTH I left for Ludhiana accompanied by my personal assistant, Acharya Sambuddhananda Avt. Doctor Rajkishan Mahendra and a group of Margis came to the station to receive us. The following day I was busy with the preparations for the DMC. In the meantime Ac. Nirmohananda Avt. and two other pracharakas approached me and said that Doctor Rajkishan Mahendra should not be allowed to come in contact with Baba. I asked them what his fault was. "He does not cooperate with us and he still follows some of the old rituals," they said. I replied that Baba had come to Ludhiana to meet with his devotees and as far as I knew Dr. Mahendra was an ardent devotee of Baba. Such external reasons were not enough. If I didn't allow him to meet Baba it would not only be wrong, it would sinful. Reluctantly I told them that even though I did not agree with such mentality, I could stop him from having personal contact with Baba but he would be allowed to join all other programmes. Nevertheless I advised them that it would be better if they changed their minds altogether, because ultimately nothing can stand in the way between bhakta and Bhagavan.

As this was going on, Dr. Mahendra was extremely busy the whole day preparing for Baba's arrival. As he was working he was often taking the name of Baba and tears would roll down from his eyes. I thought it a great offense that such a devotee would not be allowed to sit and talk with Baba.

On the eighteenth morning I went to receive Baba at the station. Hundreds of Margis were there with flowers and garlands. Accompanying Baba was our legal secretary Acharya Ramtanukjii, who was serving as Baba's attendant. In the evening, when Baba went to the bathroom, the commode broke and Baba was injured. Ramtanukjii came out hurriedly and told me that Baba was bleeding inside the bathroom. I went in and found Baba standing and the floor red with blood. I asked Baba where he was hurt. "I am not sure yet," he said. "I'm checking." Hearing this I became confounded. This great man, I thought, is so indifferent to his physical body that he is bleeding heavily and he doesn't even know where. I saw that his left leg was bleeding. I took my handkerchief, wet it, and tied it around the injured area. I then requested Baba to leave the bathroom but he said that he would take bath first. Afterward he came out and lay down on the bed.

I told Ac. Nirmohananda and others to ask Doctor Rajkishanjii to attend to Baba. But instead of Doctor Rajkishanjii they brought a quack doctor. Instead of giving Baba an anti-tetanus shot he was giving him a penicillin injection. When I objected Baba said, "Let him continue. Now it is time for General Darshan. Go as my representative and deliver a lecture to the Margis. They are waiting." I deputed Ac. Sambuddhananda to look after Baba and went to the DMC place as Baba instructed. Several thousand devotees had come to attend the DMC. My discourse was on the devotee and his Ista. The devotee is he who performs spiritual practice and Ista is his object of meditation. I also explained how through the process of yoga a devotee becomes unified with his Ista. I also clarified about samadhi. What is samadhi? It a particular state of concentration that is identical to the subject of meditation, that is, the summum bonum as well as the final goal of life.

When I was returning after completing my lecture, I saw a car with the Ananda Marga flag coming. I stopped the car and found Ac. Sambuddhananda inside. When I asked him what the matter was, it turned out that Baba's leg had started bleeding again. Baba had sent him to bring Doctor Mahendra to treat him. Hearing this I was extremely happy. I sent him to the DMC site to pick up Mahendra. The moment he informed Dr. Mahendra of Baba's injury, the doctor rushed to his house to gather the necessary medicines and then went to Baba. In the meantime I returned to Baba and sat by the side of his cot. Within a few minutes Ac. Sambuddhananda arrived with the doctor. From that moment Mahendra remained busy day and night serving Baba.

When I saw Ac. Nirmohananda I told him that he had received a proper lesson and that from then on he should not put any obstacles between bhakta and Bhagavan, the devotee and his Lord. Ultimately nothing can stand in the way of their coming together. I further told him that by taking on this injury Baba was doing penance to save us from whatever sins we had committed. A little later Baba said, "Today a good devotee and dedicated worker working in South India was on the way to his death by accident. To save his life, I underwent this injury. My little trouble saved the life of an ardent devotee. By tomorrow evening I hope my condition will be improved and I shall be able to address the Dharma Maha Chakra." Doctor Mahendra remained with Baba through the night and we left Baba's room to take rest. The next day Baba gave personal contact to some new Margis and in the evening he gave his DMC talk.

After the DMC, Baba and I took the night train to Delhi. There were programmes the whole day in Delhi and at midnight I took a train to Patna. Baba also travelled to Patna but by plane. I went straight from the station to meet Baba and then left for Purulia to attend the court. Ac. P. Saran also attended. On the twenty-second we went to Anandanagar where I met with the general secretary and completed my office work. On the twenty-fourth I left for Bermo.

95
Tattvasabha at the Colliery Area

FROM ANANDANAGAR I took a train to Marafari Station. There two devotees met me and took me by car to Bermo, where we went to the residence of the unit secretary, Gyan Vikashjii. The whole day many Margis came to meet me. Gyan Vikashjii organized a public meeting in the evening. The next evening there was another meeting at the Lion's Club. I talked for an hour and then answered the questions of the different officers.

On the twenty-sixth I went to Patratu from Bermo. A colliery foreman of Bhurkunda, Sri Muralidharjii, and a group of Margis met me at the station. From there we went to the residence of Sri L. P. Agarwal, a superintendent engineer in the electricity department. I addressed a meeting and then with Muralidharjii and others I started for Ranchi by Jeep, reaching Ranchi at midnight. Both were famous colliery areas.

Over the next two days I completed my work in Ranchi and on the twenty-ninth I started for Dhanbad. Acharya Dhyanananda accompanied me. I stayed with Police Superintendent Sri Sachidananda Srivastav and addressed a public meeting in the town hall. It was raining cats and dogs but still many people attended.

The next day I went to Calcutta where I had many pending works. In the evening I addressed a Margi meeting and the next day I went to Krishnagar for kapalik puja. I also gave some organizational instructions to the wholetime workers of that area. Then I returned to Howrah and passed one day at the residence of Sri Sailen Ghosh singing bhajans and kirtan with the Margis of that unit. The next day I returned to Calcutta.

When I reached Calcutta I started experiencing severe abdominal pain. I was forced to take bed rest but I continued my work from the bed. On April 8 my pain subsided somewhat so I was able to move slowly. Then I started for Jamalpur. I stayed there until April 19, till my pain was gone. During this period I met with Baba every day and twice on Sunday. When I desired to go to the field with Baba I would go by car. Each day I also gave necessary instructions to the wholetime workers and Margis.

On April 20 I started for Varanasi for some urgent work. Acharya Sambuddhananda and Ramashray accompanied me up to Patna. I remained at Varanasi till the twenty-sixth and then came back to Jamalpur to attend the court in Monghyr with Ramtanukjii. The next evening I went to Gaya to meet with the Margis and in the evening I left for Purulia to attend the court. Then I went to Anandanagar for two days and after that Calcutta, stopping on the way in Ranchi, Chaibasa, and Tata to supervise various works. I reached Calcutta on May 8.

96
Workshop

MY MAIN PURPOSE in going to Calcutta was to purchase the necessary machinery to establish a polytechnic workshop at Anandanagar. Baba has given me the personal responsibility of implementing this by May 15. I needed Rs. 50,000 but I didn't know how to arrange such a large amount in such a short time. When Baba gave me the responsibility to establish the Anandanagar Polytechnic workshop, I obtained his blessing and said that I would do my utmost but he would be responsible for the result. Baba said, "Yes, go and do your utmost; Parama Purusha will help you in all respects." For this purpose I remained in Calcutta for one week. Taking the help of Sri Sailen Ghosh of Salkia, a good devotee, I made a list of the different machines we needed and started investigating where to buy them at the best price. At the same time I tried to collect the money.

Finally on the fourteenth I purchased the machines along with blacksmith articles and electrical materials and loaded them in a big truck to send to Anandanagar. I sent Acharya Amritananda with the truck and took a train to Jamalpur so that I could arrive on the fifteenth, the deadline for implementing Baba's request. The next morning I reached Jamalpur and informed Baba. It was Ananda Purnima, the birthday of Marga Guru. Many devotees came to the ashram to attend this auspicious event. In the afternoon, when Baba came to the ashram, I talked with him about the shipment of machinery and my worries that the general secretary would not assist with the unloading. Then I spent time with the devotees who had come from different parts to attend the Ananda Purnima festival. In the evening I had planned on going on field walk with Baba but before then he came to the jagriti and told me that I should go to Anandanagar by the 9 p.m. train because if I were absent there might be some problems unloading the truck. I left immediately for the station.

I reached Anandanagar the next morning and the following day at 9 a.m. a worker informed me that the truck had reached the bank of the Uttara River. The driver was not ready to cross the river with such a heavy load so I went there and requested him to cross. He agreed but after entering the riverbed he got stuck. At this time there were many labourers working in different parts of Anandanagar. I collected them and with their help the truck exited the riverbed and reached the polytechnic. I spent the whole day helping with the unloading.

97
Ananda Purnima Dharma Maha Chakra

*A*MRITANANDA AND I remained at Anandanagar one more day to set up the machinery, then we returned to Jamalpur. On the twenty-third I took all the workers with me to Patna to ensure the success of the DMC programme, scheduled for the same day. Baba travelled in the same train. For security reasons the DMC committee arranged for Baba to get down at Patna City Station and then proceed by car to the DMC site. I went in the same car.

Throughout the day devotees were arriving from different parts of the country. Twelve thousand devotees attended, which broke the past record. The following day at noon Baba gave General Darshan. Then he gave personal contact to the new sadhakas and in the evening he left by car for Jamalpur. I remained in Patna for the night and then left for Ranchi with the other workers to attend the seminar.

98
Loss of Good Judgment

*A*FTER COMPLETING THE seminar classes at Ranchi I went to Anandanagar and on June 5 I returned to Jamalpur. Some local workers were waiting for me there and after giving them the necessary instructions I sent them to their areas. On Sunday Baba came to the jagriti both morning and evening, and in the evening I went on field walk. The next morning Baba came to the jagriti and directed me to go to Anandanagar to inspect the general secretary's office on behalf of the president. Accordingly I took the night train for Anandanagar. Acharya Parashivananda accompanied me from Dhanbad to Anandanagar.

After reaching Anandanagar I found that the general secretary was out. He arrived the next day, June 9. I communicated Baba's instructions and on hearing them he became reacted. He said, "The president is the symbolic head of the organization and the general secretary is the executive head. I shall not obey the order of the president."

"Our great guru, Baba Anandamurtijii, and the president of Ananda Marga, the honourable Sri P. R. Sarkar, are one and the same, working in the same physical body," I said. "How can we separate them or demarcate from whom the instruction is coming? Therefore it will be better for us to accept his instructions as the instructions of our guru. Then there will be no problem."

For two days I tried the best I could to make him understand in different ways. Ultimately, with great annoyance, he directed his office secretary to show me the items I had requested to see as per the instructions of the president. But the office secretary did not cooperate with me. I tried to implement Baba's instructions in a cordial way but could not succeed. Ultimately I sent a report of what had happened to the president at Jamalpur through Ac. Ajayananda; then I left for Ranchi. I stayed in Ranchi for three days to finish teaching the training classes. On the third day Ac. P. Saran came from Jamalpur with a message from Baba asking me to select a new office secretary for Anandanagar from among the new trainees and to send him to Jamalpur with P. Saran because the present office secretary would be transferred from Anandanagar to Jamalpur. I selected Shaktinath to be the new office secretary and sent him to Anandanagar with Ac. P. Saran.

After that Ac. Rajmohanjii from Chaibasa came to meet me, then Ac. Harishankarjii, Ac. Kshitishjii, and lastly Ac. Kedarjii. Being together with all these acharyas at the same place and time was like heaven on earth. We spent the whole day talking about the different spiritual expressions of Baba. Kshitishjii, a very good singer, sang some bhajans. Everybody was vibrated by the songs. That night I left for Calcutta.

99
Prasadjii's Request

I REACHED CALCUTTA ON June 17 and went to our office at Bhuban Banerjee Lane. At the request of Sri Sailen Ghosh, I went to his house at Salkia where the Margis of that locality organized a programme of bhajans and kirtan that lasted until 11:00 p.m. The next morning I met with Sri Raghuvir Prasad. We had some urgent work together and our meeting was the desire of the divine power. As soon as he saw me, he rose from his chair and embraced me, saying "Baba sent you to me because I was remembering you with deep concentration."

Prasadjii wanted me to consult with Baba about his problems in sadhana. I noted his problems and then took the night train for Jamalpur. Ac. Lokeshvarananda accompanied me. After reaching Jamalpur Baba gave the solutions and I wrote Prasadjii a letter and sent it to Calcutta through Lokeshvarananda. Normally, the acharya would answer the questions of his or her initiates, but Prasadjii had been initiated directly by Baba.

I remained at Jamalpur until the twenty-second and then went to Varanasi to complete some urgent office work. On the twenty-fourth I went to Patna and taught the workers classes until July 2, except for one day when I had to go to Jamalpur. After Patna I returned to Varanasi.

100
Ladies Section

*I*N ORDER TO encourage more workers to dedicate their lives to the service of suffering humanity, there was a proposal to start a Women's Welfare Section at the earliest possible date. No female had as yet dedicated her life as a wholetime worker for the organization. Hence Baba told me that at present I would have to oversee the work of both the male and female sections simultaneously.

On July 3 I arrived in Varanasi from Patna. The next day Acharya Godavari from Rewa met me at our Varanasi office. She was going to Rewa from Jamalpur after having had Baba's darshan and stopped on the way at Varanasi. She was unmarried and after passing her MA she was teaching school in Rewa. "I want to work in the organization as a wholetime worker," she told me. "I lost my parents at an early age and now I have only a guardian. After taking permission from him, I shall join your training centre next week." I told her that I would not be there that week but I would make the necessary arrangements for her training so that she would not feel any difficulty during my absence. Then she left for Rewa. A few days later she informed me that her guardian did not give her permission so she would not be able to join the training centre.

At the same time there was an aged housewife named Vimala Vashistha from Bombay who was ready to join as wholetime worker. She was a highly qualified lady. We all knew her abilities because she had been working in Ananda Marga for a long time and was very popular among the Margis. Since her childhood she'd had a desire to realize God. Though she was a housewife and mother she had spent her whole life in search of God. She had spent time at many different ashrams. She had even lived in the ashram of Papa Ramdas as a female ascetic. When I heard that she had arrived, I was extremely glad.

Vimalajii joined as a wholetime worker under my supervision and within a very short period, by the grace of Baba, she became an avadhutika and was given the name Avadhutika Ananda Bharati. During her life she had never compromised with any superstition, even where her husband was concerned. She did whatever she felt in her heart was right. Now that she was approaching sixty it was not possible for her to do hard labour. But such a well-educated lady was exactly who we needed to run the female section. My experience was that Baba's work was done by Baba — we were merely instruments. Whatever the organization needed would automatically come into the picture.

Gradually the number of wholetime workers in the female section increased. But since I was still looking after the work at the central level, it was my duty to supervise the work of both the male and female sections. Ananda Bharati used to say, "Satyananda Dada is the spiritual son of Baba." When the avadhuta system was started, Baba made me the first secretary of the Avadhuta Board. Regarding the avadhuta dress, Baba gave me instructions about the colour and the turban. He said the turban should be tied like the Sikhs and the colour of the uniform should be saffron. But as secretary of the Avadhuta Board, I designed the rest of the uniform after long research. Similarly I also designed the avadhutika uniform. The same uniforms are still used today in both sections of Ananda Marga.

101
Driver

ON JULY 3 in Varanasi I had a dream that affected me for the entire day. I dreamed about the future course of the organization. The dream was as follows: A train started from Anandanagar in a land of ups and downs with no railway tracks. But after a little distance railway tracks appeared. Baba was driving the train efficiently through all the ups and downs and Margis occupied the seats inside the compartments. I was also there among the Margis. After some time Baba called me and directed me to stand beside him so he could teach me how to drive. Anxiously I told Baba that the train always ran on the railway tracks but here it was also running without tracks. Only the Lord himself could drive such a train. Baba said, "Learn how to drive and depend on Parama Purusha; then you will be able to drive it successfully in my absence." He kept me by his side for some time and taught me the art of driving the train. Then suddenly he left the engine and after going a little distance he vanished. I was caught on the horns of a dilemma. I wanted to stop the train and run after Baba but there was no scope. I was manning the engine and the speed of the train was reaching its climax. Suddenly a dangerous obstacle appeared before the train. I cried out to Parama Purusha and surrendered at the feet of the Lord, pleading for his help. At that moment an invisible power helped me to overcome the danger. Despite the lightning speed of the train, it rattled down the railway tracks and exited the land of ups and downs. After that it became easy to drive. The trouble had been averted.

After the dream I was afraid that if I took over total charge of the organization then Baba would physically disappear. Therefore I was alert not to take total charge from Baba because I could not bear losing him under any circumstances. Never did I take total charge but Baba still disappeared one day, leaving the organization in a fragmented condition. Only he knows the future course of the organization.

On the sixth I left for Anandanagar and over the next few days I set up the machinery in the polytechnic workshop. No machine operator had come from Calcutta to set up the workshop generator and other machines as promised. On the twelfth I went to Purulia to attend the court and the next evening I entrained for Calcutta.

While there I paid the arrears for the purchase of the machines. Then I purchased some books for our schools from College Street and left for Jamalpur. Generally I tried to visit Jamalpur on Saturday and Sunday because on Saturday Baba only spent a half day in the office and Sunday was a holiday; thus there was ample time to have his darshan. It was also on the weekend that the wholetime workers in the field used to come for Baba's darshan, which gave me the opportunity to meet with them.

102
Chalking out the World Prachar Programme

WHILE I WAS in Jamalpur I sketched out a programme to propagate the ideology of Ananda Marga throughout the world. Accordingly I divided the world into nine sectors: Delhi, Hong Kong, Manila, Sydney, Nairobi, Cairo, Berlin, New York, and Georgetown sectors. Each sector would be further divided into regions, the regions into dioceses, the dioceses into districts, the districts into blocks, then panchayats, and finally villages. In this way the mission of Ananda Marga would penetrate to the grass roots. Through this system each and every person of the world would come in contact with Ananda Marga.

After this I thought about which workers could be selected to be sent abroad and where they should be sent first. I also consulted with some senior devotees in this connection. Ultimately name of Shivananda Avadhuta was selected and it was decided that he would be sent to Nairobi. He applied for a passport but some difficulties ensued and he was not able to go. Then in the coming Ananda Purnima DMC it was declared that Ac. Atmananda Avadhuta would be sent. After obtaining an international passport he took our mission abroad for the first time.

103
Baba's Ancestral Village

ON JULY 20, on the way to Calcutta, I got down at Bardhaman Station and from there by rickshaw I went the three miles to a village named Bamunpara, Baba's ancestral village, reaching there about 8:00 a.m. On the way I met a relative of Baba named Sri Ekchari Ghosh. Then in Baba's house I passed my time with his grandmother. In the meantime Sri Naresh Ghosh arrived, whom I had come to meet. In Bardhaman a residential construction for Baba was going on under the supervision of Sri Naresh Ghosh. A cement permit had been issued from Calcutta long back but Nareshjii had not yet received the cement and he did not know why it hadn't arrived. I directed him to meet me in Calcutta the next day. After that I left for Calcutta. After reaching Calcutta, Sri Shailen Ghosh and I went to the cement permit office but we could not trace the issue of the cement permit in the name of Sri Prabhat Rainjan Sarkar. The officer in-charge told us to come back the next day. The next day Nareshjii reached Calcutta and he and I went to the cement permit office. There we came to know that the cement permit had been issued in the name of Sri P. R. Sarkar but the cement had been taken by somebody passing himself off as Sri P. R. Sarkar. Therefore in the near future no cement would be issued in his name. Nareshjii left for Bardhaman and I remained in Calcutta one more day for some work with Sri Raghuvir Prasad. After completing my work with Prasadjii I left Calcutta to attend the Bhabua Dharma Maha Chakra.

104
Bhabua Dharma Maha Chakra

ON THE WAY to Bhabua a group of Margis joined me at Bhagalpur Station to attend the DMC. Baba also got on the same train in Jamalpur and when he did I shifted to Baba's compartment. At Mughalsarai Station, Baba and I got down and continued on to Bhabua by car. The next day I was busy with the DMC programme. It was raining the entire day and all were worried that the rain would cause problems, since the DMC was to take place on the open roof of a building, but by the grace of Baba the rain stopped two hours before DMC and did not resume until two hours after.

The next day, July 26, I saw Baba off, and Ajayananda and I went to the Dehri Ananda Marga school. We passed the evening at the residence of Ac. Vaidyanathjii.

105
Steering Committee

THE NEXT DAY I left for Anandanagar. A few days earlier Baba had made me secretary for the steering committee of the Education, Relief, and Welfare Section (ERAWS). Since my departure from Anandanagar, the ERAWS work had not been done properly, so now that work would be under my direct supervision. In the evening we held a meeting of the steering committee. I stayed there for two more days to attend to my work and on the thirtieth I went to Calcutta with an engineer named Suresh to contact the officers of the state council. We talked with them about the opening of the polytechnic college at Anandanagar. Then I returned to Jamalpur. On August 5 I attended a meeting of the steering committee in Jamalpur, but the meeting was unsatisfactory. The next day Baba came to the jagriti and I submitted the progress report of the meeting. After hearing everything Baba gave some specific formula how to run ERAWS in proper way. After that the work began to go smoothly.

After completing my work in Jamalpur, I visited Patna, Varanasi, Delhi, and Ambala, and then came back to Delhi on the eleventh. There I stayed with Sri Mangal Biharijii. The next day I went to Varanasi, where I completed my office work. On Sunday the fifteenth I returned to Jamalpur for Baba's darshan. In the evening Vijayananda and I went to the tiger's grave with Baba and remained there up to 10:00 p.m.

106
Indecent

THE NEXT MORNING the ashram manager Abhedananda, Vishokananda, and I went to meet Baba's wife in the Rampur Colony railway quarters. As was her custom she came to the empty quarters opposite Baba's quarters and sat on a cot. Abhedananda and I did pranam keeping a respectful distance, but after Vishokananda did pranam he embraced her around the waist and kept his head on her lap for a long time. I became reacted but since it was a matter of the guru's wife I could not object without asking Baba first, so I remained silent. I thought that both were young and therefore might not understand how to maintain purity in life.

I remembered that Swami Vivekananda had said that if the guru's wife is young then a disciple should remain at least two yards from her physical body when meeting her. Later on, Baba's wife recommended Vishokananda to be Baba's personal assistant and Baba accepted. After that they started to live together in the same quarters. Later on this would bring on the curse of their lives.

107
Dharma Maha Chakras in North India

I REMAINED IN JAMALPUR for two more days and on August 18 the North India DMC tour began, to places such as Agartala, Delhi, Chandigarh, and Jammu-Kashmir. I accompanied Baba and this time his wife also came. On the nineteenth, en route to Calcutta, we left her at Bandel Station to visit her parents while Baba and I continued on to Calcutta. Along the way a group of Margis came to have Baba's darshan at Srirampur Station. When we reached Howrah Station, hundreds of Margis were there to receive Baba and take him to the residence of Sri Manohar Guptajii. Baba gave General Darshan there for one hour. After General Darshan, Baba, Ajayananda, and I left for Agartala by plane. The Margis of that area received Baba with great jubilation at the Agartala airport and took him to the residence of the unit secretary. After reaching there I chalked out Baba's programme and started seeing to it. In the evening Baba gave General Darshan for the Margis up to 10:30 p.m. He also gave personal contact to the new Margis. The next day Baba gave personal contact, General Darshan, and in the evening Dharma Maha Chakra. On the twenty-first we returned to Calcutta by the morning flight.

At the Calcutta airport hundreds of Margis came to receive Baba. In the meantime the widowed mother of Pradip Das of Madanpur and her group encircled Baba's car and started a fray, saying that her son Pradip had joined Ananda Marga and unless and until her son was returned to her she would not let Baba leave. The public also joined her. Very psychologically we managed to get the situation under control and Baba's car was able to leave. Then Prasadjii and I and some senior Margis consoled her before going to the city.

At the time of the altercation I was running a temperature of 104 degrees, along with dysentery, and due to this I was barely able to stand. On Prasadjii's request, Baba and I went to his residence where I had to lie down. By this time Baba's wife had reached Calcutta from Bandel. Since I was sick I deputed Ac. Dhyanananda to look after Baba's programme in Calcutta. The next morning I was still very weak so I asked Baba to kindly tell me the name of some other person who could accompany him for the rest of the programme. "You will go with me up to Delhi," Baba said. "Then at Delhi I shall think over the matter." Accordingly, at noon Baba, myself, and his wife left for Delhi by plane. In the evening we completed the scheduled programme in Delhi and then late that night we cancelled the programme for Srinagar and changed our tickets for Jaipur on special request of the Margis of Rajasthan. War had just broken out with Pakistan and the Indian government was not allowing anybody to go to Srinagar or any other border area. The Margis of Jammu supported that decision.

On the twenty-third Baba, his wife, and I travelled to Jaipur by the noon flight. Baba stayed at the residence of Major Dailat Singh. I was engaged the entire day in organizing Baba's programme. We stayed there for twenty-fours hours and then returned to Delhi. That night the three of us started for Chandigarh by train.

We reached Chandigarh Station early in the morning of the twenty-fifth. Hundreds of Margis with flowers and garlands showed up at the station to receive Baba. A car took us on a tour of Chandigarh and then brought us to the residence of the Ananda Marga unit secretary, Sri Deva Vora. After breakfast Baba sat for one hour with the Margis. Then we started for Simla by car, reaching there at 1:30 p.m. We visited the sights up to 6:00 p.m. and then returned to Chandigarh. That night we left for Amritsar by train.

We reached Amritsar early in the morning and caught a flight for Jammu. On the way to the airport we visited the Golden Temple and Jalianwalabag. At the airport we met Sri Shashi Rainjanjii who was able to get a seat on the same flight. In Jammu the Dharma Maha Chakra was celebrated with great success.

The next day Baba and I, along with Baba's wife and Shashi Rainjanjii, left for Delhi by plane, reaching there in the evening. That evening there was a DMC in Delhi.

The next morning, the twenty-eighth, the four of us left for Patna by plane. The plane touched down in Lucknow, Gorakhpur, and Varanasi, and in each of these places groups of Margis came to the airport to have Baba's darshan. In Patna many Margis came from the surrounding areas to attend the programme. The whole day Baba was busy with the Margis, giving General Darshan and personal contact. In the night we entrained for Jamalpur.

While we were in Patna I noticed the same inappropriate physical closeness between Baba's wife and Vishokananda, and seeing this my mind again became reacted. This time I went directly to Baba and asked him to institute a rule for meetings between the guru's wife and his disciples. This was the second time Vishokananda had embraced her around the waist, which I considered indecent, and I was adamant that it should not be allowed. I mentioned Swami Vivekananda's pronouncement that the disciple should do pranam to the guru's wife from at least two yards distance, in which case the question of touching her physical body would not arise. Baba said that it was my responsibility to run the organization and control the workers, and if I thought that any improper or unruly activity was going on that might harm the organization then it should be stopped immediately.

Then and there I went to Baba's wife and ousted Vishokananda from the room. I also requested her not to encourage any such emotional displays from anybody in the future because it looked indecent before the public eye. For this reason, both of them became hostile to me. But I did what I did after taking permission from Baba, so they could not openly express their anger toward me. Later they joined with my rivals and hatched a conspiracy to separate me from Baba.

108
Delusion

*A*FTER COMPLETING THE long tour of North India I was feeling quite tired so I took rest for three days at Jamalpur. On September 2 I went to Varanasi and completed my pending work. From there I went to Calcutta, Tatanagar, and Chaibasa and then to Purulia on the thirteenth to attend the court. From there I went to Anandanagar to attend the steering committee meeting and on the fifteenth I went to Jamalpur and remained till the twenty-first. During this period I planned out the South India DMC tour and informed the different units of the dates and places and also the workers on whom the success of the programmes would depend.

At this time the war between Hindustan and Pakistan was going on. India is a land of saint and monks, hence Pakistan sent many detectives in the guise of sadhus to India to collect information. A few were caught red-handed in different places and for that reason the Indian government announced that Pakistani spies were moving inside the country in the guise of sadhus; therefore Indian citizens should be alert to keep a close watch on any and all sadhus moving in public. The government offered a five-hundred rupee reward to anyone who caught one of these spies. Thus it became difficult for monks and sadhus to travel. Many innocent Indian monks were mercilessly beaten by the public and some died. The avadhutas of Ananda Marga also fell victim to this. As per my programme, I went to Tatanagar and Chaibasa on September 9. On the way to Chaibasa I was at the Tata bus stand with Ac. Chandradeojii, the Ananda Marga district secretary for Tata, another WT, Acharya Suprakash, and some Margis who had come to see us off. While we were waiting for the bus several hundred people encircled us. The situation was dire but fortunately a police van happened by. I told our men that God had saved us and hurriedly flagged down the police van, which took us to the nearby police station.

After reaching the police station, the officer-in-charge sat us down and started to ask us questions. In the meantime a constable informed him that thousands of people had entered the station compound from the bus stand and were shouting slogans. They would not listen to anybody. The officer directed us to remain there and then left to remove the people from the police station campus but he could not oust them. Ultimately he called Bihar Military Police. By their joint effort they were able to oust the mob, though it remained outside the police station up to 10:00 p.m. The officer-in-charge interrogated us for a few minutes and was satisfied with our replies, but he did not allow us to leave the campus because he was afraid we would be lynched by the mob. Just one day earlier a sadhu had been beaten to death by a mob under suspicion of being a Pakistani spy.

Acharya Chandradeojii was an employee of the Tata company. To verify his identity the officer-in-charge called the chief officer of his department. Chandradeojii then requested his boss to bring his Jeep so he could take us safely to his residence. He arrived at 11:00 p.m. and the officer let us go at midnight after recording our statement. By that time the mob had dispersed.

Acharya Suprakash left the same night for Assam, while Ac. Chandradeojii took me to his residence for the night. The next morning he and his family accompanied me to Chaibasa in a taxi. In between Tata and Chaibasa there was crossroad where we were searched and then allowed to continue. I passed two days in Chaibasa with Ac. Rajmohanjii and Balendujii. Then Balendujii took me by car to Chakradharpur railway station where I reserved a first-class berth for Purulia. When the train started I locked the compartment from the inside and did not open it until Purulia. There was no such frenzy about Pakistani spies in Purulia. Therefore I had no difficulty to attend the court.

On the twenty-second I went to Varanasi and remained there until October 11 to take care of a huge backlog of office work. I also taught classes for the trainees and made a three-day trip to Ranchi, Lucknow, and Fategarh.

109
Third South India Tour

*A*FTER COMPLETING MY work in Varanasi I left for a one-month tour of South India in conjunction with the scheduled DMCs. First I went to Bhopal, meeting Ac. Ramashray, who was returning from South India. I remained in Bhopal for two days dealing with various organizational problems. I also delivered two lectures, one for the Margis and one for the public. On October 14 I started for Bombay, reaching there the next day. On request of Srimati Padma Laxmijii, I went to her residence in Khar for a short while and then to the Seva Dharma Mission office, situated near Juhu beach. The house had a very nice atmosphere. It was surrounded by trees, making it look like a garden. By that time wholetime workers from different parts of Maharastra had reached. I conducted our organizational meeting and spent the night with them.

The next day we went to visit the Ajanta caves and to see the different types of fish at Marine Drive. I also gave a lecture for the Margis of that area. From there the district secretary, Sri Anandajii, brought me by car to his house in Khar where I discussed different aspects of our philosophy with the Margis.

In the afternoon of October 17 I arrived in Surat and addressed a tattvasabha. The next morning a number of local Margis came to talk with me about different aspects of Ananda Marga. We took our noon meal at the residence of Kanchanlal, who then took me to visit the Duman seashore along with Joshijii, Devadra, and Ravi Kumar. In the evening I addressed a tattvasabha.

On the nineteenth morning I started for Baroda, accompanied by Ac. Devendra and Ac. Ravi Kumar. A group of Margi brothers came to the station to receive us. They took us to the dharmachakra where I gave a lecture for the Margis. In the evening I addressed a public meeting.

In the meantime another wholetime worker, Ac Jaykrishna, joined us. The next day I attended dharmachakra at the residence of Sri Kanubhai, where I discussed sadhana with the Margis.

On the twenty-first morning we started for Ahmedabad and reached there at noon. Sri Prananath Mehtajii received us at the station and took us to his residence. In the afternoon went to see the Gandhi ashram, and after returning we held a meeting to discuss the development of prachar work in Ahmedabad. The next day I spent with Mehtajii and his relatives discussing Ananda Marga. Then in the evening I entrained for Bombay.

The following day I remained in the SDM office near Juhu beach and in the evening I attended dharmachakra at the residence of Shyam Sundar Goenka. In the night I went to the cremation ground for kapalik puja.

110
Claimant

ON THE TWENTY-FOURTH a motor car reached our ashram gate at about 11:00 a.m. A middle-aged man and a young married woman got down from the car and I greeted them with namaskar. The man asked me if I were Acharya Satyananda Avadhuta? When I said yes, he asked me if I made the avadhutas in Ananda Marga? "I cannot make avadhutas," I said. "If a person wants to become an avadhuta and cordially requests my help then I do my best to help them. To become avadhuta or avadhutika depends on the sweet will of the interested person. My work is like a registrar who registers a couple's marriage. If someone wants to dedicate their life unto the feet of Lord and do selfless service to society, I register their name in our organization, Ananda Marga,"

"I am the principal of an engineering college," he explained, "and without informing me my wife has become an avadhutika of Ananda Marga."

"If she is your wife," I said, "then by rule she must take permission from you before becoming an avadhutika. But since it is a matter of the Women's Welfare Section, I am unaware of the circumstances. After returning to my headquarters I shall make some inquiries and inform you accordingly."

The gentleman was quite angry but I noticed that the young woman with him was enjoying the whole affair. When I asked her who she was, she told me that she was his daughter-in-law and the wife that we were discussing was Avadhutika Ananda Bharati. We talked for about an hour and eventually the gentleman calmed down. At last he said that the least she could do was to inform him through a letter that she was ending all worldly relations with him.

111
Pratapgarh

EARLY THE NEXT morning I started for Mahabaleshwar. I reached there at 5:00 p.m. Ac. Chandranathjii was waiting at the bus station to receive me. He took me by Jeep to his residence and we passed the evening narrating different stories of our beloved Baba.

The next morning I visited Pratapgarh by Jeep, forty kilometres away, passing through a solitary region of hills and jungles to get there. In this lonely place Chhatrapati Shivaji made a fort known as Pratapgarh. After reaching we climbed row after row of switchback steps to the top of the hill. There we found the Bhavani temple and a statue of Chhatrapati Shivaji riding a horse. Next to it was a marble slab on which was written some words from the prime minister of India, Pundit Jawaharlal Nehru. For as far as the eye could see stretched only hills and jungle.

On the way down, we came upon a ridge whose path was only wide enough for one person. It is said that once Chhatrapati Shivaji and Afzal Khan met here and Shivaji killed him by disembowelling him with his aptly named weapon, the Baghnokha (tiger's claw). Nearby we came upon the tomb of Afzal Khan. Then we returned to Mahabaleshwar. On the way we passed a place where a scene for a motion picture was being filmed. Out of curiosity we stopped to watch and after a few minutes we continued on our way, passing a number of rivers that cut through the hills, such as the Krishna, Kavari, Gayatri, and Koana rivers, which created a most attractive atmosphere.

The next day we left for Pune by bus. At Pune we went to the Gargi Dharmasala where a wholetime worker, Ac. Krityananda, was waiting for us. He took us to the residence of Mr. Joshijii where I delivered a lecture for the Margis. The next morning a group of Margi sisters came to meet me. I talked with them for an hour and then we started for Akola.

112
Akola and Amaravati

ON THE TWENTY-NINTH morning I reached Akola Station. A group of Margis under the guidance of Acharya Kaushal Kumar (later, Acharya Keshavananda Avadhuta) received me and took me to the place they had arranged for my stay. I talked with them for a few hours and in the afternoon I addressed a public meeting in the bar library. Then I talked for some time with the unit secretary, Doctor Usha Pradhan. She was a most enthusiastic young girl. Though she was a doctor she was still unmarried. I talked with her about becoming a wholetime worker.

The next day Ac. Shantananda, Ac. Kaushal Kumar, and I started for Amaravati by train. At Borni a group of Margis requested us to get down. We acceded to their request and from there they took us to Amaravati by car. After reaching there in the afternoon we went with them to see the historical places of that town. At the time of Lord Krishna it had been a kingdom of Vidarbha Raj. It is said that Lord Krishna abducted the Vidarbha princess Rukmini and brought her to his capital, Dwarka, where he married her. The place from where Rukmini was abducted has been preserved for visitors so we visited that place. Amaravati was the birthplace of Ac. Shantananda and he kept Kaushal Kumar and I busy meeting his relatives and friends.

113
Nagpur

THE NEXT DAY at Amaravati there was a public meeting organized in Diparchan Hall. I addressed the meeting for one hour and then left for Nagpur, where I stayed at the residence of Acharya Jialaljii, who was Assistant Collector Central Excise. I attended the weekly dharmachakra and talked to the Margis about the importance of spiritual sadhana in human life. The unit secretary, Sri D. N. Samil said, "Dada! It feels like I have known you my entire life, although we are only meeting for the first time." I told him about rebirth and how the wave from having met each other in a past life arises in the subconscious mind.

Jialaljii's eldest son, Ashok, was a very enthusiastic youth who stayed by my side during the two days I was there. His sister Bina also took care of me when I wasn't feeling well and prepared my favourite foods. She was a beautiful and well-behaved young woman. She had passed her BA exam and since her mother's death she was looking after her father. Throughout the day Margis came to meet me and in the evening I addressed a public meeting.

On the second of November, Acharya Ajay Kumar and I started for Hyderabad by train. Ac. Shantananda and Ac. Kaushal Kumar came to the station to see off us. Once we were in the train we took our meal, which Bina had prepared with much devotion.

114
Hyderabad

*A*CHARYA PATIT PAVAN and a group of Margis received us at the station and took us to the residence of an Ananda Margi. In the evening there was a public meeting, after which I talked with the Margis about the importance of sadhana. The next day I went to a doctor for a checkup and from there to see the Qutub Minar with Ac. Patit Pavan and Ac. Ajay Kumar. From the top of the Minar one can see all of Hyderabad. After visiting the Minar I addressed a meeting of the Margis.

On November 5, Ac. Patit Pavan and I started for Vijaywara, reaching there about 10:00 p.m. We stayed at the Ramakrishna Vidyalaya for the night. The next day we went to Guntur by bus. A group of Margis met us at the bus stand and took us to the residence of a Margi. In the evening a meeting was organized in the town, which I addressed. The next day Patit Pavan and I started for Anantapur by train.

115
Kurnul and Anantapur

*A*CHARYA AJAY KUMAR had reached Kurnul one day earlier to organize the programme. He and a group of Margis received us at Kurnul Station and took us to the dharmachakra. I talked about the importance of sadhana in day-to-day life and in the evening they organized a public meeting for me. The next day Ac. Patit Pavan and I went from Kurnul to

Anantapur. After reaching there we went to the residence of Sri Ranga Swami, an ardent devotee of Baba. Most of the Margis of that area were good devotees and well educated. In the evening I gave a talk for them and the next day passed in different discussions among the Margis. In the evening I addressed a public meeting in which I talked about the systematic and scientific method of spiritual practices in day-to-day life.

116
Madras

ON THE ELEVENTH, I started for Madras, stopping at Kajipet Station to catch the Madras Mail with the help of Ac. Ajay Kumar. I reached Madras in the evening. Acharya Vireshwar met me at the station and took me to the ashram where I met Acharya Shivananda and other wholetimers. It had been a long time since we had seen each other, so it was a delightful opportunity. We passed our time doing collective meditation, eating together, and talking late into the night.

117
Revenge

BABA WAS DUE to arrive in Madras on November 15 for a three-day stay. Accordingly I directed the field workers to send their reports to me at the Madras address. On November 13 I caught up on my office work, going through the letters from the different workers. Suddenly I found a typed circular sent by Ac Shantananda Avadhuta that hit me like an atom bomb. It contained a strongly worded character assassination directed at me and copies had been sent to highly reputed Ananda Margis throughout India. The moment I read that letter I felt as if I had been shot in the chest, and I felt similar pain in other parts of my body. I stopped my work and lost my mental balance, overcome by extreme restlessness. Seeing my condition the other workers became bewildered and wanted to know the cause of my sudden illness. From the time of opening that letter up to the arrival of Baba in Madras I remained extremely restless. Such a blow I had never faced in all my life.

India is such a prejudiced society that once the image of a person is tarnished in the eyes of society, it is difficult to recover. I was a monk of Ananda Marga touring India with a spiritual mission and mixing with different sections of the society, and I had become very popular among them. Such a concocted scandal could not only tarnish my image before the eyes of the public, it could ruin my life as a sannyasi. It would be very difficult for me to show my face even. As per the organizational rules, if a person committed any fault it was to be reported to the concerning higher authority; it was not to spread by a circular. This was nothing less than slander. Acharya Kaushal Kumar had accompanied me on this tour like a shadow and he had not seen any such fault in my character, whereas Ac. Shantananda who was far away had? He had concocted a fictitious girlfriend from Amaravati and made me the scapegoat of the slander.

Until Baba arrived I could not eat or sleep. My companions tried to help in different ways. They took me to the seashore and brought me coconut water, trying to take care of me as best they could, but they did not know the cause of my condition. My heart was broken and I thought I might go mad. Even the idea of suicide passed through my mind. I had previously faced many obstacles and hardships but by dint of my sadhana and my absolute faith in Baba I had always been able to overcome those critical situations.

On the evening of November 15, Baba landed in Minambakkam Airport along with the general secretary, Acharya P. K. Chatterjee. I received Baba at the airport and went with him in the car to the residence of Goenkajii, which had been fixed for his stay. After seeing Baba I got some energy. During this tour Dharma Maha Chakra was scheduled to be held in Madras, Bangalore, Cochin, Bombay, and Nagpur. My ticket had also been booked with Baba in the same plane. Sri Shashi Rainjanjii was also travelling on the same plane. A copy of the circular had been sent to him at Delhi and he did his best to console me, though Sri P. K. Chatterjee was very happy to see the situation.

Gradually I was able to recover my mental balance by reminding myself that on many occasions in the past spiritually elevated persons had faced similar character assassination through the same ruse of a concocted wicked woman, trying to tarnish the growing image of those persons before the eyes of the public. It was painful but it was not anything new. Now it was my life's boat that was facing the cyclone.

Baba decided to form a tribunal composed of a few persons from among those who had received the circular under the leadership of Sri

P. K. Chatterjee. He told me that after reaching Nagpur I would appear before the tribunal. "After getting their verdict," he said, "come to me and I shall think in what way you will be best utilized in the organization."

It was a remarkable matter that after receiving a copy of the slanderous circular, Vishokananda came to Madras from Delhi to know my mental condition. We talked and then he returned to Delhi. I came to know from Sri Shashi Rainjanjii that after receiving the circular in Delhi, Lalan, Vishokananda, Prakashananda, and Ac. Raghunath had been overwhelmed with joy and had distributed sweets in celebration.

118
Bangalore Dharma Maha Chakra

On November 16 we went to Bangalore by plane for the DMC programme. On the eighteenth we went to the Bangalore airport to catch a plane for Ernakulam. Baba, Pranay Kumarjii, and I had reservations but Shashi Rainjanjii did not and since no seat was available he was somewhat perturbed. Seeing this I decided to offer him my seat and go by train. When I informed Baba he said, "As a monk you have taken the right decision. All right, come by train." After seeing them off I headed to the train station.

119
Cochin Dharma Maha Chakra

I reached Ernakulam on the nineteenth. Acharya Pranavananda and a local Margi named Balaidhan met me at the station and took me to the residence of Balaidhan, where Baba was staying. The moment I reached there, Sri Shashi Rainjanjii embraced me and said, "You shouldn't have let me take your seat. Due to your late arrival the organizational work has been hampered. Baba was facing much inconvenience due to your absence. Please complete your bath and puja and come help to make the programme a grand success." Accordingly I spent the whole day organizing the programme. Dharma Maha Chakra took place in the evening and everyone enjoyed.

We four left for Bombay the next day. I was very happy because I had once taken an oath that I would not take rest unless and until Dharma Maha Chakra was held in each corner of the country. By Baba's grace my oath had now been fulfilled by holding DMC at Ernakulam, at the nadir point of the Indian subcontinent. Now I was ready to appear before the tribunal at Nagpur and face whatever Providence decided was in the best interest of the organization, even if it meant that the conspirators would rule the organization without any obstacle. I awaited Baba's decision. Still it was my firm faith that he would not tolerate such a wrongful act or group conspiracy. After being in close contact with him for so long I had come to know that he had no relatives and no attachment to anybody or anything. He was Purusham Mahantam. In his court justice can be delayed but it always comes. Darkness cannot prevail. Sinners were always ousted from the organization by their own wickedness.

120
Bombay Dharma Maha Chakra

ON THE WAY to Bombay the four of us enjoyed looking at the towns and other sights as we flew over the Arabian sea, chatting all the while on different topics. We reached Bombay in the evening, landing at Santa Cruz Airport (now Shivaji International Airport). The Margis of Bombay received us and took us to the residence of the district secretary, Sri Anandajii.

After completing his evening puja, Baba went for his walk. After returning he gave personal contact to the new Margis up to 10:30. Then he took supper and went to bed. The next day he again gave personal contact to the new Margis till 12:00 noon. Then he gave General Darshan for one hour and in the evening the DMC was celebrated.

121
Tribunal

ON THE TWENTY-SECOND the four of us reached Nagpur about 11:00 a.m. We went to a dharmasala where arrangements had been made for Baba and us to stay. As soon as we arrived Baba started his usual programme and in the afternoon at 2:00 p.m. I appeared before the tribunal. They asked me if the charges brought against me were true or not. I told them that it was not a question of whether they were true or not. It was a question of what was best for the organization. "In the interests of the organization, as well as to save me permanently from this group conspiracy, I accept the charges brought against me and ask for punishment." They continued to press me to know the details but I repeated the same lines over and over again. At the same time, Acharya Kaushal told the tribunal that as the pracharaka of that area he had been with me throughout the Amaravati tour and he had never seen or heard of any such unlawful action on my part, and at no time did the tribunal mention the name of that fictitious woman, nor for that matter did Shantananda's circular. In Acharya's Kaushal's opinion it was a concocted charge brought against me out of jealousy by a group of senior Margis who could not tolerate my position of influence in the organization.

When I accepted the charges without any hesitation, Ac. Chandranathjii again and again requested me to tell him what had really happened. He was close to me and loved me very much. He was a member of the High Command and I was the secretary of the High Command, and together we had discussed many previous conspiracy cases in our meetings; thus he knew the ins and outs of these internal matters. Sri Shashi Rainjanjii was also very reacted with these nasty politics. When they continued to press me, I expressed the following and then left the place: "I accept all those charges brought against me by Shantananda Avadhuta. Please take whatever action you feel necessary according to the penal code of Ananda Marga. I am fed up with this anti-social conspiracy, which has no other purpose other than to oust me from my position in Ananda Marga and to separate me from Baba."

From the tribunal I went directly to Baba and told him that I accepted the charges brought against me and awaited the judgment of the tribunal. Hearing this, Baba told me to come to him once the verdict of the tribunal was issued. After one hour the tribunal informed me that my acharyaship had been seized. I informed Baba of the decision and he told me to go to Jamalpur and take the teachers training there. "After reaching Jamalpur I will discuss this with you further," he said.

As per Baba's direction I started for Jamalpur by the evening train.

122
Dumka School

*I*TOOK THE TEACHERS training up to December 6 in the jagriti school run by Acharya Abhedananda Avadhuta. Then from the seventh to the twelfth I took the principals training at the Gaya school and then returned to Jamalpur. On the thirteenth in the afternoon Baba came to the jagriti and called me and his PA, Ac Prashantananda, asking him to bring my posting order. Baba also asked him to call Vishokananda, who was one of the conspirators. Baba directed Prashantananda to give me my posting order as the principal of the Dumka school.

The Dumka school had opened recently. It had some eight to ten students. After taking charge of the school, I went to Purulia to attend the court and from there I went to join the teachers' seminar at Dehri-on-Sone. After the seminar finished on December 24, I returned to Dumka and started to arrange the office and the classrooms. The admission of new students was due to begin on January 3.

In the meantime, Vishokananda went to Delhi, taking with him the news of my posting at Dumka. He organized a meeting of the conspirators, including Mr. Lalan and Prakashananda, in which they celebrated my demotion and distributed sweets. Acharya Rataneshjii of Lucknow was present and vehemently protested their acts. Sri Shashi Rainjanjii also protested their indecent behaviour.

Sri P. K. Chatterjee thought that now that I was removed from the scene he would have complete control of the organization and that Baba would be compelled to depend on him, but before sending me to Dumka, Baba distributed my responsibilities among some fifteen wholetime workers.

Before going to the Dumka school I had created about 150 wholetime workers and sent them to different parts of the country. As avadhuta secretary I had personally created thirty-seven avadhutas who were facing different obstacles and struggles and working in adverse conditions with firm determination based on the ideology of Ananda Marga and their absolute faith in Baba. According to their seniority, some of them were: Ac. Shivananda Avt., Ac. Sambuddhanana Avt., Ac. Pranavananda Avt., Ac. Cidananda Avt., Ac. Vijayananda Avt., Ac. Amritananda Avt., Ac. Amitananda Avt., Ac. Shankarananda Avt., Ac. Purnananda Avt., Ac. Japananda Avt., Ac. Svarupananda Avt., Ac. Cidghanananda Avt., Ac. Chinmayananda Avt., Ac. Parashivananda Avt., Ac. Nirmohananda Avt., and others.

These avadhutas had dedicated their lives to establish the ideology of Ananda Marga throughout the world. Though reproached by a group conspiracy I was internally happy because no power on earth could stop the march of Ananda Marga. Individuals cannot remain forever but the ideology can and will. It is my firm belief that a day will come when the ideology of Ananda Marga is established on this earth by these and other dedicated souls.

123
Change of Strategy

TAKING ON THE responsibility of my new assignment in the pure and calm atmosphere at Dumka, I did my best to promote the all-round development of the school. In the meantime Sri P. K. Chatterjee's arrogance continued to grow and it eventually got out of control. His audacity developed to the point that he even disobeyed and dishonoured the orders of Baba. Whatever Baba wanted, he started to do the opposite. In the month of January, 1966, Baba lost faith in him and determined that this could not continue. He sent Acharya Chandranathjii to Anandanagar to collect information and report back to him about the activities of Mr. Pranay Kumar. After hearing his report about Pranay's improper activities, Baba decided to post another general secretary in his place. In the meantime Pranay realized that his days were numbered. He shifted his wife from Anandanagar and soon afterward Baba sent four acharyas to bring him back to Jamalpur, declaring that he was posting Acharya Prashantananda in his place. At the time of his departure Pranay told his group that he would come back within two to three days. But those two to three days never came.

The day after the departure of Sri P. K. Chatterjee, Acharya Prashantananda Avadhuta was officially posted as the new general secretary. After taking the posting order, he came to Anandanagar, but due to the absence of Sri P. K. Chatterjee he could not take the charge. P. K. Chatterjee had brainwashed his followers to the point that they would not recognise Acharya Prashantananda as the general secretary, though he was officially posted there, nor were they ready to hand over the key of the office.

That same day Baba sent a special messenger to me at Dumka, directing me to go to Anandanagar. Accordingly I made plans to leave the next morning by the first available bus. That same evening Baba came to Bhagalpur on the occasion of Dharma Maha Chakra. He stayed at the residence of Doctor Suresh Verma, the civil surgeon in the district hospital. In the evening Baba telephoned me from the residence of Doctor Verma and said, "The general secretary has been removed from his post and in his place I have posted Ac. Prashantananda Avt. But to take over the charge certain problems have arisen. Therefore your presence at Anandanagar is urgently needed. Proceed by the first available bus. I am sending Acharya Sambuddhananda to Anandanagar from Bhagalpur with the necessary instructions for you. After you reach there you will act accordingly." As per Baba's direction, I started for Anandanagar early the next morning.

After reaching Anandanagar I found an unprecedented deadlock, such as one could not imagine happening in a spiritual organization. In Ananda Marga, Baba is not only the president but also the Purodha Pramukha and the Parama Guru. Disobeying the order of the guru has dire consequences for a disciple, something that is known to all true devotees.

Those who were working together with Sri P. K. Chatterjee, among them Ac. Sripatijii (Shraddhananda Avt.), had taken the charge from him and would not hand it over to Ac. Prashantananda. They said that they would challenge his authority in the Purulia court. Seeing the situation, I was in a dilemma what to do. Then Ac. Sambuddhananda arrived from Bhagalpur. He carried letters from Baba giving me full responsibility — Baba said in the letter that "the decision of Satyananda will be treated as final."

Shortly thereafter, Ac. Ramtanukjii, Ac Dasarathjii, Ac. Shiva Shankarjii, Ac. Kedarjii, and a group of Margis reached Anandanagar from Ranchi and other places. That entire day we met with the P. K. Chatterjee group and tried to make them understand Baba's decision to hand over the charge to Prashantananda Avt. But they did not acquiesce to our request. They were not ready to accept Baba's order. Seeing how adamant they had become, I told them that if they did not change their attitude and hand over the charge to the new GS by 8:00 p.m. then the organization would take its own course and implement the change with or without their cooperation. Ac. Ramtanukjii, Ac. Shiva Shankarjii, and Ac. Dasarathjii continued to implore them to listen to reason but they would not budge.

In the evening I sat for puja while the 8:00 deadline approached. Finally a representative from their group, Ac. Dhyanananda Avt., came and roused me from my meditation. "Dada," he said, "If Pranayjii does not arrive on the 8:00 p.m. train then Sripatijii will go to Jamalpur on the 10:00 p.m. train and hand over the charge there." I agreed with his proposal and told him that Ac. Ramtanukjii, Ac. Dasarathjii, and Ac. Shiva Shankarjii would accompany Ac. Prashantananda on the same train. P. K. Chatterjee did not show up and so they all proceeded to Jamalpur.

Earlier P. K. Chatterjee had left his wife at Gaya at the residence of Acharya Satyanarainjii. From Anandanagar he went to Varanasi and was moving like a vagabond. Two men from his group, Ac. Prakashananda and Ac. Vishokananda, went there and brought him to Jamalpur but never again did he come before Baba.

Upon reaching Jamalpur, Baba withdrew the discipleship of everyone in the Chatterjee group, whereupon they became mortified. Up till now they had only shown their anger and their obstinacy but now they became repentant. They fell to the ground at Baba's feet and started weeping and begging for mercy. Parama Purusha is the embodiment of mercy. Eventually he withdrew his order and excused them, saying that never again should they commit such a mistake. Ac. Prashantananda took over the charge of GS and returned to Anandanagar. I remained at Anandanagar with him for one week to put in order the office of the GS and then I returned to Dumka via Jamalpur.

In Jamalpur Ac. Abhedananda Avt. took over the charge of PA from Ac. Prashantananda. It was noteworthy that all the works that P. K. Chatterjee and myself had previously supervised for the different sections of the organization had been distributed among different workers, but due to their inexperience the entire workload now fell squarely on Baba's shoulders.

124
Admission of Students

*B*ACK IN DUMKA, I started contacting different sections of society and explaining the system of Ananda Marga education to them. I met with advocates, magistrates, government officers, businessmen, and other educated persons. Due to my efforts, students from all sections of society started to be admitted in my school. Within a short period, a positive change in the students became apparent and both guardians and the general public became attracted toward our teachings. The guardians started spreading the word about our school, and in short order all our classes were full. Still more students came to me, trying to gain admission. We had three classes by then, KG-I, KG-II, and STD-I, and ninety students.

Many Margis helped me to develop the Dumka school, but in particular I want to mention the names of Acharya Kuldipjii, Sri Biren Dutta, Sri Priyabrata Dutta, and Sri Shiva Prasad. They laboured hard on all fronts to help me build up the school.

The school was now running independently. But that year an extreme drought struck Madhya Pradesh during the summer season. Due to want of food people started to die. Many children from the affected area were sent to the Ananda Marga children's home. Of these, one dozen were sent to Dumka from Jamalpur to open a children's home. I received them and started a children's home. Sri Biren Dutta was my right-hand man in this work. Though he was a householder living with his family in Dumka, he worked with me like a wholetimer. He used to spend the entire day collecting whatever we needed to maintain the children's home and the school. His sacrifice for the Marga was unparalleled.

It was decided that the Ananda Purnima DMC that year would be held at the Patna Veterinary College compound. Baba specifically asked me to come to Patna to attend. It was in this DMC that it was announced that Ananda Marga would send a missionary abroad for the first time. Acharya Atmananda Avadhuta was selected to be that missionary and the different programmes of the Ananda Purnima Dharma Maha Chakra were celebrated with a festive air.

125
None Can Kill Those to Whom the Lord Gives his Protection

*A*FTER RETURNING FROM the Patna DMC, I was very busy with the work of the Dumka school . In the month of June at 9:00 a.m. I suddenly felt a great desire to sit for puja. At that time I lived in a corner of the school hall that I had separated with a curtain of gunny sheets. I used to sit on my cot for puja, the same cot on which I slept. While I was doing puja, I heard a loud sound just beside the cot. I got up from my puja and started to investigate. There was a small table by the side of my bed and on it a glass was lying broken, each of its shattered pieces lying together like the bloomed petals of a lotus. I searched the surroundings to find out why the glass might have broken but I could not find any logical cause.

I left it as it was and later showed it to the Margis. All were surprised but none could say how it had happened, so I decided to go to Jamalpur the following Saturday. When I reached Jamalpur and approached Baba, then and there, before I had a chance to say anything, he said, "Satyananda! You were very surprised because your glass broke on the table without anyone touching it, just at the time when you felt compelled to sit for puja." Hearing this, I pressed Baba to know the cause of the breaking glass. He told me that an Avidya Tantric had applied his power in an effort to liquidate me but since I was sitting in puja he could not succeed. Instead of destroying my physical structure, his power destroyed the glass. I knew then and there that no one can kill someone to whom the Lord gives his protection.

After that I fell ill for some time. A private doctor, Dr. Akshoy, treated me. He was a very pious man and a good doctor. He did not accept any money from me, even for the medicines he supplied me. When he came to see me, he saw our children's home and was inspired by what he saw. He expressed his desire to donate some clothes and blankets and asked our local acharya, Kuldipjii, to go to his house to collect those materials. In this way I got sympathy from all corners.

126
Advent

*I*N THE MONTH of October, during the Durga Puja holidays, Baba unexpectedly visited the Dumka school with his family, his PA, Acharya Abhedananda Avadhuta, and the security in-charge. When I got the news of Baba's arrival at the school, I hurried to reach there. It was 1:00 p.m. when I reached and Baba still had not taken his lunch. He was on the way to Bardhaman but due to car problems he had been compelled to halt at Dumka. Baba was taking his family to his newly constructed house in Bardhaman for the Durga Puja holidays. It had been a long time since I had seen Baba, thus I was overwhelmed with joy. Quickly I made arrangements for Baba's bath and meal and for the necessities of his family. Then I went to the garage to talk with the mechanics about the repairs on Baba's car. If the repairs were delayed then Baba's work in Bardhaman would be hampered. Since the car would not be ready in time I hired a taxi and sent Baba by taxi to Bardhaman with the security in-charge.

It was night before the repairs were finished. Abhedananda and I took the car to Bardhaman. It was 10:00 p.m. when we left and I was driving. We reached Suri and took rest there for the night at the Ananda Marga school. Early the next morning we continued on to Bardhaman, reaching the family's new residence at 11:00 a.m.

127
At Bardhaman with Baba

IN BARDHAMAN WE stayed in a room in Baba's house, just next to Baba's room, but Baba's brother Sudanshu didn't like Ananda Marga. He used to give Baba problems about his use of the Jamalpur railway quarters for organizational activities. Sudanshu soon told us to shift somewhere else. We decided to go to the house of a local Margi, but before going we took permission from Baba. After that we stayed with the family of Acharya Punyananda Avadhuta. They were all devotees of Baba. It was a nice place to stay and they were pleased to have us. During Durga Puja, Bengali families consider it auspicious to have holy persons stay with them so they can serve them specially prepared foods on that pious occasion.

128
Doing Mischief to Others Invites one's own Destruction

EVERY MORNING AND evening at the scheduled time I would pick up Baba with the car and take him to a different place in the area. One day we went to the residence of a relative of Baba without giving prior notice. At first they did not believe that Baba had come. Two avadhutas had also come with us. We were all talking in Bengali and since the turban used by avadhutas was like the turban the Sikhs of Punjab wear,

Baba's relatives thought that we were Punjabi. They remarked how surprised they were to hear Punjabis talking such nice Bengali. Then they turned to Baba and said, "Your prachar work has developed very nicely in Punjab, we see." We enjoyed the little drama without saying anything to disturb their feeling. We also went to Baba's paternal village of Bamunpara, near Bardhaman.

Every day I would take Baba to the Damodar River bridge for his evening walk. We would leave the car on the long bridge and walk up and down, discussing different issues. One day I told Baba that I had heard it said that by the physical touch of a Mahapurusha, or by association with him, all critical diseases were permanently cured. "But we are in your close contact and still many of us are suffering from different diseases. Why the exception?" In reply, Baba narrated a story:

"Once a king had two queens, Suarani and Duarani. Duarani was the senior queen and Suarani the junior. The junior queen was very beautiful. She was proud of her beauty and the king was more attracted to her. One day Suarani told the king she could no longer live with the senior queen and requested him to kindly send her to the forest. And so the king built a house in the forest and sent Duarani there. After that the junior queen passed her days peacefully in the palace without any rival. One day the king went to the forest to hunt. Due to unavoidable circumstances he could not return to the palace that night, so he took rest in the residence of the senior queen. When the news reached the junior queen she became angry. She decided that she needed to get rid of Duarani once and for all. She consulted with her attendant and hit upon a plan. She would pretend that she had a terrible disease that could not be cured by a physician. It could only be cured by the water of a certain pond inside the forest, a pond frequented by Royal Bengal tigers, and then only if that water was procured by the senior queen going there alone at midnight.

"Thus Suarani took to her bed and started tossing and turning, apparently in great discomfort. When the king got news of her condition, he hurried to her side and asked her what was the cause of her discomfort. The queen replied that she was in terrible pain. Whenever she moved, her bones would crack, and the pain was too much for her to bear. The king called a renowned doctor but his treatment had no effect. At last the queen told the king that she had had a dream, and in the dream she had learned of the medicine for her disease. She asked him to send the senior queen in the dead of night to bring a pitcher of water from that particular pond in the jungle. If she took a bath in that water then she would be cured. The desperate king agreed to her proposal. He sent for the senior queen and treated her with great affection. Then he told her about the medicine he needed for the junior queen. The elder queen was filled with joy at receiving once again the love of her husband, and to please him she agreed to bring the water. As she entered the forest she repeated over and again with deep emotion, *apnar lok tai to* (he is my man, that is why he is sending me). When the wild animals heard this sound they cowered in fear. As a result she reached the edge of the pond without any trouble. She filled the pitcher with water and set it down. But when she went to pick it up again she was so carried away by her emotions that instead of the pitcher she picked up a tiger who was lying there, cowering in fear. Tiger in hand, she walked back to the palace and into the room of the junior queen. She left the tiger near the foot of the bed and told Suarani that she had brought the water she needed to cure her disease. Then she left the room. Up until then the tiger had been too afraid to move. But once the senior queen left the room he let out a roar and pounced on the junior queen. He caught her in his jaws, jumped out the window, and disappeared into the darkness of the nearby jungle.

"The moment the news spread through the palace, efforts were made to rescue the junior queen but to avail. After this the king went to her room and found dry jute stalks under the mattress, the source of the cracking sound. Then he realized the truth behind the junior queen's feigned disease. From then on the king was very happy with the senior queen."

Baba then said that he had the medicine for actual diseases but there was no medicine for the sound of cracking bones as suffered by the junior queen.

At the end of the week, I took Baba by car to Calcutta to attend the DMC. Arrangements were made for Baba's stay at the residence of Mr. Handa. After completing the programme I returned to Dumka.

129
Baba's Departure for Anandanagar

DUE TO MY absence from the centre, the pressure of the organizational work fell on Baba. Therefore it was not possible for him to continue his railway service. At the end of 1966 he resigned his government service and moved to Anandanagar with his family. A house for Baba had already been constructed there. Once Baba moved to Anandanagar, devotees from different parts of the country started going there regularly to have his darshan, and at the same time the momentum of the work at Anandanagar increased tremendously.

130
Influence

*B*ACK IN DUMKA I was hard at work admitting students into my school. The reputation of the school had grown considerably and applications for admission were coming from all corners. Seats were limited, however, so I could not entertain all the applications. A number of guardians requested me to start a hostel for students from outside the area but due to want of space it was not possible. Most of the boys and girls admitted in my school were from educated families or children of businessmen. About one kilometre from Dumka, in Dudhani, there was a big Christian missionary school run by American nuns. Many of their students left that school and took admission in my school. Our English-medium school was based on Indian culture and this created a sensation in the society. A group of those American nuns came to our school and without taking my permission they started talking with their former students. I called them to my office and talked with them in a cordial and gentle manner. They were surprised how an Ananda Marga school could get so many students while their school might have to close for want of students.

After they left my school they started going from house to house to talk to the mothers of the students. They also started copying some of the things that we were doing. But they were not successful. The progress of our school was unaffected.

131
Conclusion

*A*s an ascetic monk I travelled across India several times, from the Himalayas to Kanyakumari, from Digboy to Dwarka, and found out what a variegated country it is. From one side to another, the food habits, dress, and languages are different. In North India people cook with mustard oil, whereas in South India they cook with coconut oil. But there is unity in diversity. I am Indian and India is my motherland. Lord Shiva and Lord Krishna are worshipped in different names and different forms throughout the country, but they remain Lord Shiva and Lord Krishna.

In North India both rice and wheat flour are used but in South India only rice and items prepared with rice flour. Here South India means the states of Kerala, Tamil Nadu, Karnataka, Andhra Pradesh, and part of Maharastra. The people there eat boiled rice for both lunch and dinner. For breakfast and snacks they eat idli, dosa, and bara, all made from rice flour, along with coffee, while in North India the principal food is boiled rice and bread, and for breakfast and snacks, fried rice, preparations made from gram powder, bread, and tea. In South India the white lungi is the national dress and married women do not use the vermilion mark on their forehead, nor do they cover their heads with a veil like North Indian ladies do.

In Maharastra married ladies wear the mangal sutra necklace and old ladies wear their saris like Bengali gents wear their dhotis, with the hem tucked between the legs and tied behind at the waist. Their activities and appearance are different from North India. But there is some similarity in appearance between the people of Kerala and the people of Bengal. It is said that a son of Bengal named Vijay Singh went to war with Sri Lanka and emerged victorious. Some of his soldiers settled on the Malabar Coast, which later became known as Kerala. The present inhabitants are the descendant of those soldiers. That is why the Malayalam vocabulary is sixty percent Sanskrit and only forty percent words of Tamil origin. Similarly, the food habits of the Kashmiri people are similar to the food habits of the Bengali people. They eat boiled rice and fish prepared with mustard oil for both lunch and dinner, and they consider themselves to be more intelligent than other people.

So far as language is concerned, in India has 323 languages and thousands of local dialects. There is virtually no similarity between the words used in the North and those used in the South. Therefore to impose any one language is a kind of persecution. The development of a link language is essential to the free exchange of thought between different peoples of the world. At present English with its scientific Roman script is accepted in most countries as the link language. We can note the example of the freedom movement in India. During the freedom movement, English was used to unite the multi-language people of India. That is, anti-British sentiment was supported by the English language. The whole of India was united with its help and by their concerted effort they ultimately freed India from their British rulers. Therefore English should be accepted as the link language at the present time.

So far as religion is concerned, people choose their scriptures and idols according to their preference, but often these have no relation to spiritual upliftment. They follow certain rituals imposed by their ancestors. The word "spiritual" is derived from "spirit" + "rituals." Earlier rituals were adopted to establish their practitioners in Spirit. But now Spirit has disappeared and only the rituals remain. Thus people move aimlessly in search of peace without the guidance of a realized personality (sadguru). Seeing the condition of the people, I realized that at this critical juncture only the Creator can save the society. The advent of the Maker of the age, Baba Anandamurtijii, will in the future under the influence of his spiritual ideology lead to a Sadvipra Samaj. Here is the fearless message given to the people by Lord Krishna:

> *Yadá yadá hi dharmasya glánirbhavati Bhárata;*
> *Cábhyutthánamadharmasya tadátmánam srjámyáham.*
> *Paritráńáya sádhúnám vinásháya ca duśkrtám;*
> *Dharmasamsthápanártháya sambhavámi yuge yuge*

> When dharma degenerates and atrocities to sentient people increase, I shall come again in a physical body to establish dharma and rescue the sentient people from the hands of the wicked.

Concerning mukti and moksha, liberation and salvation, he said:

> *Sarvadharmán parityajya Mámekam sharańam vraja.*

Leaving all rituals and other mental complexes, surrender unto my feet and I shall rescue you from all sorts of bondages and give you salvation.

We, the devotees, surrendering unto the feet of the Lord Incarnate, are to work without pause to establish his mission.

Dharya yasya pita, kshama cha janani
Shantischira grihini, satya mitra mohodayam,
Daya cha bhagini, bhrata manah sanjama,
Shaiya bhumitaley, navopi basanam,
gyanamrita bhojanam,
Esay yasya kutumbitam,
balo sakhey tasyat bhayam kutaha

If one practices the following precepts properly he will be free from all fears. One who has taken patience as his father, forgiveness as his mother, peace as his housewife, truth as his friend, kindness as his sister, control over the mind as his brother, the surface of the earth as his bed, the sky as his dress, the desire of acquiring knowledge as his food — for such a person, tell me my friend, can any fear exist?

www.ingramcontent.com/pod-product-compliance
Lightning Source LLC
Chambersburg PA
CBHW021053080526
44587CB00010B/234